HEROES OF THE HORRORS

HEROES OF

by Calvin Thomas Beck

THE HORRORS

COLLIER BOOKS
A Division of Macmillan Publishing Co., Inc.
New York

COLLIER MACMILLAN PUBLISHERS
London

ALSO BY CALVIN THOMAS BECK:

Ed., *Castle of Frankenstein* magazine
Ed., *The Frankenstein Reader*

Macmillan Publishing Co., Inc.
866 Third Avenue, New York, N. Y. 10022
Collier-Macmillan Canada Ltd.

Heroes of the Horrors is also published in a hardcover edition by Macmillan Publishing Co., Inc.

Library of Congress Cataloging in Publication Data

Beck, Calvin Thomas.
  Heroes of the horrors.

  CONTENTS: Lon Chaney, Sr.—Bela Lugosi.—Boris Karloff.—Peter Lorre. [etc.]
  1. Horror films—Biography. I. Title.
PN1998.A2B38   791.43′028′0922   74-18315
ISBN 0-02-508190-X

First Collier Books Edition 1975

SECOND PRINTING 1975

Printed in the United States of America

Photo Credits: Allied Artists, American-International, Columbia Pictures, Metro-Goldwyn-Mayer, Paramount Pictures, RKO Radio Pictures, 20th Century-Fox, United Artists, Universal-International, and Warner Brothers.

To my late father, Thomas Beck, the
first great SFantasy-horror film fan
I ever met, who introduced me to all
this, and without whom nothing would
have been possible.

Acknowledgments

My special thanks to Robert M. Stewart, Barry Brown, Michael Parry, and Richard Bojarski for helping to make this book possible, and grateful acknowledgment to John Cocchi, William K. Everson, Mark Ricci, Philip B. Moshcovitz, Bert Gray, Larry Ivie, Kenneth Beale, Harry Nadler, and Charles Foster Kane.

Contents

Preface

IN SEARCH OF IMAGINATION

Many an author who has written about SFantasy film history has been known to begin with: "Since the beginning of time, man has always been fascinated by monsters and horror, etc., etc." Or, more prosaically: "So you want to know about horror movies, eh?" Or, waxing profound, hoping to stun readers with his academic background: "It would take the combined scholarship of Krafft-Ebing, Freud, Jung, and existentialists such as Kierkegaard and Sartre, to explain why SFantasy films are so popular—mainly because I can't." On the other hand, the real danger is that he probably *can,* and in a preface nearly as long as the remaining chapters he will declare (as if you didn't already suspect) that SFantasy is fraught with: sexual implications (the vampire); sadomasochism (pain endured/enjoyed by monster at the hands of unrestrained scientist—or vice versa); social repression and bigotry (the villagers on the march to end the mad scientist's fun and games); phallic symbolism (the spaceship); in search of a messiah (supreme extraterrestrial being visits the earth for the first and last time). After several hundred more examples, the pedant's conclusion is:

"Besides offering a great escape valve, the genre may dissuade you from slaughtering your entire family or shooting down the President of the United States. The world may never have known about Hitler if he had been a horror movie nut."

Pedantry may froth at the mouth, while cooler heads grope for simpler interpretations, but most end in futility. Pin a gooey, cliché label on *imagination*? Ridiculous. Yet nearly everyone has the instinct to recognize and appreciate it, even though it is immeasurable.

What *is* demonstrable is that a mere handful of imaginative filmmakers glorified and brought honor to their industry during periods that teemed and ached with tripe. In later years the same breed would salvage the field from ruination. In turn, great directors have usually relied on a minority of gifted performers possessing not only incredible insight into a director's mind but the capability of embellishing his direction, benefiting good directors in their dry spells, and making mediocre directors appear to be inspired.

Though quality filmmaking has now advanced to a point where actors often appear to be subordinate, if not unessential, in certain kinds of film, the star system is still powerful. Certain *names*, in fact, have personified entire screen genres. Harlow, Monroe, and Loren: sensuality and romance. Fairbanks and Flynn: swashbuckling and adventure. Bogart, Cagney, and Robinson: crime. Laughton, Olivier, and Welles: classical drama. Harte, Cooper, and Wayne: westerns. Niven and Grant (Cary, of course, and not Ulysses S.): sophisticated humor. And where once there was Gable and Garfield, Sean Connery and Charles Bronson now deal with intrigue and the enemy in their own inimitable syles.

Synonymous with SFantasy, the *greatest* of all film genres, are Chaney, Karloff, and the other immortals covered in this book. Some may deny this out of ignorance or envy, even though SFantasy has survived numerous cycles and continues to advance after other genres have faded or met dead ends. Appreciating its total spectrum and unlimited range is to be aware that mankind's entire culture has its genesis in the myths and occult sensibility on which civilization is founded. While the cynics may scoff, more than a quarter of a century's investigation into parapsychology in several leading universities (e.g., Duke University in Durham, North Carolina), has now been superseded by advanced scientific research into the "unknown" supported by the Russian government. Not to mention phenomenal public interest in tangential subjects that has made spectacular bestsellers of books such as Erich von Daniken's *Chariots of the Gods* and William P. Blatty's *The Exorcist,* followed by their very successful screen adaptations.

SFantasy's uncanny timelessness has been too evident to warrant tedious statistics; its popularity has flabbergasted critics and flatulent snobs alike, as witnessed by the genre's mushrooming appeal in recent years and by capacity-filled revival theaters featuring titles that are nearly forty, fifty years old or older—such as *Things to Come,*

Dr. Jekyll and Mr. Hyde, Metropolis, The Cabinet of Dr. Caligari, and Nosferatu—which outgross even films from such cinema giants as John Ford, Jean Renoir, Charlie Chaplin, Buster Keaton, and D. W. Griffith.

Modern filmmakers have profited well by wisely tapping this rich heritage and creating *hybrids* that have vastly extended filmic horizons. This has been due, in part, to the critical acclaim and gargantuan profits earned by such box-office hits as *2001: A Space Odyssey,* and the James Bond and *The Planet of the Apes* series—all offshoots of *Flash Gordon, Tarzan,* and *King Kong.*

Filmic hybridization isn't very unique, and even when awkwardly manipulated, goes back several generations. But 1960 may well be the landmark year, as attested to by Hitchcock's pathological nightmare classic, *Psycho.* Roman Polanski blended *psychopathia sexualis* and autism several years later, creating the traumatic *Repulsion.* The year 1968 saw even more deviations from the genre's traditional roots, proving how Polanski's urbane *Rosemary's Baby* could yank Satanism away from familiar castles and creepy mansions and plant it on Central Park West with a Madison Avenue veneer—not to overlook monstrous ghouls in an ecological setting in *Night of the Living Dead.*

All that has passed, though, may be but prologue to other areas rarely ever touched before. Variations on the mundane are infused with scintillating introspection: reality's convoluted maze is being gradually explored, revealing other worlds beyond cardboard existences and beneath computerized superficiality.

Among some outstanding examples are Alan J. Pakula's *Klute,* Sam Peckinpah's *The Straw Dogs,* Nicholas Roeg's *Walkabout* and *Don't Look Now,* and John Boorman's *Deliverance.* Though none deal directly with traditional monsters, the supernatural, or science fiction, all have one general endowment: superb imagination.

And that is exactly what this entire genre is all about: IMAGINATION. As mankind's only redeeming virtue, spell it in big, fat capital letters, if you please.

Considered from the standpoint of intelligent objectivism, imagination demands a broad and liberal mentality, not only for enjoyment and comprehension, but for conceptualization. Ever ready to debate this are those purist die-hards who will brook no thematic intermarriage. They will remonstrate vociferously that science fiction, fantasy, and horror are totally disparate and each has its own place. They will argue with all the evangelistic fervor of a born-again Fundamentalist that "if God had ordained that S-F, fantasy, and horror should live *ménage à trois,* then the Frankenstein monster would be in outer space and Dracula would have become a tycoon or gone into politics."

As most in the 1970s would agree, that's exactly what happened anyway. Stanley Kubrick provided audiences with a Frankenstein monster in outer space personified by Hal, the fiendish computer of *2001: A Space Odyssey.* Because of the news media, and especially TV, another type of "horror show" was in full view for the first time in history in the 1960s–70s. Massacres; assassinations; monstrous, Draculan proclivities in business and government; and a cancerous economy have made the public aware of hitherto unexplored areas of the macabre. Genre awareness was no longer the monopoly of hard-core SFantasy devotees.

Benefiting from the public's heightened sensibility, highly creative directors have been stimulated into successfully capturing facets of the human condition that were formerly skimmed over, or at best compromised, by banal writing and direction. Consequently, fantasy-horror has gone beyond fangs, fright wigs, or creatures that chirp, lope, and gibber in the night: *Klute* subtly and horrifically exemplifies proof of modern executive psychosis, building up to a stunning power-charged climax. *Walkabout's* early sequences are almost in a similar vein, shifting gradually into a variation of Hansel and Gretel, and reminiscent of *2001's* "Dawn of Man." *Straw Dogs* relates the experiences of a modern David who, in an effort to escape the evils of his former environment, finds another Goliath in a world peopled by monsters in human form. *Deliverance* could very well be the adventures of another Odysseus or a Jason who, with his friends, is bound on a watery journey through a stygian land inhabited by a latter-day Procrustes and his murderous trolls.

Nicholas Roeg's masterpiece, *Don't Look Now* (released in mid-December 1973), is the quintessence of modern horror. An element of precognition is injected so slightly that it could also be construed as macabre coincidence. Typical of the director's artistry, the film relies very little on dialogue and depends wholly on Roeg's superlative visual sense and ingenious use of film grammar to transform mundane locales into poetic horror. The opening scene, set in the blissful English countryside, unexpectedly shifts from tranquility to a sudden and traumatic nightmare. Involving some brilliant flashbacks, all of the ensuing scenes take place in Venice. As lensed by Roeg, though, Venice is a cadaverous baroque monolith; funereal, at times surreal, lonely, hinting of abandonment—a creaking, moldering fungus as only Poe or Lovecraft might have envisioned. A stark contrast to the living, bustling capital described by Shakespeare, Marco Polo, and Renaissance romanticists! The ending is also unique: resembling Little Red Riding Hood from afar, a small red-caped figure scurries in the darkness by a canal, then is seen meandering along eerie, twisting alleys. The film's innocent protagonist (Donald Sutherland), believing he is witnessing the miraculous return of his dead daughter, follows the figure until it is cornered. Turning around, knife in hand, the caped figure reveals itself to be a maniac who has been wanted for a series of fiendish killings—a dwarfish monstrosity, face and form a Goyaesque fright. But it's not so much the creature's gargoylian presence as its camouflage of innocence that climaxes the horror.

Paradoxically, the "new look" in filmic imagination is rooted in the early silent era. Full orchestras were then found only in the more important theaters, and piano or organ accompaniment provided the only aural atmosphere. Without sound-tracking as a crutch, filmmakers *had* to be visually oriented from the very start, although it would take time before film grammar was universally recognized and established. As stage drama gave way to screen entertainment, filmmaking became almost an overnight industry and quickly advanced in style.

By the mid-twenties film technique had already attained such sophistication that many directors could prove and flaunt their facile dexterity by sometimes nearly abandoning screen captions and allowing images alone to tell the story. Director F. W. Murnau (*Nosferatu*) and cinematographer Karl Freund (who later lensed *Metropolis*), carried this technique to the fullest extent by creating the world-acclaimed *The Last Laugh* (1924). The film industry was amazed that a film classic could be made without a single subtitle. As noted film historian Paul Rotha puts it: "*The Last Laugh* entirely justified the position of the cinema. . . . Not a written or spoken word is needed. Cinefiction in its purest form . . . exemplary of the rhythmic composition of the film."

The transition from silents to sound came too fast and created problems for most filmmakers that would last, on and off, for many years to come. It was as if visual techniques were virtually forgotten. Much of the industry appeared to fumble, often confused as to whether the spoken word or the picture was the thing. Obviously this regression had disastrous consequences. A majority of films evinced an affinity for garrulousness, subordinating imagery and even character development to an alarmingly low level; cameras appeared to be riveted to the floor, while actors seemed to chatter endlessly when they were not walking in or out of rooms, talking on phones, or hailing cabs that would carry them to more rooms.

Until visual esthetics would again be preeminent, the successful synthesis of sight and sound proved the rare exception. It's more than historically significant that from the 1920s until as recently as the 1960s, the bulk of such exceptions have consisted of SFantasy films.

Independent of imaginative filmmakers is that handful of stellar performers who have been gifted enough to spin their own webs of fantastic imagination. Because of their *presence*, even the thinnest genre film takes on attractive life, and a good film emerges a classic.

Reminiscing sadly over Hollywood's good old days in *Sunset Boulevard*, Gloria Swanson delivers one of her great lines to William Holden: "We didn't need dialogue. We had *faces* then!"

The two Chaneys, Karloff, Lugosi, Lorre, and Price have shown the world *faces* as well as *genius*. SFantasy film champions all, they *are* among the heroes of the horrors.

——CALVIN T. BECK——

xiv

Introduction

1890–1899

It is perhaps significant that the first creative director of films was a magician. When Georges Méliès attended the historic Paris exhibition of the Lumière brothers' Cinematographe on December 27, 1895, he immediately saw what no one else in the audience saw: the potential of film to communicate ideas of the fantastic. By May 1897 Méliès had constructed his own film studio at Montreuil.

The magic began: *The Vanishing Lady, The Astronomer's Dream, The Haunted Castle, The Laboratory of Mephistopheles, Slave Trading in a Harem, Faust and Marguerite, She* (based on H. Rider Haggard's 1887 novel), *The Man with Four Heads, Cinderella.*

By 1900 Méliès had made 244 short films.

1900–1910

Méliès' 1902 masterpiece, *A Trip to the Moon,* was such a success that he found it necessary to travel to the United States to prevent pirate prints from circulating; the common practice was to opaque a company's trademark from each individual frame. The Lubin Company committed the ultimate *faux pas;* not suspecting that their screening-room guest was Georges Méliès, they attempted to sell him a duped and opaqued print of his own *Trip to the Moon!*

Méliès delighted audiences throughout the decade with films like *The Kingdom of the Fairies, An Impossible Voyage* (to the sun), *The Merry Frolics of Satan, The Palace of the Arabian Nights, Tunneling the English Channel,* and *Civilization Through the Ages.* His influence was felt in the

1

United States. For example, at the Edison Company, Edwin S. Porter employed the Méliès style of film trickery for *Dreams of a Rarebit Fiend,* and all of the earliest known film gimmicks from stop-motion to double exposures were displayed in a sequence of surrealist nightmares which continually awaken the hero.

In 1908 the Selig Polyscope Company released the first *Dr. Jekyll and Mr. Hyde* (also titled *The Modern Dr. Jekyll*), a fifteen-minute film record of a touring company performing T. R. Sullivan's play adaptation of Robert Louis Stevenson's 1886 novel. The following year, the Nordisk Company of Copenhagen produced its own adaptation, *Den Skaebnesvangre Opfindelse,* which climaxed with the idea that Jekyll had dreamed it all. Also in 1909, both D. W. Griffith and the Edison Company simultaneously released film versions of the popular play, *The Devil.*

Two men, both with leanings toward fantasy, realized that film could be used in a creative way to animate their cartoons. Émile Cohl, in France, made white stick figures dance against a black background, creating *Phantasmagorie* (1908), *Drama Amongst the Puppets* (1908), and *The Joyous Microbes* (1909). Winsor McCay, creator of the remarkable "Little Nemo of Slumberland" comic strip for the New York *Herald* in 1905, found his inspiration in his son's flipbooks (which were quite common at the turn of the century), and set to work producing the thousands of drawings necessary for the "full-animation" effect. This was not as difficult a task for McCay as some writers have assumed, since he had been drawing obsessively all his life. He described the creation of his entertaining fantastic cartoons: "The greatest contributing factor to my success was an absolute craving to draw pictures all the time. I never saved my drawings. I would give them away if anybody wanted them or would throw them away. I drew on fences, blackboards in school, old scraps of paper, slates, sides of barns. I just could

not stop. Winsor, Jr., as a small boy, picked up several flippers of 'Magic Pictures'—the ancestor of the movies—from the street and brought them home to me. From this germ I evolved the modern cartoon movies in 1909. I made four thousand drawings of *Little Nemo* move; they were flashed on the screen in Hammerstein's Theatre in old New York. Then I drew *How a Mosquito Operates.*"

The year 1909 saw the birth of the science-fiction film with the British *Battle in the Clouds* (also titled *The Airship Destroyer*). A synthesis of the ideas of Jules Verne and H. G. Wells, it shows the inventor of a radio-controlled torpedo repelling a bombing attack on London by dirigibles.

1910–1919

1910 marked the first screen appearance of Mary Shelley's *Frankenstein* monster of 1818. The film was a one-reel adaptation by the Edison Company. The hirsute monster vanishes into nothingness at the end. Sadly, so did the film itself; no print of this important step forward in fantasy-film history is known to exist. Five years later, Percy Darrell Standing portrayed the Frankenstein monster in the Ocean Film Corporation's *Life Without Soul.* It, too, was destined to become a "lost film."

The disparate *Dr. Jekyll and Mr. Hyde* personalities reappeared again in an American version (1912) made by the Thanhouser Company in New Rochelle. It starred James Cruze, Marguerite Snow, and Florence LaBadie, the trio that created a box-office sensation two years later in the twenty-three-chapter *Million Dollar Mystery* serial. Carl Laemmle produced a 1913 *Dr. Jekyll and Mr. Hyde,* and that same year the British Kineto-Kinemacolor Company produced a version in color. Yet another interpretation was released in 1914 by the Starlight Company. Also in 1914, D. W. Griffith brought Edgar Allan Poe to the screen in *The Avenging Conscience*, a treatment of "The Tell-Tale Heart" and other familiar Poe themes, starring Henry B. Walthall.

Méliès, in 1911, made *Baron Munchausen* and then his greatest foray into fantasy, *The Conquest of the Pole* (1912), featuring a frightening Abominable Snowman of giant proportions. The following year, his studio stopped production; hopelessly in debt, Méliès discovered that audiences were demanding more sophisticated products. Fifteen years later, a journalist located the Montreuil movie magician selling candy and toys at a little kiosk in the Gare Montparnasse. He died in 1938 at a rest home in Orly.

In 1913 Winsor McCay (who was now drawing a comic strip titled "Dreams of a Rarebit Fiend" under the pseudonym "Silas") presented *Gertie, the Dinosaur* to a gathering of fellow newspaper cartoonists as Reisenweber's Restaurant in New York. The film, which shows the animated brontosaurus drinking and regurgitating an entire lake, interpolated a bit of live-action magic which might have surprised even Méliès: standing at the edge of the screen, McCay used sleight-of-hand to make an apple vanish, and Gertie, on screen, appeared to eat the apple. The show at Reisenweber's made an indelible impression on a young cartoonist named Paul Terry who was present that evening. He immediately began his own experiments at home; during the next forty years he produced fourteen hundred animated shorts, including the ever-popular *Mighty Mouse*.

Dinosaurs were also present in D. W. Griffith's *Man's Genesis* (1912), and a Griffith excursion into science-fiction, *The Flying Torpedo* (1916), is unfortunately yet another entry in the columns of lost films. Abel Gance's science-fictional *The Madness of Doctor Tube* (1915) used distortion effects to show Tube's insane experiments. The following year Gance depicted cosmic destruction in *The Zone of Death*. Another French director, Maurice Tourneur, created

an outstanding American film version of British illustrator-novelist George Du Maurier's mesmerizing *Trilby* (1916), starring Clara Kimball Young. *Heaven Ship* (1917) was a Danish excursion to Mars, and, in 1919, the British Gaumont company combined a romantic triangle with the romance of space in *First Men in the Moon*, loosely based on H. G. Wells' novel.

The cinema found its first true Poet of Darkness in this decade when Germany's Bioscop company released *The Student of Prague* (1913). Produced by and starring the celebrated German actor Paul Wegener in the dual role of a man destroyed by his *doppelgänger*—in this case, a mirror reflection of himself—the film achieved great power from Wegener's performance and from Danish director Stellan Rye's use of Prague's twisting back alleyways. Wegener returned the following year as the clay statue *Golem*, brought to life in ancient Prague by a mystical sign. In *Yogi* (1916), Wegener used camera trickery to suggest the presence of an invisible character, and, in *Rubezahl's Marriage* (1916), Wegener created the frightening Giant of the Silesian Mountains who unleashes natural disasters on unsuspecting picnickers. That same year in Germany, Bioscop scored a great success with its six-chapter *Homunculus* serial about a laboratory-created superman of evil design; each chapter is about an hour in length. In 1917, Wegener filmed both *The Pied Piper of Hamelin* and a sequel to *Golem*.

In 1919 Carl Mayer and Hans Janowitz wrote the controversial *Cabinet of Dr. Caligari*, a film classic which still possesses the power to grip an audience. The story concerns murders committed by Cesar the Somnambulist (Conrad Veidt) under the spell of traveling hypnotist Caligari (Werner Krauss). Abducting Jane (Lil Dagover), Caligari flees to an insane asylum. In an epilogue (an addition by director Robert Weine), it is revealed that Caligari heads this institution and that the entire story has been the fantasy of one of the

3

inmates. The film amounted to a personal vision, communicating the angst of its creators: Mayer had suffered a series of unpleasant experiences with a psychiatrist while in the army; Weine's father was a victim of insanity; Janowitz had witnessed a respectable gentleman near the scene of an unsolved 1913 Hamburg sex murder and was convinced not only that he had seen the killer but that the city streets abounded with bourgeois criminals who were never brought to trial. The film's twisted, tortured expressionistic sets were the creation of painters Hermann Warm and Walter Röhrig, who found in *Caligari* the perfect opportunity to execute the radical visual ideas of Berlin's avant-garde Der Stürm group.

The decade ended with Lon Chaney's emergence as "the Man of a Thousand Faces," horribly contorting his body for the faith-healing drama, *The Miracle Man* (1919), and the directorial debut of fantasist Friedrich Wilhelm Murnau with *Satanas* (1919), starring Conrad Veidt as Satan.

1920–1929

Caligari's 1920 opening in Berlin theaters was a critical success. Weine, Mayer, costume designer Walter Reimann, and cameraman Willie Hameister immediately began work on *Genuine*, another tale of murder featuring *outré* sets. *Caligari* co-author Janowitz wrote *Der Januskopf*, an adaptation of *Dr. Jekyll and Mr. Hyde*, altering the screen treatment to avoid payment for the original story. Directed by F. W. Murnau, the film, starring Conrad Veidt, has regrettably vanished. There were three other versions of *Jekyll* that same year: Hank Mann starred in the Arrow Film Corporation's version; Sheldon Lewis played the dual role in a Louis B. Mayer production with another it's-all-a-dream climax; and, at Paramount, the presence of John Barrymore brought the horror film both an aura of respectability and a masterful interpretation of the role.

The following year Murnau directed the atmospheric *Haunted Castle* (*Schloss Vogelod*), and in 1922, *Nosferatu*, which he based, without permission, on Bram Stoker's 1897 novel *Dracula*. The result was a suit by Stoker's widow and a court order that *Nosferatu* be destroyed. Fortunately the film survived, and Murnau's later success with *The Last Laugh* (1925) and *Sunrise* (1927) caused a demand for *Nosferatu* in the United States, where it was eventually released in 1929. Murnau's *Phantom* (1922) characterizes a man trapped in the vortex of his own fantasy life, and in *Faust* (1926), he composed bizarre scenes strikingly reminiscent of medieval woodcuts.

Lon Chaney was firmly established as the silent cinema's great horror star in Wallace Worsley's 1922 *A Blind Bargain* (as a hunchbacked ape-man), the same director's 1923 *Hunchback of Notre Dame* (as Quasimodo), Rupert Julian's 1925 *Phantom of the Opera* (as the hideously disfigured Phantom), and in a series of films directed by Tod Browning: the 1925 *Unholy Three* (as a ventriloquist pretending to be an old lady), the 1926 *Road to Mandalay* (as a one-eyed scoundrel), the 1927 *Unknown* (as the Armless Wonder of the circus), the 1927 *London After Midnight* (as a loathsome vampire), and the 1928 *West of Zanzibar* (as a crippled magician).

Three other directors of importance in this period were Rex Ingram (the 1926 *Magician*, based on demonologist Aleister Crowley); Benjamin Christensen (the 1929 *Seven Footprints to Satan*, based on A. Merritt's novel); and Paul Leni (the 1924 *Waxworks* with Conrad Veidt, Krauss, and Emil Jannings; the 1927 *Cat and the Canary*, and the 1928 adaptation of Victor Hugo's *The Man Who Laughs* with Veidt, Mary Philbin, and Olga Baclanova). Director Weine and Veidt teamed in 1925 for *The Hands of Orlac* (remade in 1935

4

as *Mad Love*), based on Maurice Renard's novel *Les Mains d'Orlac*.

Queen Victoria's favorite novelist, Marie Corelli, was adapted to twenties films by both D. W. Griffith (the 1925 *Sorrows of Satan*) and Carl Dreyer (the 1921 *Leaves from Satan's Book*); both were based on Corelli's 1895 *Sorrows of Satan* novel.

Dinosaurs returned to the screen in *The Lost World* (1925), a film that combined aspects of both science-fiction and horror in an adaptation of Arthur Conan Doyle's novel. Wallace Beery, Lewis Stone, and Bessie Love starred in this story of an Amazon expedition that discovers a plateau where prehistoric beasts still roam. The creatures were the design of special-effects man Willis O'Brien, and all the prehistoric films to follow were based on the pioneering efforts of O'Brien in the field of animating intricate models.

Fritz Lang's *Destiny* (1921), the story of two lovers separated by Death personified, influenced both Alfred Hitchcock and Raoul Walsh, who directed *The Thief of Bagdad* in 1924. In *Siegfried* and *Kriemhild's Revenge* (1924), Lang drew inspiration from the romantic and mythological fantasies of Swiss painter Arnold Böcklin to depict the Teutonic and Norse legends. This two-part epic (intended to be seen on successive evenings), featuring Siegfried's superhuman struggles while armed with a cloak of invisibility, is one of rare achievements in the genre of the folklore film. In *Metropolis* (1927) Lang called upon his training as an architect to construct a magnificent masterwork of science fiction. Inspired by the sight of the New York City skyline during a 1924 trip to America, Lang prophetically visualized exhausted, oppressed workers rebelling against the governor of a towering sterile city. Hitler found a similarity between the rocket in Lang's *Woman in the Moon* (1928) and the rocket experiments then being conducted in Germany; he ordered destruction of the film's negative, and it very nearly became a "lost film."

Lang's films typified the growth of technology, and it was technology, in the form of fully synchronized-sound motion pictures, that altered the shape of the film industry as the decade closed. Only one man, Walt Disney, truly understood the creative asset that sound provided, and in 1929 he was hard at work synchronizing dancing skeletons to music (*A Skeleton Dance*). As the King of Animated Fantasies, his greatest work lay ahead of him.

1930–1939

Inspired by the fifteenth-century Vlad the Impaler, Bram Stoker had startled the reading public with *Dracula*. In 1923 Hamilton Deane wrote the second play version of Stoker's novel; it had a successful opening the following year. Deane then revised his play for New York, collaborating with American writer John L. Balderston (author of the fantasy *Berkeley Square* and the 1952 sociological S-F film *Red Planet Mars*). This new revised play opened in October 1927 at the Fulton Theatre and starred the then-unknown Bela Lugosi. After a year on Broadway, the touring company broke all box-office records, and in 1930, rights to the play were acquired by Universal Pictures. Tod Browning directed and Lugosi repeated his stage triumph; had Lon Chaney not died of throat cancer in 1930, perhaps he would have played the part. The success of *Dracula* gave Browning license to delve further into screen terror. Some feel he went *too* far; the film was *Freaks* (1932), a sympathetic portrait of circus denizens with a nightmarish climax of grim retribution: Cleopatra (Olga Baclanova at the peak of her beauty), a circus trapeze performer, torments her sideshow co-workers (and tries poisoning to death a midget she married for his inheritance) until they are prompted to retaliate by turning her into a giant chicken. Based on the novel *Spurs*, by Tod Robbins, the potency of this film hinges to a large degree on Browning's use of genuine circus freaks (since the story would be ineffectual if acted in any other fashion). Theater managers, distributors, and audiences reacted negatively, and in some countries it was banned, with the result that Browning's last efforts, *Mark of the Vampire* (1935), *The Devil Doll* (1936), and *Miracles for Sale* (1939), were tame affairs. He disappeared from the film industry and died in 1962 at the age of eighty.

Zombies were introduced for the first time in *White Zombie* (1932), considered by some as *the* definitive horror film of at least the thirties and Bela Lugosi's greatest role.

Frankenstein (1931) by British director James Whale, featuring the Boris Karloff interpretation of the Monster, is the most famous horror film ever made. Its success has prompted dozens of sequels and variations, beginning with Universal reteaming Whale and Karloff for the 1935 *Bride of Frankenstein*, considered by many critics as the best of the series. In 1932 Karloff appeared as *The Mummy*, and played a murderous mute in Whale's *Old Dark House*. The next year Whale directed a fine atmospheric adaptation of H. G. Wells' *Invisible Man*, a striking film debut for Claude Rains.

Rains followed this film with an equally powerful performance in *Crime Without Passion* (1934). Written by Ben Hecht and Charles MacArthur, the story opens and closes with spectacular fantasy scenes showing the Furies which possess mankind swirling about in the heavens, gliding over Manhattan, and diving into the soul of a lawyer (Rains), prompting him to commit murder. Montage expert Slavko Vorkapich was responsible for many of the film's best moments.

Merian C. Cooper's *King Kong* (1935), with its marvelous Willis O'Brien special effects, is as popular today as when it was first released. The commercial windfall immediately prompted a pallid sequel, *Son of Kong*, which was rushed to completion and released only ten months after the original. Cooper's memorable 1935 *She*, one of the seven different screen adaptations of H. Rider Haggard's supernatural romantic adventure, still towers over all the other films based on this novel. Directed by Irving Pichel and Lansing C. Holden, spectacular sets and costumes surrounded actors Randolph Scott, Nigel Bruce, and Helen Gahagan (who later married Melvyn Douglas and became a congresswoman; she was deposed by Richard M. Nixon after a bitter insidious campaign in which he convinced voters that she was a Communist). But of all the hidden kingdom fantasies of the thirties, the best remembered is Frank Capra's *Lost Horizon* (1937), with its utopian visions of a peaceful world.

Lycanthropy was introduced as a theme in *Werewolf of London* (1935), starring Henry Hull as the werewolf who turns on his own wife (Valerie Hobson). Another common theme of the period was Death in human form and commonplace situations, as seen in *Death Takes a Holiday* (1934), with Fredric March as Death; and *Outward Bound* (1930), a Warner Brothers film version of the Sutton Vane play about passengers on an ocean liner sailing toward their own destinies. (A 1944 remake of *Outward Bound* and a 1971 remake of *Death Takes a Holiday* were not as effective as the originals.)

Science-fiction spectaculars of the thirties included the Bauhaus burlesque of *Just Imagine* (1930); the battle between construction workers and management in *Transatlantic Tunnel* (1935); the tidal-wave wreckage of New York City in the 1933 *Deluge* (based on the novel by S. Fowler Wright); the sociopolitical speculations of H. G. Wells, Alexander Korda, and William Cameron Menzies in *Shape of Things to Come* (1936); the sputtering rockets and ray guns of Universal's *Flash Gordon* (1936) and *Buck Rogers* (1939).

1940–1949

The decade began with Technicolor brightening the fantasy film: Ernest B. Schoedsack's *Dr. Cyclops* (1940); Walt Disney's *Fantasia* (1940) and *Dumbo* (1941); Arthur Lubin's 1943 *Phantom of the Opera* (with Claude Rains in the Lon Chaney role); and certain scenes of Albert Lewin's 1945 *Picture of Dorian Gray*.

The horror film sunk to a B-level in the forties, but one producer, Val Lewton, found that production costs were not necessarily synonymous with quality. He based his low-budget horror thrillers on a realistic approach and a premise quite similar to H. P. Lovecraft's idea of "the monster unseen." Lewton began as a story editor for David O. Selznick and soon found himself assigned to head an RKO unit planned for the production of double-bill programmers. The first film was *The Cat People* (1942). Lewton called his staff into his office for a conference outlining the approach to be taken. He then turned out the lights and proceeded to tell them a story in the dark. (This anecdote achieved its own degree of fame when it was incorporated into the 1952 film, *The Bad and the Beautiful*, with Kirk Douglas portraying a Lewton-like producer making a horror film.) The result of that initial conference was a tight suspenseful drama, directed by Jacques Tourneur, with sounds and shadows suggesting that the feline Simone Simon has the power of lycanthropy and can (when sexually threatened) change into a cat. The film is highlighted by its memorable scene of reverberating echoes in an indoor swimming pool blending with sounds that *might*—but not *quite*—be a screaming panther.

Praised by critic James Agee, the film opened a path for a new type of psychological thriller. Its "sequel," *The Curse of the Cat People* (1944), offered not only the directorial debut of Robert Wise but also a different kind of story that had nothing to do with cats; instead, it presented a subjective view of a child's "invisible playmate," all the more powerful because the adults are treated as insensitive and incapable of grasping the world of childhood fantasy. Lewton's *Leopard Man* (1943), again directed by Tourneur, has one of cinema's greatest moments of pure fear: a child, chased through the streets by a leopard, arrives at the door of her home only to find that her mother doesn't *believe* her and won't let her in. The scene ends with a sickening thud against the door as the mother stares at the slow seepage of blood under the door and into the room. The attack is never shown. The film is based on a Cornell Woolrich story, "Black Alibi."

Richard Dix and Russell Wade starred in Lewton's *The Ghost Ship* (1943). Directed by Mark Robson, it presented a psychological portrait of an authority-obsessed captain. Robson also directed for Lewton the 1943 *Isle of the Dead*, with its powerful scene of a woman buried alive. The poetic *I Walked with a Zombie* (1943), directed by Tourneur, perhaps will always remain the definitive "zombie" film, second only to *White Zombie*; it captured the imagination of a generation that had been enthralled by William Seabrook's classic study of Haiti, *The Magic Island*. Lewton said, "They may never recognize it, but what I'm going to give them in *I Walked with a Zombie* is 'Jane Eyre in the West Indies.'" The title derived from a Hearst Sunday newspaper series. In Lewton's *The Seventh Victim* (1943), directed by Robson, evil lurks in the cityscape as a girl searches for her sister and stumbles onto a cult of Greenwich Village devil-worshipers.

Robert Wise returned to direct Karloff and Lugosi in the now-classic *Body Snatcher* (1945), based on the Robert Louis Stevenson short story. The Lewton cycle ended with Karloff as the sadistic headmaster of an eighteenth-century London insane asylum in *Bedlam* (1946). Lewton's influence was strongly felt in the later films of Robert Wise, particularly *The Haunting* (1963), and in Tourneur's 1958 *Curse of the Demon*. *The Uninvited* (1943) directed by Lewis Allen (who later produced *Lord of the Flies and Fahrenheit 451*) is an unpretentious ghost story that seems to borrow the Lewton style.

Universal continued to exploit their thirties' horror creations during the forties with such sequels as *The Wolf Man* (1941), *Ghost of Frankenstein* (1942), *Frankenstein Meets the Wolfman* (1943), *House of Frankenstein* (1944), *House of Dracula* (1945), and eventually sputtered out with *Abbott and Costello Meet Frankenstein* (1948), in which Karloff sadly burlesques the character he made famous.

A key film of the decade is the brilliant British *Dead of Night* (1945), an Ealing Studio anthology of stories by H. G. Wells, E. F. Benson, John V. Baines, and Angus MacPhail. The cast included Michael Redgrave, Sally Ann Howes, Miles Malleson, and Mervyn Johns. Outstanding are the tales of a ventriloquist controlled by his dummy, and a mirror that reflects another room where a murder was once committed. All the stories are linked together in the finale.

The decade ended with the triumphant return of Willis O'Brien, who won an Academy Award for his special effects on *Mighty Joe Young* (1949), an animated gorilla who holds Terry Moore aloft while she plays "Beautiful Dreamer" on a grand piano. Assisting O'Brien on this film was Ray Harryhausen, who continued to develop and polish the art of animating model creatures throughout the fifties, sixties, and seventies.

1950–1959

Puppet producer George Pal entered feature-film production with *The Great Rupert* (1950), about an animated trained squirrel, and the prophetic *Destination Moon*, released in the spring of 1950, right in the middle of the postwar science-fiction boom. Now outdated by history, the film gained a great deal of authenticity from its moon-fissure settings by Ernst Fegté, the background paintings of S-F illustrator Chesley Bonestell, and the technical advice of German rocket expert Hermann Oberth (who had, with Willy Ley, also served as advisor on Lang's *Woman in the Moon*). Although preceded by the more imaginative low-budget *Rocketship S-M* (1950), Pal was immediately enthroned as the King of Hollywood Science-Fiction, and studio personnel went scurrying through story departments in search of optioned S-F properties. Howard Hawks delivered *The Thing* (1951), based on a pulp fiction story (that originally appeared in *Astounding Science Fiction* magazine) "Who Goes There?" by Don A. Stuart (pseudonym for *Astounding Science Fiction* editor John W. Campbell). Robert Wise at Fox directed *The Day the Earth Stood Still* (1951), based on Harry Bates' "Farewell to the Master." To this day the film remains a powerful antiwar statement and is a popular favorite of young people.

Pal returned with *When Worlds Collide* (1951), an Edwin Balmer–Philip Wylie novel purchased by Paramount in 1932 when its serialization in *Blue Book* magazine stunned readers. The film was, in fact, announced by Paramount as a 1934 Cecil B. De Mille production and was then shelved until Pal saw the special-effects potential. The talents of Bonestell were once again employed in designing the production. A sequel—written in the thirties by Balmer and Wylie to satisfy the demands of *Blue Book* readers—has, oddly, never been filmed. Arch Oboler made a small gem, *Five* (1951), on the end-of-the-world-survivor theme later explored by *On the Beach* (1959) and *The World, the Flesh and the Devil* (1959). In 1953 Pal produced *Houdini* and an adaptation of Wells' *War of the Worlds*, another property that had been collecting dust for years in the Paramount story department. With this motion picture, Pal found the perfect director for his concepts—special-effects expert Byron Haskin. The two worked closely in the years to come; in 1954 they lensed *The Naked Jungle*, starring Charlton Heston as an Amazon farmer who battles a horde of ants. Based on Carl Stephenson's short story "Leiningen vs. the Ants," a radio adaptation on CBS' "Escape" in the forties had made the tale a popular favorite. The Haskin–Pal *Conquest of Space* (1955), which takes viewers on a not-too-convincing Mars trip, is based on the Willy Ley–Chesley Bonestell nonfiction speculative book of the same title. In 1958 Pal released *tom thumb,* a project that had interested him for over a decade.

Another fantasist to make his mark in the fifties was Jack Arnold. In 1953 he directed the 3-D *It Came from Outer Space,* based on a story concept by Ray Bradbury about peaceful space visitors harassed by hostile Earthmen. Arnold's *Creature from the Black Lagoon* (1954) introduced a monster that equaled Universal's creatures of the thirties. The *Revenge of the Creature* sequel (1955) explored further the combination of fear and eroticism that had delighted audiences in the initial film. *A Creature Walks Among Us* (1956) brought about a definite loss of interest in this character by both the audience and Universal; it was the last film in the series. Arnold's great triumph is *The Incredible Shrinking Man* (1957), which, even today, retains an epic and philosophical quality with its intense concentration on survival and its ambiguous and inconclusive ending. Arnold's *Space Children* (1958) not only expresses an antiwar statement but also seems as antiadult as *The Curse of the Cat People. The Monolith Monsters* (1957), from a Jack Arnold script, is something of a surrealist nightmare with its giant stone blocks shuttling across the countryside. Arnold's *Tarantula* (1955) was preceded by the first and best of the giant insect movies, *Them!* (1954).

Vincent Price established himself as a major horror star during this decade in *House of Wax* (1953), *The Mad Magician* (1954), *The Fly* (1958), and *The Return of the Fly* (1959).

The Blob (1958), like *The Fly* and *The Thing*, was launched with an equally bloated publicity campaign, exciting audiences before the release of the film; but promoters avoided mention of the fact that the concept of an all-devouring bloblike entity had been previously introduced to films in *The Creeping Unknown* (1955), based on the popular BBC-TV serial, "The Quatermass Experiment," by Nigel Kneale. *Invasion of the Body Snatchers* (1956), based on a Jack Finney novel, was directed by Don Siegel with uncredited work on the screenplay by Sam Peckinpah. An imaginative thriller concerned with aliens who are able to counterfeit zombie-like human beings, the film owes its thrust to a conviction by Siegel that most human beings are, indeed, quite zombie-like. *This Island Earth* (1955) took filmgoers on a guided tour of an outer-space civilization, as did the magnificent *Forbidden Planet* (1956), a loose S-F translation of Shakespeare's *Tempest*, featuring special effects by Disney craftsmen.

In 1956 George Orwell's pessimistic vision of political oppression, *1984,* became a tightly directed, handsome British film of overwhelming power. (Orwell's novel has never been filmed in the United States— where, no doubt, it would seem too much like an outdated version of the real thing. Closed-circuit cameras already monitor street activity in Mount Vernon, New York, and other American communities just as described by Orwell.) Other British science-fiction came from Hammer Studios and director Terence Fisher in *Spaceways* (1953) and *Four-Sided Triangle* (1952), in which two scientists who both love the same girl create an exact living replica of her. The success of Fisher's *Curse of Frankenstein* (1957) led to a recharting of previously explored territory; virtually any idea filmed in black-and-white by Universal in the thirties was presented in large-screen color: *Horror of Dracula* (1958) was followed by *The Revenge of Frankenstein* (1958), and in 1959 *The Hound of the Baskervilles, The Man Who Could Cheat Death, The Mummy,* and *Stranglers of Bombay.*

After a decade of big bugs and streamlined spaceships, horror had returned, with a British accent.

1960–1969

In 1960 Terence Fisher directed *The Two Faces of Dr. Jekyll* (with Mr. Hyde as a young smiling psychopath whom women find attractive), *Brides of Dracula,* and *Sword of Sherwood Forest.* But *Curse of the Werewolf* (1961) shows Fisher at his peak. Adapted by producer Anthony Hinds (under the pseudonym of John Elder) from Guy Endore's *Werewolf of Paris* classic, the film is strengthened by a grim combination of realism and fantasy in its opening scenes that depicts the birth of the werewolf after its mute mother is raped by a crazed degenerate dungeon prisoner of twenty years. Oliver Reed's magnetic screen presence in this film was the best portrayal of lycanthropy ever filmed.

George Pal directed H. G. Wells' *Time Machine,* winning a 1960 Academy Award for special effects, and in 1964 the Haskin–Pal team went to Death Valley to make the visually viable *Robinson Crusoe on Mars,* which closely parallels the episodes in Daniel Defoe's famed 1719 novel. In *The Power* (1967), Pal and Haskin, in tandem, soft-pedaled the special effects for a well-acted tense drama adapted from Frank M. Robinson's novel about the battle against a malevolent supermind.

"*Psycho* all came from Robert Bloch's book," said Alfred Hitchcock. "Joseph Stefano contributed dialogue mostly—no ideas."

Bloch detailed the film's creation this way: "When Hitchcock bought the book he bought it blind from my agent in New York. I was not told who bought it. All I received was a flat offer. He asked if I was available to do the screenplay. The person he talked to was an MCA agent. And it took that agent three seconds to say, 'No, Bloch is not available.' Because at that time MCA was in the talent business and wanted to sell one of their own clients. Well, someone else got the assignment and gave Hitchcock a treatment which was turned down. He then hired Mr. Stefano who worked three weeks on the screenplay. Hitchcock did the rest. Nobody from the start, except Hitchcock, wanted this picture. It was an aggravation to Paramount. It was considered too far out, too shocking, too daring for its time. They wanted to change the title, the story, everything. But, fortunately, Hitchcock had the kind of contract by which he could exercise control."

The control Hitchcock exercised is, perhaps, his peak achievement in audience manipulation. The 1961 film benefited from a shrieking Bernard Herrmann score and a gifted interpretation of the lead character by Anthony Perkins. (His impact in this part was so lasting that he found himself typecast in similar roles until the 1972 *Play It as It Lays.*) *The Birds* (1963) created terror from the inexplicable as thousands of birds attack humans on California's Bodega Bay. Adapted by Evan Hunter from a short story by Daphne Du Maurier (granddaughter of the author of *Trilby*), the film has many memorable moments, particularly a bird's-eye overhead traveling matte shot as a service station erupts in flames.

Roman Polanski limned a terrifying intimate portrait of schizophrenia in *Repulsion* (1965) by filming his subject's hallucinations as if they were stark realities. Polanski's *Cul-de-Sac* the following year treats the transferral of fantasy and reality in a Samuel Beckett-like fashion. In *The Fearless Vampire Killers* (1967) he brought a combination of atmospheric suspense and subdued parody to the classic vampire theme. *Rosemary's Baby* (1968), adapted by Polanski with almost no changes whatsoever from Ira Levin's novel, proved to be an immense popular success, engaging the sensibilities of many filmgoers who usually ignore fantastic films.

The decade was also notable for the Roger Corman adaptations of Poe: *The House of Usher* (1960); *The Pit and the Pendulum* (1961); *Premature Burial* (1961); *Tales of Terror* (1962); *The Haunted Palace* (1963—advertised as a Poe story but actually based on H. P. Lovecraft's "The Case of Charles Dexter Ward," with a brief fragment of a Poe poem seen during the end titles); *The Raven* (1963); *The Masque of the Red Death* (1964); and *Tomb of Ligeia* (1964). Vincent Price starred in each of these films; by the time the series ended, his preeminence as the reigning horror star was firmly established.

Lovecraft received his first "official" adaptation in the disappointing *Die, Monster, Die!* (1965), a laughable variation on "The Colour from Out of Space," that appeared originally as a pulp magazine story in the '30s. The film's only noteworthy point was the casting of Karloff in his first dramatic monster role since *Son of Frankenstein* (1939). *The Shuttered Room* (1966), based on a Lovecraft–August Derleth collaboration, is the only film to truly capture the fetid essence of Lovecraft's eldritch fiction. It was followed by *The Dunwich Horror* (1969), an unfaithful and specious translation of one of his greatest stories. All of these films, however, plus several later television adaptations ("Cool Air" and "Pickman's Model" on "Night Gallery") popularized Lovecraft among young people and brought about a belated literary acceptance for the works of this great master of weird writing.

Led by a desire to make "something like *King Kong*," producer Arthur P. Jacobs filmed *Planet of the Apes* (1967), based on Pierre Boulle's novel. Oddly, Ja-

cobs encountered much of the same initial resistance to this project that Merian C. Cooper had faced before beginning *Kong*.

The Innocents (1961) was based on William Archibald's play of the same title (which, in turn, was based on Henry James' famous 1897 short novel). This story has been adapted to almost every media, including an opera by Benjamin Britten, but none has succeeded as well as this Jack Clayton film in dramatizing James' sense of lurking evil. Truman Capote was part of the screenwriting team.

Burn, Witch, Burn (1962) is a superb British production of Fritz Leiber's story "Conjure Wife," first filmed in 1944 as *Weird Woman* (an "Inner Sanctum Mystery") and later seen as a live television drama starring Larry Blyden. Screenwriters Richard Matheson and Charles Beaumont obviously sought to retain feeling for black magic. Director Robert Wise raised the spirit of Val Lewton in *The Haunting* (1963), a story of mediums, lesbianism, and the supernatural based on Shirley Jackson's *The Haunting of Hill House*. Peter Bogdanovich made his directorial debut by starring Karloff in *Targets* (1967), which hit the bull's-eye with effective social comment on American middle-class violence. Had it not been for *Psycho*, there might have been more interest in Michael Powell's *Peeping Tom* (1960), a British psychological thriller about a film-maker who commits murders and simultaneously documents them on film.

The sixties saw science-fiction protagonists grappling with thought-provoking ideas rather than big bugs. Joseph Losey's *The Damned* (1961) for Hammer concerns a secret government project in which children are bred to survive nuclear radiation. The film was cut by Columbia, given a 1964 United States release, and retitled *These Are the Damned*, perhaps in an attempt to make audiences believe it was somehow connected with the excellent *Village of the Damned* (1960), loosely based on John Wyndham's *Midwich Cuckoos*,

11

and its superior sequel, *Children of the Damned* (1963). *Creation of the Humanoids* (1962), about the leader of an anti-android faction who learns that he is already an android, received a great deal of attention after Andy Warhol called it the best movie of the year. Chris Marker's highly praised short, *La Jetée* (1963), uses still photographs to tell a story of World War III underground survivors and a trip backward in time. *Panic in the Year Zero* (1962), directed by, and starring, Ray Milland, as a response to the Civil Defense controversy of the early sixties, follows one man's efforts to save his family during a nuclear attack. Jean-Luc Godard in *Alphaville* (1965), inspired by Richard Matheson's vampire novel *I Am Legend*, outlined an oppressive computer-ruled society where any nonconformity or display of emotion results in execution. Exterior scenes were shot at night on present-day Paris locations. Godard stated, "I do not know whether I have made a film about the world of tomorrow or the world of today." This theme received a different kind of treatment from another French director, François Truffaut, in *Fahrenheit 451* (1966), based on Ray Bradbury's 1950 novel about a book-burning future in which intellectuals are subjected to political persecution. Both are remarkably prophetic works.

Ikaria XB1 (1963—also titled *Voyage to the End of the Universe*), a Czech film about life aboard a giant starship, seems reminiscent of a Richard Matheson short story, "Third from the Sun" (filmed during the fifties as an early episode of television's "Twilight Zone"). *Planet of the Vampires* (1965), directed by Mario Bava from a Deke Heyward–Ib Melchior screenplay, employed a skilled visual flair in its story of space visitors under attack by an alien entity beyond their comprehension. In John Frankenheimer's *Seconds* (1966), a middle-aged New York commuter learns of an organization that offers a technological Fountain of Youth; oddly, Frankenheimer denies that this film is science-fiction. Richard Fleischer took viewers on a *Fantastic Voyage* (1966) through the inside of a human body. *Barbarella* (1968), directed by Roger Vadim at a cost of three million dollars, gave cinematic life to the comic-strip fantasy of Jean-Claude Forest; the story is an ultimate extrapolation of man's hedonistic tendencies. The last of the British "Quatermass" serials was filmed in 1967 by Hammer. Titled *Five Million Years to Earth,* the film gains a great deal of power from lead actor Andrew Keir and Roy Ward Baker's convincing directorial treatment of Nigel Kneale's premise: demon legends are revealed to have some validity after the discovery of an alien spaceship in a London subway excavation.

In 1963 Stanley Kubrick directed *Dr. Strangelove or How I Stopped Worrying and Learned to Love the Bomb*, a cynical and satirical riposte at the military meat-heads who could easily plunge the world into nuclear disaster. In 1969, Kubrick unveiled his masterwork, *2001—A Space Odyssey*, a statement on tools, technology, and the next step in man's evolution. Heightened by Kubrick's brilliant choices of soundtrack music, the film will undoubtedly still be revered by the year 2001, especially if restored to original Cinerama form.

HEROES OF THE HORRORS

Lon Chaney, Sr.

1883-1930

Superior and, undoubtedly, more fantasy-horror films were produced by Germany, from World War One through the twenties, than anywhere in the world, including the United States, which was ahead of everyone in general film production and profits. Germany even had some of the world's finest horror artists ever seen on the screen: Werner Krauss, Conrad Veidt, Paul Wegener, Max Schreck, and especially Rudolf Klein-Rogge—the grand archetype of all diabolical intellectuals and mad scientists that followed.

Great as they all were, Lon Chaney made the most indelible impression in America, not so much because of his roles but because of what he *did* with them.

His understanding of pathos and his ability to humanize even the most bizarre characterization emblazoned portrayals upon the screen that were among the most unique of their time; to this date, nearly all remain unforgettable.

The late Irving Thalberg, who worked with Chaney since his early MGM days, and later was in direct charge when he became the head of Universal's production office, offered the following touching eulogy at Chaney's funeral:

"The actor is a very special human being. There are only a few who possess his peculiar magic, that extraordinary ability to make us feel, to lift us out of our own existence, and make us believe in the

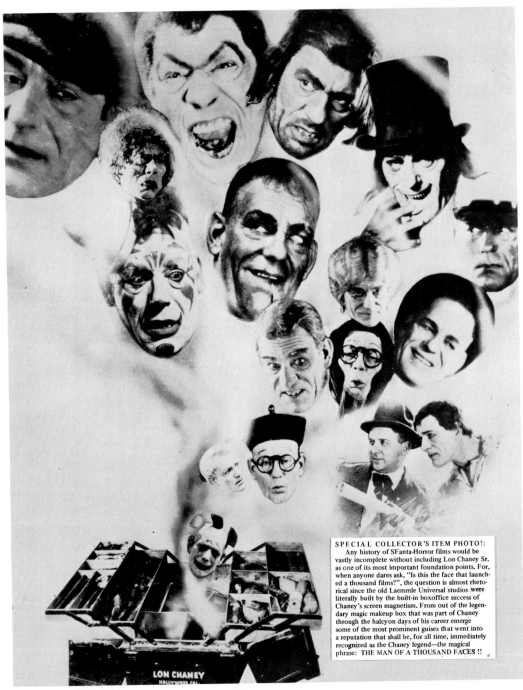

Some of the characterizations originated by "the Man of a Thousand Faces."

16

world of make-believe. I am speaking of the great ones, those whom audiences selected and set apart, some no longer here to enchant you, but who will always be remembered.

"We cannot replace these personalities. There can be only one of each, born out of their own personal joys and sorrows, like precious stones reflecting the warmth and color in their particular origins. Life shapes them in wondrous ways, often beautiful—sometimes with flaws—but all quite rare. When that stone is polished and given a proper setting, it shines brightly, casting its star-glow and warming the hearts of the people of the world. Such a one was Lon Chaney—a diamond in the rough—for he could be very hard. But let's examine him closely, look behind the makeup, the many masks, and see what happened to this strange and interesting man to give him those sharp edges, those facets that made him glitter, that made him great! Great not only because of his God-given talent but because he used that talent to illuminate certain dark corners of the human spirit. He showed the world the souls of those people who were born different than the rest.

"To understand why he was destined for this, we would only have to go back to any day of his boyhood in the town of Colorado Springs—not a very easy boyhood—for his parents were . . . different."

And both being deaf mutes, they were unusual parents, indeed, for a baby called Alonzo Chaney, born on April Fool's Day, 1883. Although his maternal grandmother had given birth to four offspring who were all deaf mutes, Lon's mother had four normal children, of whom Lon was the second.

Theater was in Lon's blood from practically the very start of his life. Despite her handicap, his mother was in charge of children's school projects that also involved pantomime plays and one-act sketches, many "starring" little three-year-old Lon. Responsibilities began piling up for the youngster at a very early age; before he

was ten he quit school because his mother became disabled by crippling inflammatory rheumatism, requiring him to care for her and his little sister and brother. By the age of twelve, Lon secured work as a prop boy in a local Colorado Springs theater where his older brother John had a job. But his father—a barber who appreciated the value of a dollar more than the average unhandicapped man—felt that one member of the family in the theater was enough and consequently financed Lon to take an interior decorating job in Denver. The youngster had already done other odd jobs, including summer work as a Pike's Peak guide.

Lon never regretted these varied experiences. Being the child of deaf-mute parents taught him patience and gave him the ability to communicate with all of his mind and body; working as a stagehand and as an interior decorator taught him to appreciate the sensitivity, importance, and soul of hardworking craftsmen, and to the very end of his life he proudly retained full membership in the stagehands' union.

But after three years as one of the best men at Cortdez and Feldhauser's (Denver's largest drapery house) the theater beckoned again through his brother John. He wrote Lon that he and the local stagehands' union were going to stage a comic opera called *Said Pasha* and they wanted Lon to assist them. Lon charged out of his room like a racehorse from the starting gate, gave immediate notice of resignation to the drapery firm, and joined his brother.

If *Said Pasha* had gone the way of most amateur productions, the screen might never have had its "Man of a Thousand Faces." But the operetta was a success, and it made money. The Chaney brothers were enthralled by the results, and mental gears began whirling around various other "ideas." Lon was a natural dancer. His agile mind and sharp eyes, which, during his film days, could snatch an idea from another's mind before it was even articulated, could then grab a routine from beneath the very toes of any vaude-villian. Buck and wing, tap, soft-shoe came easily to him. Lon polished his repertoire of dances and cultivated his comedic talents.

With their small funds and great ambitions, the Chaney brothers produced another show. And with much self-confidence they did Gilbert and Sullivan's *The Mikado*, were cocky enough to engage professional actors as their principals, and astute enough to limit the local talent to chorus and walk-on roles. This production was an even greater success! Self-assurance now covering them like a tent, the boys felt every bit like professional producers, and they decided to take their company on the road.

Their chief effort was to be an opera called *Fra Diavolo*, but they were perfectly willing to stage anything else that the cast could sing. They hired a prima donna named Mabel Day; her husband, Leslie Stowe, was their character man, and Charles Holmes, their tenor. They also wrote down on their books "L. Chaney," who, in addition to playing the principal comedy roles, was in charge of wardrobe and transportation.

So, in 1901, as vaudeville and legitimate theater flourished all over the country, even in the most remote towns and hamlets, the Chaney brothers felt that the world was now their oyster. But unhappily, after a long tour through nearly every region of Colorado, they began running into financial adversities, and brother John decided to sell out to Charles Holmes. Lon, however, remained with the company as it traveled even farther afield through the South and Florida. Twelve dollars a week was his average paycheck in those days—nothing by future cost-of-living standards, but enough to keep a young man comfortable and well fed at a time when room and board didn't cost more than $1.25 a day, and often less. Four years of perseverance and work in his brother's former company had given the resource-ful Lon tremendous experience. And romance at last came into his life when in 1905, during engagements with another company in Oklahoma City, he met the lovely Cleva Creighton, a fifteen-year-old choir singer who had sought work with his troupe. With the approval of Cleva's parents, they were married three days after their first meeting; a year later the Son of Chaney, Creighton, was born.

Now with three mouths to feed, life could have been an ordeal if Cleva wasn't also employed in various singing roles. The next few years resembled a Cook's tour of North America, and the young Chaney family found itself cruising with one stock company after another from the Carolinas to Halifax, Nova Scotia, and westward through mining and lumber camps to Vancouver. Lon claimed that he probably got to know every good and bad rooming house *alive* . . . with roaches and bedbugs. As was so often the case, a company would fold unexpectedly, and when this occurred Lon would have to count his pennies. Even under such financial hardship, providing food for his family presented little difficulty, since local saloons supplied all the free lunch one could cadge on a nickel's worth of beer and—like a scene from a Chaplin comedy—Lon could be seen walking away, overcoat pockets bulging with a variety of wrapped cheese, meat, and bread, after eating a hefty lunch himself.

Following a lean period and a stage-managing job in Chicago (then stock-company booking headquarters for the entire country), he signed a contract to do musical sketches seven times daily, seven days a week, for the Olympic Theater in Los Angeles. After half a year of this—in addition to working for the Grand Opera House Company, where he met such upcoming luminaries as Roscoe "Fatty" Arbuckle and future film star and director Robert Z. Leonard—he was engaged as a stage manager by several vaudeville and comic-opera companies, and this job took him from one end of California to the other.

Lon's marriage, however, was gradually disintegrating. Perhaps he was too engrossed in his own career; certainly, in later years, when he had attained stardom, no one could deny that he was self-centered and almost antisocial, though he must have been well-intentioned and sincerely thought that he wasn't hurting anyone. In the final analysis, there could only be one star in the Chaney family, and rivalry developed between him and Cleva when, because of her beauty, talent, and charms, she was earning better wages and excelling in show business while he was still unrecognized and struggling. Petty quarrels developed into bitter harangues and drawn-out fights over Lon's insistence that she should be more of a homemaker and mother than a glamor queen. Pressure mounted and, finally, driven almost out of her mind by aggravation, Cleva tried taking her life backstage one night while Lon was performing. Feeling contrite, Lon remained constantly at her bedside in the hospital, but on her complete recovery he left immediately. He then assumed complete custody of Creighton and never went back to Cleva again.

By 1914 Lon had been making a complete transition from stage to movie work for two years, and was happy to realize that they needed a versatile character actor in the young film colony. The pay, also, was much better—and steady. He could see the handwriting on the wall—to lure audiences, theaters in which he performed were becoming more dependent on fast-moving featurettes and, later, on little Chaplin comedies and hundreds of other one- and two-reel programmers and gradually cutting down on their live stage acts; a few of the smaller theaters even switched over entirely to films.

In April of that year Lon divorced Cleva and the next year married an old friend, Hazel Hastings. Cleva's own career was wrecked, her suicide attempt having permanently injured her voice; but, gallantly, she showed no resentment and even seemed heroic by accepting most of the blame for the breakup of the marriage. All the while Hazel was trying to be a devoted mother and wife, Creighton was misled into believing that his real mother, Cleva, had died. The boy never forgot his beautiful mother and how much he had loved her, and when he learned a few years later that he had been deceived, his relationship with his father was seriously impaired for a very long time.

Lon joined Universal Studios, and though he appeared in dozens of comedies and action shorts, his true fame was still years ahead; yet he was being recognized as a very gifted and above-average supporting player. *The Universal Weekly* (Universal's trade journal) remarked in its April 25, 1914 edition that in *The Tragedy of Whispering Creek*

> Mr. Chaney has used his own ideas in working out the character, a pervert, in this play, and what he has given us is startling to an unusual degree. True, he paints a horrible picture for us—one that is apt to cause a feeling of revulsion. But that is as it should be. In fact, Mr. Chaney has created a *new* character— one that will live long—that will be copied as a newer standard by others.

Stardom wasn't of prime importance to Lon—he was working steadily and for better pay than at any time before in his life; he thought that only a handful of film people like Chaplin, Fairbanks, and Mary Pickford emerged as reigning and wealthy celebrities. So long as the world of film entertainment required good character players, he felt he would always be in demand, and this satisfied him. But his wife Hazel wasn't so easily pleased; she knew he was an extremely talented man, far more than the majority of featured players reaping bigger harvests. At her urging he requested a special conference with Universal's studio manager, William Sistrom; the topic of conversation: a better salary—fifty dollars a week more than his seventy-five dollar average. Sistrom's reaction was negative; he pointed out in great detail that character actors of Lon's "ilk" weren't worth more than one hundred per week . . . take it or leave it. For the first time Lon was fully cognizant of how the studio management had been short-changing him; all along they had realized how unusually competent and gifted he had been, not only as a fine performer but also as a director and writer of many neat one- and two-reelers. Unable to ever forgive or forget Sistrom's unconscionable action, Lon, years later, made it a moral point of getting fifty dollars a week more added to his contracts, regardless of how much he was offered.

It was late in the year of 1918 that Lon, no longer an unknown, made his decision to leave Universal for greener pastures, thinking that other doors would now open to Lon Chaney the artist. At that particular time, however, the film industry was in a state of upheaval: major companies were fighting for dominance while smaller ones were trying to stay alive, and the flurry of such excitement and competitive warfare created a tight job market for many freelancers. Lon found it rough going and nearly regretted walking out of Universal. He was almost on the brink of returning to the studio's unappreciative, low-paying grind when William S. Hart, one of the screen's biggest money-making stars, asked for Chaney to appear opposite him in *Riddle Gawne*, Hart's next major production. Hart had for some time been aware of Lon's unusual ability and, despite his studio management's insistence that a short (approximately five feet, five-and-a-half inches) Chaney might not measure up too well against Hart's more than six-foot height, he insisted on having Chaney for *Riddle Gawne*, and told management their arguments were ridiculous.

Chaney's appearance in the prestigious Hart film paved the way to roles in many

other productions. Within a short period Lon began to be in demand as one of Hollywood's most versatile and unusual character players for a variety of characterizations that ran the gamut from gangsters, cowboys, and pirates, to comedy, beggars, straight types, and cripples.

Around mid-1919 Lon was summoned by director George Loane Tucker to audition for an extremely offbeat role in *The Miracle Man*—that of Frog, a twisted cripple who is restored to normalcy through faith-healing. Tucker felt the demanding role could be played only by a contortionist. Lon experimented in various positions the night before the audition, trying to sink into the character's personality to understand him better; while mulling over the role, he unconsciously crossed his legs, looked at them, and suddenly realized that with a slight twist here and there he could easily assume the desired effect. The next day the part was his. The film was not only a box-office hit but it also brought Lon greater recognition, even though his $125-per-week salary (better, of course, than anything he had ever had) was hardly commensurate with his success and the studio's profits. Consequently, when he demanded $500 to appear in *The Penalty*, he got it without any argument.

Lon's roles were now bigger and more colorful in far more important films. He scored triumphantly in the part of Ricardo, the pock-marked villain, in *Victory*, adapted from Joseph Conrad's novel and directed by Maurice Tourneur (father of Jacques Tourneur, director of *Curse of the Demon* and other memorable screen fantasies). Again under Tourneur's direction, Lon played *two* pirate roles in a thrilling version of Stevenson's *Treasure Island*, appearing as the blind, evil Pew and as Merry.

The remarkable fact of Lon Chaney's film career was that while he didn't appear in more than seven or eight films which could be classified as "pure" horror, he himself was such a strange and involved personality that most of his roles were of a profoundly macabre character. Perhaps it may have been the very nature of silent films that inspired such mood and qualities, at least in an actor so fanatically dedicated to his art as Chaney; for, as has been said by many a film historian, once sound took over, actors were using their voices a lot more and their bodies less. Before sound, directors had to make fullest use of the visual to overcome the limitations of silence. And only the most expressive performers could survive. Chaney went a great deal further; and though early film audiences and production executives would have scoffed or have been appalled by the very thought, Lon was in all sincerity limning his weird, offbeat, and villainous roles with all of the facets that would be one day regarded as basic ground rules for horror-film acting.

Appropriately, Lon's next film under Tourneur was, "officially," his first excursion into horror—*The Glory of Love*, the first of its kind and the precursor of filmic essays in the mold of *Mystery of the Wax Museum* and *House of Wax*. As the mad owner of a waxworks exhibition, Lon has evil designs concerning a young man he hopes to convert into one of his wax models. The finished movie was considered so grim that its release was held up for three years; finally, in 1923, it was distributed under the title *While Paris Sleeps*.

Twenty-two years later an evil surgeon would purposely amputate Ronald Reagan's legs in *King's Row* without seriously distorting his victim; but in the 1920 movie, *The Penalty*, the same treatment turned Chaney into a warped criminal leader who made audiences gasp as he hobbled about in leather boot stumps. Swearing vengeance on all his enemies, particularly the surgeon who had crippled him, Lon's hateful visage was aided by severe pains he actually endured to play the role. To achieve the desired effect he had to fold his legs behind him and hold them in position by binding them;

The Penalty (Goldwyn, 1920). An evil surgeon purposely mutilated Lon in early life. His condition turns him into a revengeful criminal.

then he added leather padding on his knees. He suffered excruciating pain when he was required to jump down on his "stumps," land on his knees and *walk* around.

In 1922 Chaney surprised and pleased his growing legion of fans in one of his finest and warmest roles. In *Shadows*, he

21

As a gangster in *Outside the Law* (Universal, 1921).

Lon in one of his many Oriental roles in *Bits of Life* (Associated First National, 1921).

Poster ad for *The Night Rose* (Goldwyn, 1921).

The Trap (Universal, 1922), a Northwoods melo-drama.

enacted with profound sentiment the story of a Chinese laundryman who, through kindness and wisdom, teaches others in his adopted American community the essence of love and brotherhood. One of the few early Chaney films that has managed to survive, it was seen by millions over PBS-TV's "Film Odyssey" series in 1972.

Lon chalked up another success in 1922 as Fagin in Dickens' *Oliver Twist*, starring the child-star wonder of that era, Jackie Coogan, as Oliver. Because the film industry did not have the foresight to guarantee

preservation of at least its more outstanding and unusual productions until the past few years (even today there are some witless firms not giving a damn), *Oliver Twist* must be counted among the shockingly large number of lost films.

In less than eleven months Chaney was seen in three outstanding horror films, notwithstanding those cavilers who prefer evaluating *The Hunchback of Notre Dame* as a historical romance. The first of the three shockers, *A Blind Bargain*, was a true progenitor of films in the tradition of

23

A rare poster ad for *Oliver Twist* (Associated First National, 1922).

A Blind Bargain (Goldwyn, 1922).

Island of Lost Souls, Dr. Renault's Secret, and *Terror Is a Man.* Lon essayed two roles —a mad scientist and his pathetic creation, a sympathetic ape-man. As a noted surgeon, he has reached the borderland of insanity through his experiments to prove the theory of evolution, concluding that he can turn a man back into his ancestral prototype by implanting in him live monkey glands. In a number of previous experiments he has already wrecked the minds and bodies of several victims. A young struggling author sells himself to Chaney in return for medical aid that will restore his dying mother to health. Before the day arrives when he must stick to his bargain, the author falls in love with the daughter of a rich publisher who has accepted his book. In vain he attempts to buy his release from the mad Chaney, who proceeds to strap him down on an operating table. But the doctor has not counted on the superhuman strength developed by one of the animal-men in his private dungeon, and when he goes to obtain a monkey, the man breaks out of his cell and crushes Chaney to death.

A few months later came the delayed release of *While Paris Sleeps,* and then Lon finalized a contract to star in *The Hunchback of Notre Dame,* returning to Universal in full glory as a number-one box-office

Poster ad for *Flesh and Blood*
(Cummings, 1922).

luminary. He was now being paid more
than ten thousand dollars a month by the
company that five years before didn't think
he would ever be worth more than one
hundred dollars a week.

A whole year was required for the pre-
planning, the construction of the massive
sets that entailed duplicating early Parisian
buildings and the great facade of Notre
Dame Cathedral (so well constructed that

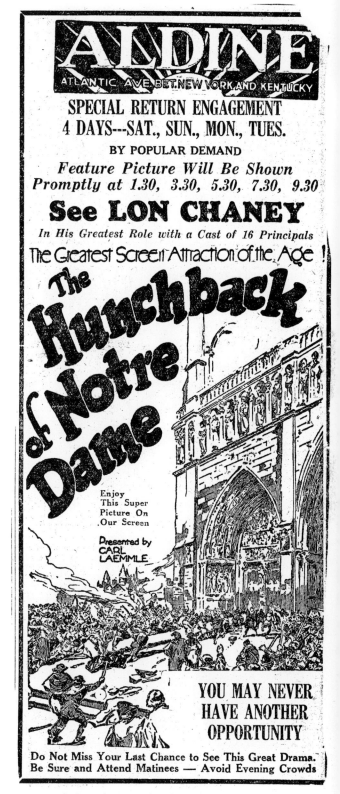

Poster ad for *The Hunchback of Notre Dame*
(Universal, 1923).

it stands to this very day), and the actual shooting time of nearly four months. Military tactics were used to mobilize the cast of three and a half thousand supporting players and extras, under the command of former Armed Services officer Charles Stallings, who would get everyone costumed, loaded on trucks, and ready for location shooting in one hour. Handling mob scenes in other productions had always been of grave concern to producers, but Universal solved the problem with one of the most up-to-date means then known: public-address speakers, placed every twenty-five feet, were connected to one radio transmitter. From a lofty platform, director Wallace Worsley could bark out orders through a microphone to the thousands spread out nearly a quarter of a mile around him.

Lon had to be on the lot each morning four hours before the rest of the cast, for he needed every moment of four and a half hours to transform himself into Quasimodo. For this he harnessed on his back a mound of heavy rubber weighing seventy-two pounds (this was long before the discovery of lightweight plastics and foam rubber), and wore a breastplate and shoulder pads not unlike football gear. A corset-like leather harness held both back and front plates together, and on top he had to wear a flesh-colored rubber suit. Utilizing his full knowledge of makeup, Lon manipulated modeling putty around his features to achieve the face of a gargoyle; animal hair was made into a wig that looked like Orphan Annie's hairstyle—if she'd gone stark-raving mad. Tufts of hair were glued to the rubber suit, one ghastly eye disguise and a set of terribly deformed

The Hunchback of Notre Dame. Esmeralda (Patsy Ruth Miller) offers kindness and water to the tormented and thirsty Quasimodo.

The Hunchback of Notre Dame. Now it is the loyal Quasimodo's turn to repay Esmeralda for her kindness by saving her from certain death.

One of the better torture scenes in *The Hunchback of Notre Dame.*

teeth were added and . . . a super-geek was born—a masterpiece of hideous deformity. Lon had little difficulty playing the crablike Quasimodo, walking and running, in a perpetual Groucho-style crouch—he couldn't have stood erect under all that load if his life had depended on it.

Enormous liberties were taken with this bowdlerized adaptation of Victor Hugo's monumental work (although Lon's make-up adhered faithfully to the author's description of Quasimodo) which, when published in 1830, was too bold and frank in its descriptions of atrocious social and religious aberration for neurotic 1923 film-makers. In Hugo's original work Quasimodo occupies only a small portion of the story; trimmed of numerous details, the film adaptation makes the Hunchback the central character who assumes heroic stature as he saves Esmeralda (the gypsy girl who was kind to him when he was tortured) from injustice by bringing her within the inviolate sanctuary of the great cathedral.

The 1923 audiences found it a unique experience, and though Chaney was already an acknowledged celebrity and favorite, *Hunchback of Notre Dame* made him a box-office giant. Utilizing virtually all of the original sets and, of course, the gigantic one representing Notre Dame, the 1939 version (starring Charles Laughton), under William Dieterle's excellent direction, was outstandingly superior, emphasizing macabre elements eschewed in the original. The last version (made in France in 1957, starring Anthony Quinn) lacked some of the dramaturgy and scope of its predecessors, but dared to articulate for the first time a number of Hugo's ideas that included alchemy, necromancy, and astrology.

But no subsequent Quasimodo compared with Chaney, who suffered so badly for his role that he was hospitalized for three months after the film's completion. His suffering paid off, though; his performance was acclaimed a masterpiece, and the film was selected among the ten best of 1923.

Charles Laughton as Quasimodo rescuing Esmeralda (Maureen O'Hara) in the 1939 version of *The Hunchback of Notre Dame* (RKO Radio Pictures).

The Hunchback of Notre Dame (1939). Laughton as Quasimodo confronts the evil seminarian (Sir Cedric Hardwicke) in a fight to the finish.

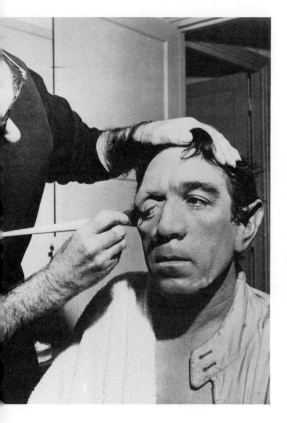

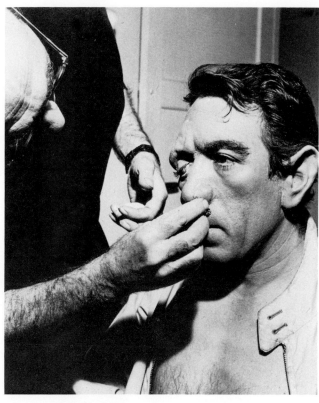

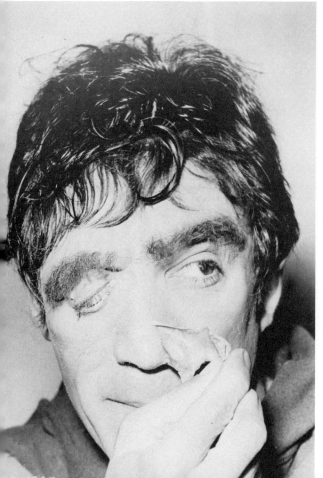

Anthony Quinn being made up as Quasimodo for
the French-based 1957 version of *The Hunchback of Notre Dame*.

Taking a well-needed vacation, Chaney found it difficult to isolate himself for even a few days of peace and relaxation in the country, where he usually engaged in his favorite pastime, fishing. He was now one of Hollywood's hottest properties, and he knew it. Offers by the dozens were coming in from everywhere, and if various producers could have had the power to work him into a film each day without let-up, they would have done it. But he was now under special contract to Universal, better paid than ever, and for some time exercised an option to refuse appearing in productions he felt were beneath him.

His only two films for 1924 were prestigious "art"-styled productions, each one under the command of two of the most respected directors. *The Next Corner* had already been a Broadway and road company hit, based upon Kate Jordan's novel and play, and received respectable reviews in its filmic form. Its director was Sam Wood, who had assisted Cecil B. De Mille with a number of silent hits before going out on his own to carve an enviable reputation in future years with such acclaimed classics and Award winners as *Goodby Mr. Chips, Our Town, Kings Row, For Whom the Bell Tolls,* and more. But the kind

Four shots of Lon Chaney, Sr., showing how he could change his face with virtually no makeup.

reception accorded *The Next Corner* was slight compared to that given Leonid Andreyev's excellently adapted *He Who Gets Slapped*. Two years earlier it had had a successful Broadway run, with Richard Bennett in the lead. In the lead role of the movie verson, Chaney plays an aristocratic and distinguished man of letters who becomes disillusioned with life because of the faithlessness of his wife and the treachery of his best friend, who has stolen his writings. Fleeing from these sordid conditions, Chaney alters his appearance by removing his beard and professional trappings, and then gains employment as a clown, believing he may find happiness and freedom in a world of total make-believe; instead, he learns that the circus world has its own griefs hidden beneath the grease paint and tinsel. Production was under the direction of Victor Seastrom of Sweden who, at forty-five, had achieved an eminent international reputation as a brilliant actor, designer, and stage and film director. (Later at the age of seventy-eight, he won the highest praise as the elderly star of Ingmar Bergman's masterpiece, *Wild Strawberries* [1957]; he passed away three years later.)

Seastrom's film and Chaney's performance elicited accolades from some of the most influential critics, typified by this review in *The New York Times*:

> It is a shadow drama so beautifully told, so flawlessly directed, that we might imagine that it will be held up as a model by all producers. Throughout its length there is not an instant of ennui, not a second one wants to lose. Never in his efforts before the camera has Mr. Chaney delivered such a marvelous performance. . . . He is restrained in his acting, never overdoing the sentimental situation, and is guarded in his makeup.

Chaney returned to the world of the macabre with three awesome films, mindbending for 1925 audiences, two of which were acknowledged *classics*. In a semiparody of 1922's *A Blind Bargain*, Lon appeared in *The Monster* as the maniacal Dr. Ziska who controls a terrifying sanitarium inhabited by his creations and other assorted ghoulish types. The victims are usually innocent travelers led astray to his house of horrors. Using almost no makeup, Lon amazed everyone by his ability to distort his features adequately enough to impress early horror fans. The big problem with *The Monster* was that early audiences were unprepared to fully understand a film parodying a genre that had scarcely started to exist!

The same year Chaney and Tod Browning formed a liaison that endured through some of the most memorable productions of their careers. Browning was the almost perfect director for Chaney's more bizarre films, and it's quite natural to assume that had he been in charge of Chaney's other horror essays, they might have had fewer glaring flaws. At the very least, Browning would been able to inject in them subtle moods and maintain Gothic touches and

Lon as the maniacal Dr. Ziska in *The Monster* (MGM, 1925).

The Monster. Lon is at far right.

Another menace-filled scene from *The Monster,*
with Lon (*center*) pointing a gun.

Poster ad for *The Monster*.

A rare ad showing Lon in his most famous Oriental role, *Mr. Wu* (MGM, 1927).

feeling for suspense that other directors frequently ignored or mishandled. Lon and Tod were already good friends for a number of years and had worked together in 1919 when Tod had directed *Wicked Darling* with Lon in an impressive supporting gangster role. Their first joint effort, *The Unholy Three,* was one of 1925's film sensations; but just as fantastic was the year 1925 itself, perhaps the greatest in American film-making history in that no other year gave to the world so many outstanding productions at one time, many of them still unchallenged classics: *The Big Parade; The Lost World; A Kiss for Cinderella; The Gold Rush; The Merry Widow; The Sea Beast; Peter Pan; Grass; Lady Windermere's Fan,* and many more.

The Unholy Three was so unusual, so unique, that it had to be remade five years later, again starring Chaney in the same role. At this time Hollywood was well aware that crime paid big dividends at the box office. But unlike its contemporary counterparts, this film strove hard to be a serious and imaginative presentation of the diabolical, and not a collection of stock crime situations and cliché shock effects so typical of numerous underworld programmers of this period. An inventive and dedicated craftsman, Browning liberated the cameras and moved them freely within the dramatic framework of his story with exciting artistry. The story's sinister plot involved a perfidious triumvirate of circus exiles—Victor McLaglen as Hercules the strongman; thirty-three-inch-tall Harry Earles as Tweedledee the midget; and Chaney as Echo the ventriloquist. The three, hiding behind the peaceful facade of a pet shop by day, decide to turn their talents to more fruitful pursuits in crime. As the brains of this operation, Chaney masterminds each job (disguised part of the time as the old lady proprietress of the shop), by utilizing the dumb but useful McLaglen's muscle power and the midget's ability to sneak into small spaces. But conflicts arise —Chaney cannot control the strongman and

33

Poster ad for *The Unholy Three* (MGM, 1925).

Publicity shot of Lon from *The Unholy Three*.

Lon as Professor Echo, stage ventriloquist, who finds crime more profitable than show biz in *The Unholy Three*.

34

midget's individual actions when they commit a murder during a robbery, nor the midget's diabolical mind and sadistic streak that he uses to plague the strongman. Unable to withstand the midget's scorn and derision, McLaglen kills the midget. He, in turn, is killed by Chaney's pet gorilla. Chaney attempts to undo these dreadful events by using ventriloquism in the courtroom to clear a young man charged with the murder, even though the freeing of the defendant means he can now marry the girl whom Lon loves.

But if *The Unholy Three* garnered huge praise and high honors, Chaney's crowning achievement that year was *The Phantom of the Opera,* his most famous film —the one that would immortalize him forever more. It was based on a novel of the same name by Gaston Leroux, and Chaney starred as Eric, the mad organist of the Paris Opera House, who is so hideous to behold that he dares not live in the outside world; instead, he has found a world hidden deep beneath the honeycombed structure of the Opera House that he feels befits his appearance and strange mind— a frightening and intriguing subterranean region, labyrinthian as the dark Cretan maze of the Minotaur, accessible solely via complicated passageways leading to odious-looking canals. Upon these fetid waterways Chaney guides his gondola like Charon upon the River Styx, bringing with him

The three versions of *The Phantom of the Opera:* 1 and 4: Lon Chaney and Mary Philbin in the original 1925 Universal production; 2 and 5: Claude Rains and Susanna Foster in Universal's 1943 version; 3 and 6: Herbert Lom and Heather Sears in the 1962 Universal/Hammer production.

Here and opposite page: three different and rare poster ads for *The Phantom of the Opera.*

The Phantom of the Opera. Lon, as Eric the Phantom, haunts the Paris Opera House like a ghost.

The Phantom of the Opera. Merrymakers gathered at the Opera House's bacchanalian Mardi Gras stand back in awe as they watch Lon pass, garbed as Poe's "Red Death."

the abducted Christine, a young singer whom he loves madly, to share this Purgatory. Regarded by many as a ghost, feared by those who know of him, he has long haunted the Opera House, sometimes seen only in shadows, once attending a gigantic opera Mardi Gras party garbed as Poe envisioned Death in "Masque of the Red Death."

As a disembodied voice, speaking behind a secret panel in Christine's dressing room, Chaney as Eric pretends to be the Spirit of Music instilling confidence and inspiration in the young ingenue, promising her that under his guidance and unseen presence she will rank as the leading prima donna of all Paris. To further these ambitions, Chaney terrorizes the Opera House's management; then, when they continue to ignore his threats, one evening he brings down the auditorium's immense chandelier upon a packed house. In the confusion that ensues, he leads Christine away on a white horse, down complex ramps, to his macabre world, like Pluto guiding Proserpine to Hades. Shifting Christine from horseback to his gondola, Eric brings her at last to his mausoleum-like "home." Ecstatic over his accomplishments and victory, Eric begins to play the organ with great passion, still wearing the mask that thus far in the film has not been removed. Christine's curiosity to see his face is piqued, but Eric plays away, unaware of her intent. Hesitating briefly, Christine creeps up behind him and rips off the mask. With an outraged roar Eric turns to reveal a face of horror that adheres completely to Christine's description of him in Gaston Leroux's novel:

"Yes, if I lived to be a hundred, I should always hear the superhuman cry of grief and rage which he uttered when the terrible sight appeared before my eyes. . . . You have seen death's heads when they have been dried and withered by the centuries, and, perhaps, if you were not the victim of a nightmare, you saw *his* death's head at Perros. And then you saw Red Death stalking about at the last masked ball. But all those death's heads were motionless and their dumb horror was not alive. But imagine, if you can, Red Death's mask suddenly coming to life in order to express, with the four black holes of its eyes, its nose, and its mouth, the extreme anger, the mighty fury of a demon, *and not a ray of light from the sockets*, for, as I learned later, you can not see his blazing eyes except in the dark. . . . Leaning over me, he cried:

"Look! You want to see! Feast your eyes, glut your soul on my accursed ugliness! Look at Eric's face! Now you know the face of the voice. . . . Oh, you women are so inquisitive! Well, are you satisfied? I'm a very good-looking fellow, eh? . . . When a woman has seen me, as you have, she belongs to me. She loves me forever. I am a kind of Don Juan, you know!' And drawing himself up to his full height, with his hand on his hip, wagging the hideous thing that was his head on his shoulders, he roared, 'Look at me! *I am Don Juan triumphant!'* "

The Phantom of the Opera. This is the scene in which Lon, for the first time in the film, reveals the most memorable face of horror ever to be projected on a movie *scream*.

38

The Phantom of the Opera. Lon, as Eric, puts Christine (Mary Philbin) to a nerve-wracking test.

A publicity shot of Lon as the exhausted and broken-hearted Eric in *The Phamtom of the Opera* —a film classic for all time!

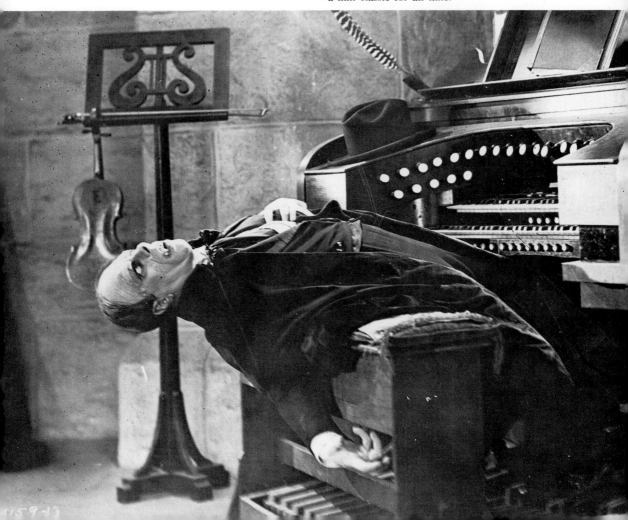

Picking up her trail, Christine's lover Raoul and a detective almost lose their lives, trapped below in a fiery furnace; but giving in to Christine's pleas—and putting her to a test which she passes—Eric frees the nearly doomed men. Meanwhile, the Parisian mob is enraged and dares to explore the fearsome passageways beneath the Opera to mete out vengeance upon the murdering Phantom. They ferret him out of his lair (Christine, Raoul, and the detective are now safe and sound), and Eric flees aboveground, steals a hansom, feverishly whips the horse down boulevards, past Notre Dame, until the coach overturns when he loses control. His back to the River Seine, he holds the mob temporarily at bay, telling them he has a terrible bomb in his fist ready to blow them all to kingdom come; actually he holds nothing and has fooled them. Infuriated, they beat him to death and throw his body into the river.

Though somewhat altered from the original 1911 novel for screen adaptation, *The Phantom of the Opera* owes all its power and grandeur to its author's fertile imagination, and especially to Chaney's inspired performance and makeup ingenuity which manages superbly to draw attention away from acute production problems and flaws, one of them unbelievably permitted to remain uncorrected: the famous Opera House chandelier-crash sequence is badly botched up and lasts but a few seconds, instead of being a memorable highlight that could very obviously have been heightened by the suspense of seeing Chaney hacking away at the cables, cross-cutting scenes showing the stage, audience, Chaney again, cables being slowly severed, chandelier swaying—and, finally, the ultimate in terror as it falls, pinning scores of victims underneath. Director Arthur Lubin was keenly aware of this deficiency when he remade the film in 1943, with Claude Rains as the star, by developing the chandelier sequence to its fullest potential. The Chaney version had problems from the very beginning;

it was started under one director, Rupert Julian (who was fired or "quit"), and was completed by assistant director Edward Sedgwick. Before scheduled for general release, the film was prescreened with several sequences that were omitted in the final print; consequently, it may be assumed that negligent editing is to be blamed. And, of course, there is no doubt that director Julian's well-known thickheaded stubbornness, his quarrels with his staff and Chaney, created serious impediments.

On the plus side, and unknown to the public, was that Chaney controlled a number of scenes under his direction, and undertook incredible steps to create the Phantom makeup. To achieve the most memorable face of horror in screen history, he used an intricate combination of makeup and devices that remain, like most of his made-up characterizations, among the many secrets that he carried to his grave. When he was once queried about his secret technique, he said:

"There are tricks in my peculiar trade that I don't care to divulge any more than a magician will give away his art. In *The Phantom of the Opera* people exclaimed at my weird makeup. I achieved the death's head of that role without wearing a mask. It was the use of paints in the right shades and the right places—not the obvious parts of the face—which gave the complete illusion of horror. My experiments as a stage manager, which were wide and varied before I jumped into films, taught me much about lighting effects on the actor's face and the minor tricks of deception. These I have been able to use in achieving weird results on the screen. I've never worn a mask in my life, save at Halloween parties. It's all a matter of combining paints and lights to form the right illusion. Since falling heir to the odd and ugly roles of drama in pictures, I'm supposed to have evolved some magic process of malforming my features and limbs. It's an art, but not magic."

The 1943 Technicolor version of *The Phantom of the Opera* is, under Lubin's direction, almost a classic in its own right, but it does not capture the original's Gothic flavor, for Rains as the Phantom is less a figure of mystery and more human. Nearly all action centers around the upper sections of the Opera House; although all of the original 1925 sets were used, the labyrinthian subchambers appear less macabre and more minimized. Rains' disfigurement comes about as a consequence of acid being tossed in his face during an argument with a crooked music publisher—his face is badly scarred as if by fire, but less repelling compared with Chaney's. While the Phantom is not quite the monstrous genius and tower of insidious power he was in 1925, Lubin compensates for some of his own directorial weaknesses by excellently developing suspense in areas that were flawed or improperly handled in the original version (particularly, as already mentioned, the dynamic Opera chandelier sequence), and by taking full advantage of sound and advanced Technicolor. The Chaney version did, in fact, employ early three-color Technicolor and tints for some sequences; and in 1930 Universal re-released it with the addition of a musical score and sound-effects track.

The third and last version, created by Hammer Studios in 1962, was a colorful, music-laden mishmash, evincing this company's often blatant carelessness and disregard for logical and consistent film plot construction. Hardly bearing any resemblance to Leroux's beautiful Gothic classic, it is not only an insult to its honored predecessors but an unconscionable fraud and a demeaning production for a company that has occasionally—even though erratically—measured up to certain standards of excellence.

Nearly forgotten in the excitement generated in 1925 by the release of *Phantom* and *Unholy Three* was an offbeat and altogether different Chaney vehicle, *The Tower of Lies*, made under Victor Seastrom's artistic and subtle direction. Lon played an old Swedish peasant who is happy with his family and dreams; but, being too sensitive and caught up in his own fancies, his mind breaks when his daughter (Norma Shearer), abandons the old family homestead for city life. In this instance, father-love proves stronger than a mother's. Consumed by guilt, and thinking he is to blame for his daughter's desertion, he goes out into the world searching for her, growing more deranged and, finally, imagining he is an emperor, a King Lear figure misunderstood and abandoned by his loved ones. Perhaps Seastrom's subtleties were a bit ahead of the times for mass audiences unaccustomed to stylized art films, because the movie did poorly at the box office though Chaney's performance was among his finest.

In *The Blackbird* (1926), based on a story written and directed by Tod Browning, Lon was cast in a dual role that, according to at least one critic, was "one of the most difficult acting feats ever attempted by an actor . . . accomplished without resorting to any false noses, whiskers, or facial deformities of any kind." Lon played the part of a London East End crook, feared and sought by Scotland Yard, and in his other characterization (in "disguise" to foil the law) appeared as the "Bishop of Limehouse," a kindly and charitable cripple, loved and pitied by everyone. The true test of Chaney's ability is that the two characters appear entirely dissimilar to each other, even though they bear the same features. Eventually good overcomes evil when Chaney's nobler alterego starts taking over. Another prominent reviewer who praised the role said, "Mr. Chaney's depiction of the two types is one of the finest exemplifications of screen artistry one would hope to behold."

Outside the Law, also directed by Browning, exposed Lon in another fine gangster role; but his most popular film for 1926 was *The Road to Mandalay*, in

Poster ad for *The Road to Mandalay* (MGM, 1926).

which he begins his adventures as a starry-eyed young seaman but falls upon bad times. In a few years he degenerates into a sinister, battle-scarred ruler of an Oriental underworld known as Singapore Joe, hiding in a strange dive on the Singapore waterfront. From afar he adores his orphaned daughter, who knows nothing of her strange father. Lon's special makeup was one grotesquely blind eye that he created by painfully covering his eyeball with the inside membrane of an egg. His

reputation as a wizard of makeup went up another level, not only for the way he looked as the older, battered gang leader, but primarily because of his appearance as the *handsome* young Joe, who, at the start of the story, looks like a matinee idol. According to Chaney, his role as Joe represented more of a problem than changing to Quasimodo, Eric, and most of his other bizarre personifications.

"Most of my makeups depend on weird grotesqueries, colorful foreigners, and on duplicating age," he said, "and to try to put on youth proved much like trying to write with my left hand."

Besides Chaney, the film combined the expertise teamwork of writer Herman J. Mankiewicz—who architectured most of the story line of *Citizen Kane* (1941)—and co-author director Tod Browning. In an interview he gave during *Road to Mandalay*'s publicity campaign, Browning revealed some of his personal film-making philosophy:

"The background of a motion picture should never be depended upon for entertainment, but should merely be atmosphere, and assist in the creation of a mood. A magnificent background or setting may fascinate the audience, but it should never be allowed to predominate; rather, it should always be the setting for the drama of a few characters. Many directors believe that any audience would rather look at a story laid in a luxurious setting, but that is not my impression. I believe that if the story is sound and interesting, any kind of audience will like it, even if it is played before a backdrop.

"All of Shakespeare's first productions were produced in the crudest form of stage setting, yet because their philosophy was sound and the story entertaining, they succeeded. People of meager circumstances may prefer to watch entertainment with a luxurious setting, but they forget about it when a real story is unwound."

Chaney's marvelous attributes as a great artist immortalized him as one of the finest

42

actors who ever lived, and audiences were undoubtedly engrossed by his art—but, more than anything else, they loved to see him *seem* to suffer. The studios and exhibitors were aware of this, and Chaney had known for a long time that "art" or no, and even if "the play's the thing," they *paid* to see him go through all of the pains of a latter-day Prometheus chained to a box office by an interminable, unbroken wreath of tickets.

Mightily did he suffer in 1927, after completing *Tell It to the Marines* (in an unforgettable role, sans makeup, as a tough Marine sergeant); in *Mr. Wu* he was seen as an Oriental from young manhood to middle-age and, finally, senescence. Among his most bizarre roles, Lon appeared in *The Unknown* (directed by Tod Browning), returning to circus life as a man pretending to be an *armless* knife-thrower whose agile footwork compensates for his handicap. The only one aware of this incredible hoax is his loyal dwarf assistant who helps Lon in and out of a painful harness that pins his arms underneath a costume. Estrelita (Joan Crawford), the circus owner's daughter, has a loathing for most men, dating from numerous past experiences when they attempted to grab and kiss her; she is repelled even if they seem about to *touch* her. Lon misconstrues her phobia and imagines that she is romantically interested in him. One night Estrelita's father discovers Lon's true identity. Fearing exposure, and filled with hate, Lon strangles the man to death—the only clue being Lon's anomalous double-thumbmark on the corpse's throat. Realizing the danger he leaves the circus, pretending to need a vacation but in reality to seek surgery—and not to amputate just the incriminating double-thumb . . . *but to remove both arms*. He feels that in this way he will truly be able to win Estrelita's complete love. Returning to the circus after having recuperated, he's horrified to learn that Estrelita is married to Malabar, the strongman, who has taught her true love's meaning and to be unafraid of a

Poster ad for *London After Midnight* (MGM, 1927).

good man's arms. Feeling cheated, and maddened with a desire for revenge, Lon plots to have Malabar killed during one of the strongman's famous performances involving two large horses on treadmills pulling him in a test of strength. His plan to fix the treadmills, so that the horses pull Malabar apart, backfires when Lon falls under the great steeds and is trampled to death.

The seemingly untiring Chaney went on to create an even more outstanding reputation that year in *London After Midnight* in a role that can easily rank with Quasimodo and Eric, yet is not as well known or appreciated today since prints of the film are apparently nonexistent. Chaney played several roles under Tod Browning's direction, but considered this movie —the *first* American film dealing with vampirism—as their greatest collaboration. An ominous curse and a history of terrible tragedies hang over the great Gothic mansion known as Balfour House, which has been deserted for many years. Now the young Balfour heirs, Harry and Lucille, desire to claim their estate and restore it; but their guardian and neighbor, Sir James, who had reared and financed the parentless

Lon and H. B. Walthall in *London After Midnight*.

youngsters since their childhood, confronts Harry with an itemized list of expenses he's incurred in their upbringing. Harry protests when Sir James suggests mortgaging the estate over to him to satisfy the debts. Even Sir James' secretary, Hibbs, cannot impress the penniless young man with the folly of his sentimental attachment to property that is beyond his means and "shadowed by disaster."

Harry continues with his own plans, nevertheless, anticipating that he and his sister will be soon occupying their estate; but his dead body is found several days later bearing two strange puncture marks on the throat. An investigation uncovers nothing concerning the circumstances of this terrible event, and now Lucille, the last of the Balfours, appears to be in danger of being afflicted by some horrible ancestral curse. Seven months later, Chief Inspector Burke (Lon Chaney) of Scotland Yard steps into the case, convinced that he can unravel the mystery through the scientific use of hypnotism.

The mystery deepens when Balfour House is leased out by Hibbs to a weird-looking couple (after their references have been approved by mail). They are frightening to any who meet them by chance in the still of the night—the only time they move about. The woman is wraithlike and alien; the man, looking somewhat like Mr. Hyde, wears a top hat and a cape resembling huge bat wings, and his face has a deathlike pallor, abnormally large, burning eyes, and a mouth ridged by sharklike teeth. Sir James is especially shocked to find that the lease's signature bears the name of Roger Balfour, who had committed suicide more than five years before. Strange and startling events follow, all leading up to the possibility that Roger Balfour has come back from the grave as a vampire. It is, therefore, with open arms that Sir James greets Colonel Yates, recently returned from India, an old friend whom he hasn't seen for years. With its terrifying tenants, Balfour House has become a place

London After Midnight. Lon in the first film ever to bring a vampire theme to the screen.

of horror, frightening Sir James' household, his secretary, and Lucille, who is still his ward.

By now the baffled and worried Sir James leans heavily on his friend and houseguest, Yates, for succor, hoping he will aid him in breaking the mystery and dispelling the horrors of Balfour House. Yates tells Sir James to meet him that evening at the Balfour estate; Sir James assents without a word, his eyes staring strangely, glassily. At Balfour, Yates quickly changes his makeup and clothes, adopting the appearance of the allegedly undead Roger Balfour, and carefully instructs Lucille (who has been part of this deception for some time) to remain calm and collected lest his plan be ruined at this crucial period. In a hypnotic state and unaware of preceding events, Sir James arrives at the mansion, thinking that he is back in time *reliving* the very hour, more than five years ago, when he had met the real Roger Balfour up to the very moment he had shot him and made the murder look like a suicide. Now he meets the false Roger Balfour, who exposes his insidiousness. At a command, accompanied by the snapping of his fingers, "Yates-Balfour" brings the evil Sir James out of hypnotic control and reveals himself as none other than Inspector Burke of Scotland Yard—the genius behind one of the most elaborate plans ever devised in the history of criminal investigation!

The complex and ingenious plot of *London After Midnight* (too richly detailed in its entirety for this space) was considerably superior to the usual simple-minded mystery shockers proliferating from that time to the present. Had it been published in story form, instead of merely being a screen vehicle of director Tod Browning's conception, it might well have served as a creditable addition to Conan Doyle's more colorful and intricate adventures of Sherlock Holmes.

Above all, Chaney revealed himself as an infinitely more multifaceted artist, using not just his bag of makeup wizardry to create a vampire (and enduring great pain by creating a "popping-eyes" effect with a wire tightened around his head across his eyelids), but by subtly developing *two other roles* that were complete opposites: Inspector Burke and Balfour-Yates—actually, almost four roles in one film!

Chaney had apparently, by then, climbed the highest mountain, and as the Alexander of mystery and macabre films he would have been justified in wondering if there was one more area left to be conquered. And, of course, there *was* one more—but it would have to wait more than two years for the world to realize it.

With radio booming and sound motion pictures a reality and about ready to replace silent films, Hollywood's experimental "horror cycle" sagged for awhile, even

Lon Chaney, Sr. in 1928.

though there would be a resurgence of the genre in three short years. Consequently, Chaney's films fell mostly within the school of realism throughout 1928 and 1929. He played a tough but genial gangster implicated in big-town crime in *The Big City*. Circus life involved him as a broken-hearted Pagliacci type in love with a young ingenue named Loretta Young in *Laugh, Clown, Laugh*—but this doesn't last long: while balancing on his head during a high-wire routine, he falls and breaks his neck.

West of Zanzibar, one of his most colorful films, surrounded him with a prominent cast that featured Lionel Barrymore and Warner Baxter. Lon played Dead Legs Flint, a former suave stage magician, who

46

Lon starts off in *West of Zanzibar* (MGM, 1928) as a suave stage magician who falls upon bad times.

West of Zanzibar's director, Tod Browning, almost exactly duplicated this Chaney promotional scene four years later, when he directed *Freaks'* horrific ending. However, whether a publicity stunt or deleted in the final cut, it does not appear in any existing print.

becomes paralyzed in a fight with the man (Barrymore) who stole his wife. Later his wife dies, leaving a baby daughter whom Chaney believes to be Barrymore's. In a vengeful search for his rival, Chaney goes to Africa and leaves the baby with a good-hearted whore who runs a dive in Zanzibar. Years later, when the girl has grown to beautiful womanhood, he locates the man he seeks and plans a terrible revenge that will include both the girl and the man he believes to be her father. Before he is able to execute his awful plan, however, he discovers that the girl is his own daughter. His hate and bitterness now nullified, he mellows and becomes a changed man. Chaney was again a strange sight, dragging himself over the floor with his useless legs, ruling the local jungle natives with sleight of hand, magic, mysticism, and other stage tricks.

Hurled back into the world of crime once more in *While the City Sleeps*, Lon played a crack metropolitan detective at odds with the underworld; but the film hardly measured up to his presence and was little more than a programmer.

Where East Is East starred Lon as Tiger Haynes, a mysterious animal trapper caught up in yet another eternal decadent triangle set in a jungle. The public had by now grown to love Chaney-in-the-jungle movies, even if they were all variations of the same plot. But all were under Browning's expert direction; and Chaney—unlike some others of "star status"—could never

Poster ad for *West of Zanzibar*.

The crowning disaster arises, though, when he loses his colleagues' respect and is heaped with disgrace by being held responsible for a serious train wreck. In a moment when the railroad faces a terrible crisis, Chaney redeems himself by nearly losing his life during his efforts to resolve the situation, and he is reunited with his family in happiness. Railroad stories were not unusual and had been done either as straight dramas or—under Buster Keaton and others—as a setting for high comedy. But *Thunder* was particularly important and seemed heavily influenced by Jacques Feyder's classical *Crainquebille*, produced in France and released to the United States in 1923.

Thunder was Lon's last *silent* film and, like many others of its kind that were released in 1929, it didn't do well at the box office since *sound* films had been in existence more than a year. Chaney was among the last few big stars who held out

Chaney as a city detective in *While the City Sleeps* (MGM, 1928).

be accused of rendering *similar* characterizations, and was once even dubbed "the Man of a Thousand Performances."

Thunder was part silent, but had a quota of sound effects and music, as did many other films from various studios that were anxious to compete (often with sad results) with Warner's now-pioneering, technically superior "talking pictures." Chaney played "Grumpy," a crusty and lovable veteran railroad engineer whose two sons also work on trains. He becomes bitter when one of his boys, after falling in love with an actress, gives up his work and pursues another career; the father then goes practically out of his mind upon learning that his other son was killed in an accident.

48

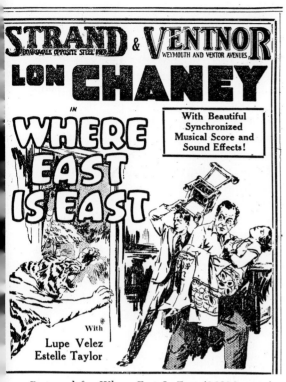

Poster ad for *Where East Is East* (MGM, 1929).

But Lon was fully aware that he had to make a choice: to take the plunge and go "talkie," or announce his retirement which, at age forty-six, seemed out of the question for a man who had been constantly on the move since early childhood. When he finally made his decision, early in 1930, Lon gave notice to MGM and the press: "No, retirement is the bunk. And, yes, I am going into talkies!"

In an exclusive interview in March 1930 concerning his momentous decision, Lon sat back in a huge easy chair, wearing his inevitable cap—he once claimed he wore it for "good luck" even though others thought this ill-mannered—and being seen for the first time wearing horn-rimmed eyeglasses:

"I'll tell you frankly that my first talking picture is going to make me—or break me! Inside, I mean; in here . . ." He tapped his breast. "Now, listen. I hope they like my first talkie. I'm going to try my darndest to make them like it. I'm going to make it the sound picture I want, even if it takes a year to get it that way. And I hope they like it.

"If they do, that will be fine. But if they don't—well, it will do something to me. It will make me what I've never been since I went into pictures—a man whose sole interest is the money he's being paid. I'll just go ahead, making the required talkies under my contract terms, and collecting my pay. And at the end of five years, I'll step out of the picture, and that will be all. I'll probably retire then, anyway. I'll have enough to take it easy."

Explaining the reason for his decision, Lon said:

"Well, at the outset, I didn't think talkies were any good at all. You can make a picture *move*, yes. But simply because it *is* a picture, a picture *cannot* talk. To make it talk is all wrong. And, anyway, you know, talkies were pretty awful at first. And it got so that *everybody* was making them. So, since it was the thing to do, I did it too."

from making a transition to sound films; he had watched the careers of long-standing silent film stars wiped out overnight. While a few like Greta Garbo and Ronald Colman bridged the sound barrier only to achieve higher stardom, others, such as John Gilbert, once the idols of millions, were destroyed as soon as they opened their mouths by the very public and studios that had made them potentates. Lon had wholeheartedly dedicated himself too many years to his art—perhaps more than any performer of his time—to chance watching his career go down the drain simply because of a mechanical innovation which some authorities believe contributed little to films and took away much of the enchantment and glamor.

Lon repeats his 1925 roles for MGM's 1930 version of *The Unholy Three*. This was his first sound film and, tragically, his final screen appearance.

For some time Chaney was immersed in technical research around the sound rooms, studying recording devices at the studios. He had been in the mixing rooms, not only watching the sound mixer do its stuff but occasionally doing the mixing himself and experimenting. He wasn't discussing the extent of these experiments, but everything he said betrayed the fact that he was studying sound techniques with the same devotion and intensity that he had previously applied to the intricacies of facial and physical makeup. He wouldn't even admit he had voice tests made, and he was so emphatic in his denials that he couldn't be doubted:

"No, I haven't taken a single sound test. I'm not going to. What's the good of them? I'm going to start shooting my first talkie without making a single test in advance."

He said he would not bother taking voice culture either. "It ruins voices," he snorted. "That's what's the matter with John Gilbert!"

The film that concerned Chaney so much and that was to be his first talkie was, of course, a completely new version of one of his biggest box-office moneymakers, *The Unholy Three*. But the *other* reason he had held up making his sound debut was that he had been ill; in fact, he was a sicker man than either he or the press realized. Before he was to make his film, rumors were rife that he would be too ill to ever make a film again. Finally, after much trouble in trying to find him, he was located in a Hollywood hospital bed, after having undergone surgery for what was officially termed a tonsilectomy.

"Going off the screen?" he retorted. "Humph! Not by a jugful. I'll be out of this place in a week, and the doc says that after a rest to get back my weight, I'll be a new man. And believe me, they've got a strenuous program laid out for then, for I have to catch up on the time I've lost being sick. You know, under my contract, if I'm sick I have to make up the time and deliver productions by intensive work.

"Say, what are they trying to do to me? First they report me laid up, even say I have TB, and now they rumor me out of pictures! I wish you'd tell 'em for me that any guy's got a right to be sick once in his life, and I'd appreciate it if they'd let me do it in comfort. Not that comfort's the right word for this kind of thing. Do you know they had to fatten me just like a pig getting ready to be butchered? They sent me off to the Hot Springs to eat and lie in the sun so I could get ready for the butcher. But I put one over on 'em. I sneaked across the border for some hunting."

He started to grin, then remembered hospital orders.

"Put one over on 'em here, too. Nobody knew I was coming. Had 'em out and didn't tell a person. I don't remember the first night. Good thing, I guess. When a fellow gets to be in his forties, the knife is sort of unnatural to him. And ether!

"How did I get sick? I had pneumonia. Went over to Wisconsin and played around in the snow for my last picture. *Thunder,* they called it. *Snow* would have been better. I wasn't used to it or the cold, either. Living in California sort of makes you forget that you come from Denver. Pneumonia! I guess that's sort of likely to be serious. People tried to tell me to stay in bed, but I'm not much of a sick person. The nurse, there, will verify that statement. I went back to finish the picture and then it sort of started all over again."

He wasn't too explicit about what had started "over again," but studio personnel had mentioned that his already weakened bronchial area was further aggravated by slivers of the synthetic snow (used in interior sequences) that had accidentally gotten into his throat, resulting in a relapse.

He said, "Nobody is ever sorry for a man who is sorry for himself. If I'm playing a pathetic part on the screen, I never get to feeling it so hard that I'm sorry for myself even in character. I always tell the director, 'If I start lookin' as though I'm feelin' sorry for myself, stop me.' That's no way to get sympathy from people, even in pictures.

"I squawked my head off about this operation. I didn't want flowers and telephone calls and letters."

He just wanted his wife, who had been beside him every moment. Dressing down with mock irritation the young lady who was interviewing him, he said, "Say, I told you once before that if I had my way I'd never have an interview. I want to be a mystery. Don't you remember? And here, I can't even be sick. . . ."

Asked if he really intended doing more films:

"I never even thought of leaving pictures. Illness is all that prevents me being at the studio right now. I ought to be there. The last picture I made is already being released, and I'll have to hustle like the dickens to keep 'em up to schedule."

And his feeling about "talkies":

"I've said my say about them pretty often, but perhaps they misunderstood my meaning. They seem to take it for granted that I won't talk at all. I didn't ever say that, but I wanted to wait awhile. I didn't think the thing was perfected so that a man could get a real human quality into it. They say that they've done wonderful things lately. I want to see, when I get back. But I'm not afraid of the talker. Dean Immell, of the University of Southern California, is an expert, and he listened in on my squeaking. He says my voice is okay. I was on the stage before I ever thought of pictures and my voice seemed to get across there without any trouble.

"Taking these lumps out of my throat ought to help it. Sort of difficult to talk across a couple of baking-size potatoes. My leaving the screen is just about as silly as that rumor about my having tuberculosis, which I haven't. TB bugs like young and tender meat. I'm too old and tough for them to pay me any attention."

In 1957, in one of the finest, most moving film biographies Hollywood has ever put on the screen, Universal paid a tribute, and its debt, to Lon Chaney with its release of *Man of a Thousand Faces*, starring the great James Cagney in one of his best roles.

James Cagney as Lon Chaney, Sr.

The young reporter told him that it was also rumored he had held out for a more remunerative contract.

"Say, young woman, you ask too many questions. Don't you know I'm a sick person? My old one isn't up for a year. If you know so much, why do you ask me about it?"

"To get your answer," she retorted.

"Well, you got it, didn't you?" He started to smile, then remembered his throat operation. He had recently written the *Encyclopedia Britannica*'s official entry on makeup. The reporter asked, "Why didn't you show yourself being made-up instead of Johnny Mack Brown?"

He replied: "I wrote the piece, didn't I? Should an author show his own mug on what he has written? Do you print your own picture? Besides, I've told you before that it's my business to keep being a mystery. I didn't care about having them see Lon Chaney go through all his secrets. They looked different on another fellow."

The reporter wondered why they also showed Conrad Veidt and Emil Jannings in the *Encyclopedia*. He answered:

"Because I admired their makeup and they made good illustrations. I don't see any sense in hogging the whole show. . . . Say, young lady, you asked enough questions."

Released in July 1930, *The Unholy Three* was an instant success. Old fans and new ones were anxious to hear Chaney talk for the first time; and he proved how good he was by not only using his own natural voice and imitating an old lady, but playing three more parts as well. One of many glowing reviews said:

Mr. Chaney has made a further contribution to the modern motion picture—although it may be a bit indelicate to mention it here. Like the two dozen students who swam the Hellespont and so ruined the beautiful legend forever, he has destroyed the effect of the phrase, "See your favorite actor—he speaks." For while others were loudly proclaiming the finding of a forgotten note, he quietly went fishing and came back with five. The industry will never be the same again.

Having exhibited vocal qualities that exceeded everyone's expectations, he was now being touted as "The Man of a Thousand Faces is also The Man of a Thousand Voices!" Among the productions the studios were now busy lining up for him were *Cheri Bibi, The Sea Bat, The Bugle Sounds, Dracula,* and undoubtedly *Frankenstein*.

No one realized how ill he really was while filming *The Unholy Three*. On at least several occasions he could hardly muster up enough strength to leave the dressing room after finishing his makeup; yet, some-how, he found some mysterious and un-tapped source of energy. True trouper that he was, he knew the show had to go on.

He went immediately to New York after completing *The Unholy Three* to un-dergo special medical tests. After consult-ing with several leading specialists, he returned to rest up in his mountain retreat in the High Sierras. His strength was fail-ing rapidly; he and his family knew that his days were numbered. He was finally brought into a Hollywood hospital on August 1, 1930, for what was described as "acute anemia." A number of blood transfusions were given to him and he was placed on the critical list for awhile, but he suddenly appeared to have safely passed the crisis after a ten-day battle. Monday morning, August 25, he was reported in much better condition—in fact, he had quite an appetite and was taking his first nourishment in more than three days. At midnight a lung hemorrhage oc-curred so suddenly that physicians failed to reach him before he passed away at 12:55 A.M.

On the day of his funeral, Thursday, August 28, all work ceased throughout the film colony for five minutes when members of the Marine Corps fired off their rifles as a tribute to his memory, while their chap-

One of the many people in Universal's art depart-ment who were engaged in creating the pieces of art used in the film.

lain, Lieutenant Colonel Dyar, rendered a touching prayer. Celebrities came from all corners of the film world, and theaters throughout California and elsewhere gave their tributes.

At his death Lon Chaney was said to be worth around two million dollars. Every-one—except his first wife—was provided for by his will and heavy insurance policies. His wife Hazel passed away several years later, and his first wife, Cleva Creighton, died of a stroke, at the age of seventy-eight, in a Sierra Madre nursing home in No-vember 1967.

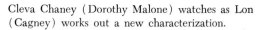

Cleva Chaney (Dorothy Malone) watches as Lon (Cagney) works out a new characterization.

In this scene Jim Backus visits Lon (Cagney) on a movie set where he is working as an extra.

WARDRO

PROD. 1844

PART OF `CH

PLAYER JAME

CHANGE NO
Sc. 5

WORN L

DESIGNER

CH#12

SUIC

WARDROBE TEST

PROD. 1844   DATE 10·24·56

PART OF   CHANEY

PLAYER JAMES CAGNEY

CHANGE NO. 1

WORN SC 1 THRU 10

DESIGNER EXT + INT THEATRE

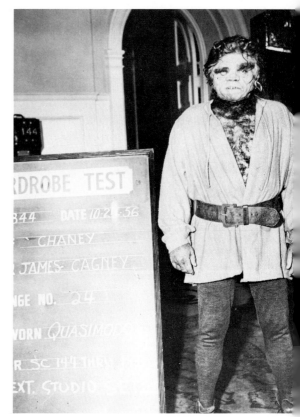

RDROBE TEST

1844   DATE 10·24·56

CHANEY

JAMES CAGNEY

NGE NO. 24

WORN QUASIMODO

R SC 144 THRU

EXT. STUDIO

54

Man of a Thousand Faces. Here and on opposite page James Cagney's re-creations of some of Lon Chaney, Sr.'s most famous roles.

Bela Lugosi
c. 1884-1956

"I—am—Dra—cula. I bid you—welcome." And: "I never drink—eh—wine." Undoubtedly the most famous lines in the history of horror films, spoken by one of the greatest actors in the genre: Bela Lugosi.

For most of the world, the story of Bela Lugosi's life, from his birth in Lugos, Hungary, until his death in Hollywood, was surrounded in mystery almost as thick as the mists that permeated the atmosphere of some of his movies.

More than is generally the case with actors—although many are reticent enough about some areas of their private lives—Lugosi's early years seem to be shrouded in secrecy. But this is more easily understood when Lugosi's personality is considered. In the first place, he communicated poorly with the "outside" world, and preferred the company of other Continentals, spending all the time he could in what passed for the Los Angeles area's Eastern European-Hungarian colony. And in those five short years when his name was still potentially "hot copy," he was, as will be seen, inaccessible to the important producers, publicists, and journalists who, failing to get much material about him, usually devised their "Lugosi stories" through padding and imagination. Tragically, it wasn't until the last years of his life, when poverty and need forced him out into the open, that more began to be known about Lugosi; and more tragically

56

still, further knowledge and a truer appreciation of this great star only began to surface posthumously.

Knowing also the area from which he came should create some sympathy for the number of writers who, in attempting to research Lugosi's life, might have done better covering the life and times of Tibet's Dalai Lama. The task of uncovering any significant details about the origins of an uncommunicative Eastern European artist, now deceased, is a formidable one, even for the most demon-driven archivist. Unlike the majority of known screen performers who emerged from accessible and familiar areas of America, England, and Western Europe, Lugosi came from Hungary; where —in addition to the usual language barrier— some half dozen wars and revolutions have made the country and its adjacent territories virtually impenetrable for the past sixty years. With this in mind, we can consider it fortunate that there is any Lugosi "story" at all to be told and that we are privy to at least some of the sadnesses as well as the joys of this very individual artist.

Even assuming that October 29, 1884 is Lugosi's birthday, as reported in *The New York Times'* obituary, dates of his birth have been at variance; the years 1880, 1882, and even 1889 have been listed at one time or another. But since 1882 or 1884 appear to be the most frequently mentioned, this would have made him forty-nine or forty-seven when he appeared in Dracula —an unusual age to achieve stardom.

His full name was Bela Lugosi Blasko (the "Lugosi" part of his name was taken from the village of his birth). His parents Paula (von Vojnics) and Stephen Blasko came from an affluent background and could well afford to give their only child the finest education. As soon as he was old enough, young Bela was enrolled in the Budapest Academy of Fine Arts, one of the world's most respected institutions specializing in dramatic arts. Participating in numerous recitals and full-dress plays, Bela

started gaining the attention of Budapest producers at an early age, and by 1900 he had appeared as Romeo in *Romeo and Juliet* at the Royal National Theater. In addition to his success in various Shakespearean dramas, he continued building an enviable reputation as a star in many Hungarian plays—translations of Shaw, Ibsen, Wilde, and many others adapted for the Budapest stage.

Though America was eventually to be the leader in the quantity and quality of film production by the time World War One was in full bloom, Europe had already proven its abilities through William Friese-Greene's pre-twentieth-century experiments and the magical delights of Georges Méliès; therefore it was only natural that film-making caught on fast, spreading like wildfire through every important capital on the Continent and turning Budapest into a major film center. By 1910 enough work was being created by Hungarian filmmakers to utilize the services of its country's struggling stage actors; this was also the year young Lugosi first broke into films —mostly in one- or two-reel dramatic shorts, but in enough of them to keep him busy for the next couple of years. In addition to these short films, he also undertook a considerable number of stage roles. As was the practice with many film productions, names of actors were often unlisted or else appeared under pseudonyms. But one more important fact about Lugosi's hazy early film career is that he appeared in a number of Hungarian films under the name of Arisztid Olt! Full data are, of course, unavailable; but according to *Magyar Filmografia* (an index of Hungarian films from 1901 to 1961) the Olt list includes *A Leopard* (1917) and *Casanova* (1918).

One of the many directors under whom Lugosi worked was Hungarian-born Mihaly Kertesz, who in 1928 continued his career in Hollywood under the name of Michael Curtiz. In less than eight years Curtiz would establish himself among the most notable film directors of the world

57

Rare photo of Bela Lugosi in a Budapest stage
role as Jesus Christ, around 1915.

with such gems as *Captain Blood* (1935), which made an overnight star of Errol Flynn; *The Walking Dead*, starring Boris Karloff; and later, *The Mystery of the Wax Museum; The Sea Hawk;* and *Yankee Doodle Dandy;* to name just a few. At the time of his death in 1962, Curtiz was eulogized for not only being one of the greatest film directors of all time but also as an important driving force that raised Warner Brothers to its position as a major studio and film distributor.

When World War One broke out, Lugosi answered the call to arms by enlisting in the Hungarian army. His commanding officers were so impressed by him, even at this early stage, that he was advanced at once to an officer's position; after serving for two arduous and harrowing years on the Serbian front, he was reassigned to lead his platoon into Russia. They came under heavy fire and Bela was severely wounded at least three times; once, in attempting to save a friend from death, he narrowly escaped the same fate.

He departed from the armed forces with full captain's honors after receiving the Hungarian equivalent of the American Purple Heart for action "above and beyond the call of duty." But then the Hungarian government, badly weakened by corrupt, internecine politics, was easily taken over by Communist revolutionaries, under the direction of the notorious Bela Kun, who destroyed their idealistic goals in a bloody reign of terror that even included some of their own comrades. Fearing for his own life because of his opposing political views, Lugosi fled to Germany.

Significantly, his first German role was in a horror film, *Necklace of Death*, made in 1919; next, in the role of Uncas, he appeared in *The Last of the Mohicans.* Postwar Germany was seriously burdened by refugees, and work was scarce in all fields, especially in film-making; but F. W. Murnau —already planning his immortal *Nosferatu*— liked Bela's personality and gave him a meaty part as a butler in *Der Januskopf*, an

Bela in a 1917 Hungarian film role.

adaptation of Stevenson's *Dr. Jekyll and Mr. Hyde*, starring Conrad Veidt in the lead dual-role. The adaptation veered substantially from the original Stevenson novel so that Murnau's company could avoid paying royalties. Prints of the film vanished long ago—a pity, since Murnau went on to become one of the most laureated directors. He went to America to continue his career, but a car accident ended his life in 1931 at the age of forty-two.

Having taken political sides in Hungary, Lugosi still feared reprisals, and with Germany in the throes of financial depression and his funds running perilously low, he secured work as an assistant engineer aboard an Italian freighter in order to work his passage to the United States.

Not knowing one word of English, friendless, and a total nonentity in the States, he immediately declared himself a political refugee to United States immigration authorities when he arrived in New Orleans. After the horrors of war, revolution, and the sadness of a depressed Europe, no obstacles appeared to him impossible to overcome. America was the land of promise, and after what he had experienced, seemed like a Paradise. Before long he found himself in New York City—managing, producing, directing, and starring in his own Hungarian stock company.

There was, however, a limit to the number of times he could profitably do Hungarian dramas in New York, and he realized that impoverishment was certain unless he made efforts to learn English. Still, he had the guts to try out for a Greenwich Village drama group which was producing *The Red Poppy*. The director was stunned when he found that Bela could only articulate in pidgin-English, using his hands or lapsing into occasional German when words failed him. *Incredible—this would never do.* Bela was astounded, therefore, when the director said that he was so impressed by Bela's appearance and felt he had so much potentiality that he would take a gamble on him—provided Bela *learned* to say his lines for the lead role of Fernando!

During the next three months preceding the play's opening, Bela probably worked harder at learning the basics of English than at anything he had ever done before. Under the tireless tutelage of one of New York's finest drama professors, he finally learned his lines to perfection. Yet on opening night Bela was so worried, he was certain that after he opened his mouth and said a few lines, they would "bring out the hook." But nothing happened. Could it be that they were saving all the eggs and tomatoes for the last act? Not at all. Indeed, when the final act was over and the curtain dropped, Bela and the rest of the cast had to take repeated bows—the

audience was ecstatic! The following day's notices were good and the play had a good run. And in all that time neither audiences nor critics ever realized that Bela had memorized his lines phonetically and had only a superficial knowledge of his part. He had, quite simply, been a human recording machine!

A variety of stage roles were now available to him, but, aware of his limitations and recalling his pleasant experiences in European films, Bela grabbed at his *first* United States film offer—a spy role, in Fox's *The Silent Command,* released in 1923. Bela's aristocratic manners and Continental charm not only impressed his colleagues but made the hearts of many young ladies flutter; and it was not long before Beatrice Weeks, who had also been involved in theatrical production, fell hopelessly in love with the handsome actor and became his wife.

Coping with English was still a trial for Bela, so he was happier whenever silent film work was available, though strong character roles on the stage kept him busy, such as the part of the Sheikh of Hamman in *Arabesque*; playing opposite Fredric March as Father Petros in *Devil in the Cheese;* and as Sergius Cheroff in *Open House.* Directors found at last that Bela was also an appealing-looking heavy when they cast him in his earliest known horror stage play, *The Werewolf.* Meanwhile, in 1925, ripples that would eventually affect him were being made clear across the ocean in England: a revival of *Dracula* was having a successful run in London, and though it had been presented on the stage for nearly thirty years since first opening in London in 1897, it had never before enjoyed such popularity nor so much acclaim. Horace Liveright, publisher of the book's American edition, was so impressed by the play's London success that he at once laid out production plans for its New York presentation. The pruning of the novel's 56,000-odd words for the stage adaptation in the 1890s had been neatly and professionally done; but the play still seemed talky and had begun to look a little dated. Consequently, a fresher version was created by John L. Balderston and Hamilton Deane.

When casting started, Liveright took one look at Lugosi and immediately advised his staff that this was *the* man—the *perfect* choice for the role of Dracula. Liveright was not only intrigued by Bela's unique personality and the sense of mysticism conveyed by his every movement and facial expression, but realized as well that Bela's background could create other residual benefits, for he had come from an area near the original vampire country, Transylvania; in the publicity and reviews that followed, this fact gave the play a colorful aura of mystery and suspense. Opening on Broadway on October 27, 1927, *Dracula* was an instant success; it ran for five hundred performances, and road companies of the play traveled all over the country, with the original Broadway cast (starring Lugosi) appearing in major cities for the next two years.

Lugosi's career suddenly slumped badly when the play's tour ended, however. Returning to Hollywood he learned that there had been a drastic change of climate in the film colony during his more than two years' absence. Silent films had given way to sound and had died out almost overnight. And Bela's English had an accent which diction-crazy Hollywood could not only cut with a knife but which it found highly undesirable. This attitude was to change eventually when film-makers came to realize that audiences loved actors more for their ability than for good looks and pear-shaped tones, especially when foreign actors with a Continental sound—such as Paul Lukas, Charles Boyer, Greta Garbo, Akim Tamiroff, and Elizabeth Bergner, for example—became numbered among the screen's highest-paid performers. Bela starred in a few unimportant roles, but his only film at this time worthy of note was *The Thirteenth Chair* (1929), mainly because it brought him to the attention of

Bela in 1930.

Universal Studios' producer-director, Tod Browning.

Paradoxically, the role and film that would raise Lugosi to stardom—*Dracula*—wouldn't be handed to him on a silver platter, despite his great credentials after three years in the stage version. Universal had an obsession about using in their productions only those actors who had made their mark in films—an obsession shared by other major studios that has, surprisingly, continued to the present time, resulting in lesser actors appearing in roles made famous and perfected by others on the stage—Audrey Hepburn instead of Julie Andrews in *My Fair Lady,* and Peter O'Toole instead of Richard Kiley in *Man of La Mancha,* to name but two. Originally considered for *Dracula* were Conrad Veidt, who had already starred in about a half-dozen fantasy-horror films (*Caligari, Student of Prague,* etc.); Ian Keith, established as a versatile screen hero and sometimes heavy since silent films; Paul Muni; and William Courtenay, who certainly must be considered the most unusual: Courtenay was primarily famous in theatrical work for his roles as Billie in *Trilby,* as Jules Beaubleu in *The Wolf* (1909), as Christian in *Cyrano de Bergerac* (1898), and as a matinee idol in dozens of other plays. More unusual yet is that Courtenay was a hero-lead in *Miss Jerry,* a two-hour film made in New York City in 1894—a full generation before full-length features films would even be attempted by studios! Though he was a renowned stage personality till the time of his death in April 1933 at age fifty-seven, Courtenay's film work was virtually nonexistent.

Whatever reason made Universal first consider such a distinguished but unsuitable array of talent in lieu of Lugosi is a mystery. Suffice it to say that sanity was restored and Tod Browning finally overrode others' dictates. Universal at last signed Lugosi to a five-year contract and began production on *Dracula* in early October 1930; after some three months of shooting and editing, the film was released in February 1931 to the accompaniment of typically brilliant Universal publicity. Overall costs amounted to about $400,000, the equivalent of some two million dollars in the seventies.

As the film begins, a coach, rushing its occupants through a mountainous countryside, attempts to reach its destination before sundown. One of the passengers is Renfield (Dwight Frye), a dapper young Englishman who has been commissioned through correspondence with Count Dracula to arrange for the shipment of the Count's personal effects to his future English residence, Carfax Abbey. On Renfield's arrival at the remote Transylvanian village, the townspeople's hospitality gives way to agitation when he explains his presence and says that a private carriage will

An unusual photo showing the small-scale model used in long shots of the Count's castle in *Dracula* (Universal, 1931).

A NIGHTMARE OF HORROR!

DRACULA

with
BELA LUGOSI · DAVID MANNERS
HELEN CHANDLER · DWIGHT FRYE
and EDWARD VAN SLOAN

A TOD BROWNING PRODUCTION
FROM THE FAMOUS NOVEL AND PLAY BY
BRAM STOKER

A UNIVERSAL RE-RELEASE

47/140

One of the lobby cards for *Dracula*.

Program cover and cast guide of the very first presentation of *Dracula*, given at the Royal Lyceum Theatre in London on May 18, 1897.

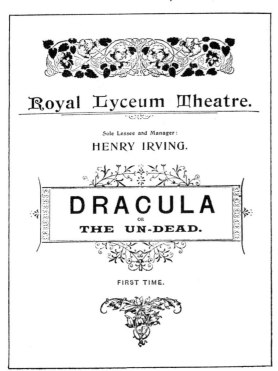

Royal Lyceum Theatre.

Sole Lessee and Manager:
HENRY IRVING.

DRACULA
OR
THE UN-DEAD.

FIRST TIME.

TUESDAY, MAY 18, 1897, AT A QUARTER-PAST TEN O'CLOCK A.M.,
WILL BE PRESENTED, FOR THE FIRST TIME,

DRACULA
OR
THE UN-DEAD

IN A PROLOGUE AND FIVE ACTS
BY
BRAM STOKER.

Count Dracula	Mr. JONES.
Jonathan Harker	Mr. PASSMORE.
John Seward, M.D.	Mr. RIVINGTON.
Professor Van Helsing	Mr. T. REYNOLDS.
Quincey P. Morris	Mr. WIDDICOMBE.
Hon. Arthur Holmwood (*afterwards Lord Godalming*)	Mr. INNES.
M. F. Renfield	Mr. HOWARD.
Captain Swales	Mr. GURNEY.
Coastguard	Mr. SIMPSON.
Attendant at Asylum	Mr. PORTER.
Mrs. Westenra	Miss GURNEY.
Lucy Westenra	Miss FOSTER.
Mina Murray (*afterwards Mrs. Harker*)	Miss CRAIG.
Servant	Miss CORNFORD.
Vampire Woman	Mrs. DALY.

63

Bela as Count Dracula.

arrive soon to carry him through Borgo Pass to Dracula's castle. He scoffs at their superstitions and vague warnings, and before long his coach arrives, attended by a strange coachman wearing a large hat, his features hidden by a heavy coat collar and winding scarf. Off goes the carriage down an incredibly tortuous mountain road, gathering momentum and dashing on at breakneck speed—like a rollercoaster gone wild. Frightened by the ride, Renfield peers out the window to signal the driver to slow down; but the driver seems to have vanished. Instead, the horses are being led by a huge bat flying over them! The carriage approaches the path leading to the castle, which is atop a precipice, surrounded by high mountains. The very Stygian look of the area is rather as Hades must have seemed to Orpheus.

Passing through the castle's huge creaking doors, Renfield is witness to five hundred years of desolation and decay: ancient drapes hang in black tatters around a great hall crawling with vermin and odious-looking creatures; large sections of stonework lie broken and crumbled beneath huge pillars that support vast archways fronded by a jungle of cobwebs. The little light that seeps in spectrally through the huge broken windows does not help to dispel the unbridled gloom by making the room more visible.

Renfield turns in his amazement to find that this huge mausoleum does indeed house a tenant. Standing upon the great stairway and clutching a lit candelabrum is the tall, caped figure of the castle's owner:

"I—am—Dracula. I bid you—welcome."

Renfield introduces himself, somewhat detailing his bewilderment; Dracula shows Renfield the way to more comfortable quarters upstairs. The disquieting howls of strange-sounding animals from outside further unnerve Renfield—he pauses while Dracula explains in his own inimitable way:

"The children of the night. What music—they make!"

Another shot of Lugosi as Count Dracula.

As Dracula goes up the steps, an eighteen-foot-wide spider's web presents no barrier to him; he passes through it without breaking it. But Renfield must sweep aside the sticky web's strands to go on, hardly becalmed by Count Dracula's ironical metaphor:

"A—spider—spinning its web for the unwary—fly."

Dracula's upstairs quarters are opulent and well kept, in stark contrast to the ferment of neglect below. Renfield, while finalizing the contract covering the shipment of the Count's personal effects, accidentally cuts his finger on a paper clip. At this, Dracula's face takes on a satanic expression, and it is only the sight of a crucifix hung around Renfield's neck that forestalls a compulsive attack on him by the Count. Dracula feigns hospitality by offering his guest some vintage wine. Renfield cheerfully accepts, for his arduous travels have left him tired and thirsty. When he asks his host if he too will quaff the exotic wassail, Dracula cryptically responds:

"I—never drink—eh—*wine!*"

Dracula leaves his guest to retire for the night, but not before saying in a mocking tone:

"Good night—*Mis-ter*—Renfield."

The wine has been drugged; it is Dracula's intention that Renfield be not only his traveling and real-estate agent but his slave as well. Renfield falls unconscious to the floor and three wraithlike women enter to make him their prey. Livid with rage, Dracula rushes in to thwart them before they can begin their sanguinary repast. Henceforth Renfield becomes Dracula's personal creature.

Once Dracula leaves his Transylvanian environs, there is an almost abrupt change in the pacing and quality of the film. After destroying the entire crew of the ship in which he crosses to England, the Count is seen as a man of culture on his way to a concert at Albert Hall—but not before

having a refreshing diversion during his stroll: a poor flower-girl near the concert hall joins the list of his victims. During the concert he introduces himself to Mina, Lucy, and their escorts. He is courtly, charming, and for the first time seems very human but terribly melancholy. His new friends invite him to their home, never suspecting the evil that Dracula will bring into their lives. Renfield meanwhile has been incarcerated in Dr. Seward's asylum for the insane after being discovered babbling and laughing aboard the death ship that carried Dracula to England. But Professor Van Helsing, an antiquarian and a specialist in the occult, sees more sinister implications in Renfield's ravings. Tragedy befalls Lucy when she becomes Dracula's victim, but this provides Van Helsing with additional clues that form links in the chain exposing Dracula's true horrible identity. Even while Dracula is gradually ensorceling Mina, Van Helsing prepares to unmask him before Seward and the others. Whipping out a mirror, Van Helsing holds it up before Dracula's face: it casts no reflection of the Count. Dracula snarls in rage, then quickly recovers; but realizing

The insidious Count Dracula (Lugosi) attempts to place the lovely Helen Chandler under his spell.

Simultaneously with the Lugosi version, and using the same sets, Universal shot a Spanish version of *Dracula* with an actor strongly resembling Bela in the title role and a different cast.

Another scene from Universal's Spanish version of *Dracula*.

Time for Bela's coffin-break in the Carfax Abbey sequence of *Dracula*.

Publicity shot of Bela and Helen Chandler for *Dracula*.

that Van Helsing is now on to him, he apologizes curtly to the incredulous company and departs. Dracula returns to deal with Van Helsing, but the Professor's will is too strong for Dracula to overcome, and now Van Helsing becomes the hunter.

While attempting to save Mina from Dracula and from becoming one of the undead, Van Helsing and Mina's fiancé (David Manners) temporarily lose track of the Count and his victim. At last, after an exhaustive search through the very bowels of Carfax Abbey's catacombs, Van Helsing finds Dracula in his coffin and, driving a stake through his heart, destroys him. Happily, they discover that Mina is alive, and with the Count's death, is released from his spell and again free.

Though it spawned several dozen sequels and hybrids, including the excellent though more commercial-looking *Horror of Dracula* (1958), there has never been anything to surpass Lugosi's *Dracula* or, for that matter, its brilliant predecessor, *Nosferatu* (1922). It may even be said that, for sheer and inimitable terror, *Nosferatu* is superior and that director F. W. Murnau's literate understanding of a nightmare's essence is vastly more sensitive and Gothic than Tod Browning's. *Horror of Dracula* (aided by an effective but cornball score) proved the advantages of stimulating the senses through Technicolor, physical action, and by accentuating what others eschewed: violence and gore. At

the very least, it elevated a fine actor, Christopher Lee, to stardom; however, vampire roles have haunted him ever since, involving him also in several execrable productions under witless directors.

What distinguishes the Lugosi *Dracula* from *Nosferatu* and all the others is . . . Lugosi. Certainly *Dracula's* screen treatment cannot be the reason for its surviving for two generations as an acclaimed classic; for, once action leaves Transylvania and moves to London, production values decrease sharply, and the camera is no longer used very imaginatively except for several short scenes—such as Dracula's appearance outside Seward's asylum as he communicates mentally with Renfield, and the Carfax Abbey sequences. Comic touches by an idiotic maid and a silly, moustached hospital orderly who look like Sennett comedy-factory refugees are almost clumsily intrusive, and Renfield's unrestrained, cavorting, wheezing antics all but ruin sev-

Dracula. Bela leading Helen Chandler to Carfax Abbey.

eral of many embarrassingly stagebound scenes. The other supporting actors are stock types, particularly David Manners, whose wooden-Indian style adds nothing; but Helen Chandler as Mina is quite good and most attractive, and Edward Van Sloan as Van Helsing is the film's second most important and best performer.

For all of the superiority of *Nosferatu*, Max Schreck as the vampire Count is such a consummate apparition of horror and evil that he is too unclean and unreal—rather like a monstrous malignancy that should only be seen among the things that chirp and gibber in the dark. At the opposite extreme, Christopher Lee's portrayal in *Horror of Dracula*, under Terence Fisher's sometimes utilitarian direction, has him appearing in his first scene somewhat like a troubled but handsome Byronic anti-hero; though he becomes magnificently dramatic under provocation and when his blood-lust rises, he is physical rather than cerebral in a milieu that is more mundane than occult.

Lugosi, on the other hand, is evil but elegant—an unworldly alien, but one who is not completely divorced from human activity. His deeply set eyes mirror well the agony as well as the ecstasy of vampirism. The way he speaks in a slow, steady, Hungarian-accented but individualistic Lugosian voice *is* the way Dracula would be expected to speak. Notwithstanding their redoubtable talents, Schreck and Lee reached their most frightening peak because of makeup and special effects. Lugosi used his whole body and inimitable face to achieve the same results—a face that could be satanically malevolent but flexible enough to express loneliness and understanding with dignity.

In spite of some great moments and unpardonable flaws, *Dracula* is an undying masterpiece solely because of Lugosi. For Lugosi *is* Dracula!

Even while Universal was scheduling *Dracula* for release, plans were already set in motion to film *Frankenstein*. Lon Chaney had originally been scheduled for the Monster role at the time *The Unholy Three* went before the cameras; his untimely death, however, delayed production plans. Lugosi now seemed to be the natural choice. Test-footage was made with Lugosi wearing a costume and makeup somewhat resembling the Golem, and completely different from the monster later portrayed by Karloff. The story is that Lugosi finally rejected the role because it lacked dialogue and seemed a comedown after *Dracula;* but it is more logical to assume that James Whale, who replaced Robert Florey (the original director), made the final decision. The rest, of course, is history.

Appearing next in *Black Camel*, Bela was the red herring in this Charlie Chan mystery with its very quaint Egyptian setting, replete with macabre touches, hidden tombs and treasure, curses and murder, all neatly resolved and rationalized by the finale. Bela turns out to be the strange but friendly swami who eventually helps Chan.

Chandu the Magician (1932) seemed miscast with Edmund Lowe, of the rough-and-tumble school of acting, starring as the famous magician, and Bela in a good but hardly sensational villain role that many others could have played. The roles should have been cast the other way around.

Murders in the Rue Morgue (1932) adhered closer to Poe's original tale than the majority of films bearing the celebrated author's name. Combining top-drawer talent, it could not help but emerge a classic: Karl Freund, the cinematic genius of *Metropolis* and director of *Mad Love*, was the photographer; a young John Huston wrote part of the script; and Robert Florey was the versatile and imaginative director at the helm. Obviously influenced entirely by Robert Wiene's *Cabinet of Dr. Caligari* (which probably did more to influence film-making than any other film), it gave plenty of room for a beetle-browed and tousled-haired Lugosi to enjoy his Caligari-mad-scientist role. As Dr. Mirakle he runs

Dancing cheek-to-cheek with Thelma Todd is Bela, in a supporting role opposite Joe E. Brown (*right*) in the comedy, *Broadminded* (First National, 1931).

That's Arlene ("What's My Line?") Francis being crucified by Bela in *Murders in the Rue Morgue* (Universal, 1932).

Seated near each other like underground-film-society buffs, Bela and his murderous ape worked as a team in *Murders in the Rue Morgue.*

As Sydney Fox lies unconscious, Bela receives bad news from Noble Johnson in *Murders in the Rue Morgue.* Johnson appeared in many horror-shock features, such as *The Mummy* (as the Nubian), *Ghost Breakers* (as the frightful zombie), and *The Most Dangerous Game,* to name but a few.

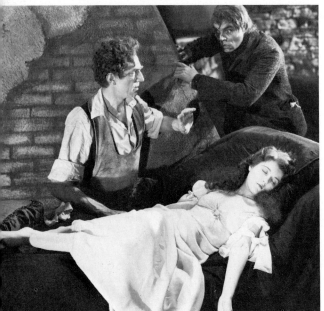

an offbeat carnival attraction by day, regaling audiences with his theories of evolution and man's proximity to apes, using his own private giant orangutan to spice up the act. By night though, Bela is engaged in diabolical experiments, transfusing the great ape's blood into unwilling females. When they die he howls, "I've failed again!" Back to the drawingboard, assisted by Noble Johnson (the famous "Nubian" of *The Mummy* and the unforgettably horrific zombie of *Ghost Breakers*), Bela sends the ape out to bring back more victims. In between, in a rather Mr. Hyde-type gaslit street scene, Bela entices a sidewalk hostess (Arlene Francis) to visit his homey spider-webbed domicile; she, too, doesn't survive a hideous ordeal (though she was reincarnated years later on "What's My Line?"). For shocks and Grand Guignol horror, *Rue Morgue* was quite ahead of its time, only equalled three years later by *The Raven.*

There is general agreement that *Dracula* was Lugosi's most important film; but too often disregarded is the lesser known *White Zombie.* Lugosi's role as M. Legendre, the evil master of zombie slaves, is easily as good as Count Dracula—if not better. The main problem is that to appreciate the film's classical impact and Bela's grandstand magnificence the film has to be seen, and to the utter despair and growing disgust of cineastes, *Zombie* is rarely shown in revival houses and now never seen on TV, though local stations continue proving their tastes by offering such disasters as *Ghosts on the Loose* (starring the Bowery Boys!) that Lugosi was reduced to playing in—but still more enjoyable than most of "The Beverly Hillbillies" or "I Love Lucy" episodes.

White Zombie is among the few horror classics which, like *Destiny, Caligari, Nosferatu,* and Universal's *Black Cat,* gains supremacy with age; each, literally, is one of a kind. What they and lesser horror-fantasy film classics have is a common heritage rooted in Gothic Romanticism which

Bela as the murderer Legendre in *White Zombie* (UA, 1932).

grew out of European mythology and folklore—or, more simply put, fairytales. Trolls, warlocks, and *Beowulf*'s Grendel remind one of *Dracula*—indeed, *Nosferatu*'s Schreck does resemble an elf king or a goblin-gone-wrong. In *White Zombie* the facets of several famous legendary archetypes combine to create this Faustian-like drama: Lugosi's Legendre is a synthesis of the *Odyssey*'s Circe; the witch and sorcerer of innumerable children's fantasies; the Mephistophelian nemesis, or tempter, found throughout the Bible, epic poetry, dramas, and opera. Legendre, therefore, is not a character accidentally thrust into his role or a victim of "durance vile," but the master of evil practices by choice and destiny.

White Zombie begins as Madeline journeys to Haiti to meet her fiancé and get married. Well-to-do Beaumont befriends her aboard ship and is soon head over heels in love with her. She informs him of her betrothal, but soothes Beaumont by prom-

ising to have her wedding take place on his inland estate. Later, as Madeline and her fiancé, Neil, travel by horse-drawn carriage down a lonely road through the interior, they witness a strange funeral—under special rites, a corpse is being interred in the midst of the road so that it cannot be unearthed and turned into a zombie. Lugosi's presence is soon evident as his eyes loom gigantically, superimposed over the scene. Moments after, the travelers see the bizarre figure of Lugosi standing silently by the roadside; his mere presence frightens them, particularly Madeline, who recoils when he comes closer. As in the climax of Ingmar Bergman's *The Seventh Seal* (1957), when Death leads his victims across a rise, so in this film does a procession of zombies appear atop a nearby hill, evoking a cry of "Zombies!" from the carriage driver; he drives away in terror, but not before Lugosi snatches Madeline's shawl to keep for his own mystical plans.

Zombies in *White Zombie* toiling away for Lugosi as cheap labor—"cheap" because the evil Legendre never paid them a cent!

Soon Madeline and Neil arrive at Beaumont's estate and are welcomed as his house-guests; but their host can barely disguise his frenzied love for Madeline. Driven nearly out of his mind, he decides to seek Lugosi's aid even though he loathes him and has been forewarned about him by a faithful servant. In a little while Beaumont is driven away in a carriage (sent by Lugosi) with a zombie at the reins. Arriving at Lugosi's sugar plantation, he witnesses a scene that seems more suitable to Dante's *Inferno* than to this earth: pushing long oarlike handles around a huge sugar mill are zombies, staring vacantly without feeling or emotion and unconcerned when one of their number loses his balance and topples into the immense vat where cane is being crushed. Only the moaning and creaking sound of large wooden gears is heard.

Lugosi is slighted when he extends his hand and Beaumont refuses to clasp it in greeting. Lugosi speaks:

"I've been on a journey—getting men—for my mills."

Appalled, Beaumont asks, "Men?"

"They work—faithfully. They are not worried about long hours. You could make good use of men like mine—on your plantations."

"No, that's not what I want," Beaumont answers.

"Then perhaps you want to talk about the young lady who came to your house this evening."

"You've seen her?" Beaumont asks. "When?"

Then slowly, in gloating irony, Lugosi answers:

"There—was a young man with her."

Beaumont says, "They're to be married tonight. If *she* were to disappear. . . ."

"What do you hope to gain by her disappearance?" Lugosi asks.

"Just give me a month—one little month. . . ."

Lugosi says, "Not in a month nor even a year. I have looked into her eyes. She is deeply in love—but, not with you."

Frantically, Beaumont says, "They are to be married within the hour. There *must* be a way!"

"There *is* a way," Lugosi replies with evil determination.

The scene shifts momentarily to the zombies—the sound of the crushing sugar mill is now louder, almost unbearable. Baumont cringes in terror: "No, not that!" Eyes blazing diabolically, Lugosi holds up a potion: "Only a *pinpoint*, Monsieur—in a glass of wine—or—perhaps—a flower?" Placing the vial in Beaumont's hand, he says, "You must do your share if I am to help you." Beaumont at first refuses. "Keep it, Monsieur," says Lugosi. "You may change your mind. . . . There is no other way."

Later, just before the wedding, Beaumont once more begs Madeline to change her mind. Failing again, he hands her a rose touched by the potion; she sniffs the flower, thus beginning her entrapment in a circle of evil. Even while Madeline and her beloved stand before the altar, Lugosi is casting his spell, whittling away at her waxen image from afar; then, wrapping the effigy in her shawl, he holds it over a lantern's flames and lets it melt away. At the wedding feast, Madeline reads her fortune in a wineglass: "I see happiness. I see love, far more than I deserve." Neil asks, "Is that all?" The wineglass grows upon the screen to giant proportions, with Lugosi's diabolical eyes blending in. She says, "I see—I see—death!" and she falls dead, while her husband cries out her name repeatedly in agonized despair.

The next sequence finds Beaumont, Lugosi, and his "special" zombie attendants at the cemetery near Madeline's mausoleum. Lugosi's evil powers are never more clearly evident than when he points to his "servants" and says: "In my lifetime they were my enemies. The witch doctor, once my master. The secrets I tortured out of him. Von Gelder, the swine, swollen with riches—he fought against my spell even to the last. Scarpia, brigand chief. And this—this is Chauvin, the high executioner, who

Madge Bellamy is stolen from her tomb by Robert Frazer, Bela, and his zombie legion in *White Zombie*.

Bela, Madge Bellamy, and Robert Frazer in another scene from *White Zombie*.

almost executed me. I took them—just as we will take—this one."

"But what if they regain their souls?" Beaumont asks.

Lugosi smiles sardonically. "They would tear me to pieces; but that, my friend, shall never be." They then proceed to carry Madeline's body away.

Trying to douse his sorrow in a tavern, Neil imagines he sees Madeline's silhouette moving on a wall. Tearing himself away, he goes to the cemetery only to discover to his horror that her coffin is missing; his screams echo and re-echo through the mausoleum chamber.

There is a cut into the next scene —Lugosi's castle. Staring vacantly, Madeline is playing the piano like an automaton, not comprehending what Beaumont is saying. Consumed by remorse over his deed, he says almost prayerfully, "I must take you back." Lugosi says scornfully, "Back to the grave, Monsieur?"

"Anything's better than that awful expression," says Beaumont. "You must put the light back into her eyes and bring laughter to her lips. She must be gay and happy again."

Lugosi answers, "You paint a charming picture, one that I should like to see myself."

When Beaumonts reiterates, "You must bring her back!" Lugosi logicizes, "How do you suppose those eyes will regard you when the brain is able to understand?"

"Better to see hatred in them than that awful emptiness," answers Beaumont.

Lugosi feigns sympathy, anticipating trouble. "Perhaps you're right. It would be a pity to destroy such a lovely flower. Let us drink to the future of this flower. A glass of wine?" Both men toast each other, but Lugosi's face seems to change into a satanic mask. Noting that his drink tastes odd, Beaumont gasps, "What are you trying to do to me?"

"I've taken a fancy to *you*, Monsieur," Lugosi answers in a sinister tone.

Beaumont's degeneration doesn't take long; fighting in vain against the potion's effect, he reaches out in supplication for Lugosi's hand. "You refused to shake hands with me once—I remember," Lugosi says. Beaumont is reduced now almost to the level of a gibbering idiot, and his will vanishes.

White Zombie. Bela's zombie legion consists of former associates—once allegedly normal men who have become his slaves.

One of Bela's zombie elites in *White Zombie.*

As Bela makes a wax figure of him, Robert Frazer gradually turns into a semi-zombie in *White Zombie.*

White Zombie. Joseph Cawthorn (*left*), assisted by John Harron (*right*), bring Bela's evil career to an end.

Driven by some mysterious power, Neil passes through desolation until he locates Lugosi's mountaintop eyrie. Before he is even within the main hall, Lugosi senses his presence and formulates his evil plan: Madeline will kill her own husband under the necromancer's direction. Neil is rendered unconscious under Lugosi's hypnotic will. Madeline approaches, clutching the very knife Lugosi has just used to create Beaumont's wax image. Just as Madeline is about to plunge the knife into Neil, a missionary (who has already helped Neil a short while ago) wrests the weapon from her hand. Neil quickly revives, but finds himself threatened by Lugosi's four "special" zombies who chase him to the cliff's edge. With demonic fervor, Lugosi delivers his ultimatum in answer to Neil's query about the zombies: "To you, my friend, they are the angels of death!" Overconfident and drunk with his sense of power, Lugosi doesn't notice the missionary who catches him off guard and hits him on the head. Without orders from their leader, the four zombies who have been pursuing Neil walk mechanically off the mountain's edge, plunging down to their final resting place.

Regaining consciousness, Lugosi attempts to escape, but his occult power has diminished. Beaumont dredges up his last ounce of will during the confusion and lunges at Lugosi; in a fatal embrace, both men hurtle down the precipice to oblivion. Madeline returns to normal as she and Neil are reunited, love once again proving itself strong enough to overcome all evil.

White Zombie has received more coverage in this book than any other film because it could very well be *the best* in the genre. Certainly few horror-fantasy films have so smoothly and artistically blended the basic principles of *sight, sound,* and *imagination* with such classical effect. Strikingly rich and beautifully *antique* in visual details, *camerawork* tells the entire story; dialogue serves only supplemental—with dramatic force—but very sparingly, with practically all the best lines said by Lugosi. Original horror-film scoring has often been good or adequate, but it has rarely been created with so much dedication and obvious quality for the sole purpose of enhancing the macabre. Supremely decadent, limned by rich symbolism and esoteric overtones, *White Zombie* is Lugosi's finest film.

H. G. Wells' science-horror novel, *The Island of Dr. Moreau,* was adapted for the screen by Philip Wylie and released in 1933 as *Island of Lost Souls,* starring Charles Laughton as a mad scientist whose experiments involve trying to turn beasts into men—with horrific results. In a small but imposing role, Lugosi (in wolfman-like makeup) plays the troublemaking leader of the animal-men who (after years of painful experimentations) revolt against their tyrannical Prometheus and destroy him. The theme, especially that of the latter sequence, was altered extensively but used with great success by director Georges Franju to create his relevant socio-horror essay, *The Horror Chamber of Dr. Faustus* (*Yeux Sans Visage,* 1960).

In the interim Lugosi coasted along in his erratic career; then Universal considered the tremendous advantage of uniting two great horror names in one film: *The Black Cat* (1934), co-starring Boris Karloff (further detailed in the Karloff chapter). Karloff seemed somewhat more dominant simply because he was the main heavy, while Lugosi played an eccentric but highly sympathetic role. As a man haunted by the scars of war and tragedies, Lugosi, en route through Hungary aboard the *Orient Express,* meets a young couple (Jacqueline Wells and David Manners). Chance brings them together again when the shuttle bus in which they are riding overturns in a storm. With the aid of Lugosi's burly major domo, Thamal, they all head on foot to Marmaros, Karloff's fortresslike chateau, Lugosi's original destination. Later on it becomes evident that Karloff is a warped genius who has benefited by betrayal (he sold out to the enemy in the war) and

Bela plays an Eastern swami in *Night of Terror* (Columbia, 1933), with Wallace Ford (*right*), of *Freaks'* fame, and Sally Blane.

Bela, with Egon Brecher as the major domo, Thamal, in *The Black Cat* (Universal, 1934).

SHOOTING AT THE STARS

PLAYED COUNT DRACULA IN "DRACULA" ON BOTH STAGE AND SCREEN

HEIGHT 6 FT. 1 IN. WEIGHT 179 LBS. EYES DARK BLUE HAIR DARK BROWN

ALSO PLAYED IN "MURDERS IN THE RUE MORGUE"

Bela Lugosi

PLAYED IN EARL CARROLL'S STAGE PLAY "MURDER AT THE VANITIES"

STARRING WITH KARLOFF in "BLACK CAT"

FOREST AGES McGINN

BORN IN LUGOSI, HUNGARY, OCT. 29, 1884, SON OF BARON LUGOSI A BANKER

Biographically slightly inaccurate (Bela's father was not a baron), this is nevertheless interesting "Believe It or Not" style material on *The Black Cat*, syndicated in newspapers in 1934.

others' lives. Lugosi bides his time; but even his patience comes to an end upon learning that—apart from heading a sacrificial devil cult—Karloff had married his (Lugosi's) wife (who died under mysterious circumstances) and is now married to Lugosi's daughter! Overwhelmed by the enormity of Karloff's depravity, Lugosi later goes completely berserk on discovering his daughter's dead body. Isolating Karloff in his underground laboratory with the help of Thamal, Lugosi has Karloff stretched out on a rack and disrobed. His face contorted by the passion of vengeance, he says:

"Do you know what I am going to do with you now? Did you ever see an animal skinned? That's what I'm going to do—tear the skin from your body—slowly—bit by bit!"

True to his word he proceeds to flay

80

Karloff alive with a sharp scalpel—Lugosi laughing insanely, Karloff screaming in pain. David Manners misconstrues Lugosi's good intentions (while helping Jacqueline Wells escape) and shoots him. Dying, Lugosi says: "You poor fool . . . I was only trying to help. Now . . . go. Please go." As David and Jacqueline are leaving the building, Lugosi, with his last bit of strength, limps over to a jungle of relays and switches on the wall. Facing Karloff's shredded but semiconscious figure, he says:

"Five minutes—and this switch ignites the dynamite. Five minutes and Marmaros, you, and I—this whole rotten cult will be no more. . . ."

Out in the open and at a safe distance, David and Jacqueline turn to see Marmaros explode, lighting up the skies like an angry volcano.

Black Cat stands out as a landmark in the genre—many buffs have even dubbed it the best of Universal's "Golden Horror Films" of the thirties—with Lugosi in one of his several finest roles.

It was also during this time that Lugosi tried making ends meet by appearing in his second serial, *The Return of Chandu*

Bela as the heroic and mysterious Chandu in the 12-chapter serial, *The Return of Chandu* (Principal, 1934).

(1934), in the title role. (His first, *The Whispering Shadow*, was shown in twelve chapters in 1933.) Scarcely any serial ever made rose above the self-imposed limitations of two-dimensional cardboard characterizations and monosyllabic dialogue. And the greatest of the cliff-hangers, *Flash Gordon*, was little more than a vehicle for the capable and handsome Buster Crabbe and the special-effects department. Bela had neither Buster's Greek-god looks nor athletic build, nor were his five serials a great challenge to the special-effects technicians. But they were styled well and thrillingly enough to make Saturday matinees pass pleasantly, and were often better made than the double-feature programmers on the same bill; moreover, they probably paid Bela more than the five hundred dollars he said he had received for *White Zombie*.

The other Lugosi serials were: *S.O.S. Coast Guard* (1937); *Shadow of Chinatown* (1937); and *The Phantom Creeps* (1939). In their own way they had—besides Lugosi—enough charm and allure to warrant profitable re-release in edited feature-film form within two to three years; and *Chandu*, the best of the lot, was even made into two carefully edited separate features consisting of different sequences from the first and second half of the twelve-part serial—the first under its original title, *The Return of Chandu*; the second, *Chandu on the Magic Isle*.

Tod Browning returned with a remake of *London After Midnight* (1927)—which was also directed by him—titled *Mark of the Vampire*; it was in the typical Browning tradition of being an excellent but gigantically flawed minor masterpiece. The combination of stunningly macabre scenes, Lugosi looking more Draculean then ever, and a Vampire Girl (who seems to have stepped out of a Goya print) airborne on bat wings, work so well—and indeed still remain among the most outstanding moments in fright-film history—that they offset an atrociously hokey ending: Lugosi and the Vampire Girl go off into a dressing room to take off their makeup; they were

Bela in 1935.

Publicity shot for *Mark of the Vampire* (MGM, 1935). The girl is Carol Borland; Lugosi is on extreme right.

81

Bela and Carol Borland in an eerie scene from *Mark of the Vampire*.

The concept of basing a film story line on a collector of Edgar Allan Poe memorabilia was used only twice: in *The Raven* (Universal, 1935), with Bela in the lead, and in *The Man Who Collected Poe* segment of *Torture Garden* (Columbia, 1967.), written by Robert Bloch and co-starring Peter Cushing and Jack Palance.

Irene Ware rebuffs Bela's romantic proposal in *The Raven*.

only hired actors helping to unravel a murder mystery. Out the window flew the bats, imaginative sensibility, and Browning's reputation. But a small and devoted cult has grown around his films—primarily because of *Dracula* and *Freaks*, which are undeniably unique, and, though all gravely flawed, are above most of the then-current product.

Though Bela would continue working for another twenty-one years, one of his last starring roles in a major quality production was in *The Raven*, a film that inspired a long spate of similarly oriented horror films that made a fortune for American International in the sixties and seventies. Lugosi plays Dr. Vollin, an Edgar Allan Poe fanatic, who makes his living by day as an eminent surgeon but, by night, gloats in the privacy of his home over his *special* Poe artifacts. His mania for Poe has reached such extremes that his entire house is outfitted with Poe memorabilia and devices: a bedroom that sinks into the basement; a torture chamber; walls that move crushingly together, and a giant, razor-sharp pendulum.

One night, while attending an interpretive ballet version of *The Raven* (staged à la Isadora Duncan), he falls madly in love with the star dancer. Lugosi finds his golden opportunity to prove his affection when the young girl is almost killed in a terrible auto accident and he saves her by his ingenious surgical skill. Even though the only payment he wishes is her affection, he is brokenhearted to find she is already engaged. Further, he is stupidly rebuffed by her father who believes his daughter is better off with a colorless young man than with the great doctor who saved her life. The notorious killer and criminal, Boris Karloff, is on the loose and seeking a hideout; unfortunately he lands in Dr. Lugosi's sanctum sanctorum for a plastic-surgery job. After the operation Karloff looks in a mirror to see himself horribly disfigured. Lugosi promises he will restore Karloff to "normality" if he helps carry out Lugosi's plan of vengeance. Karloff agrees, and before long the dancer, her fiancé, and the dumb father are Lugosi's prisoners—and probably getting everything they deserve for their callousness. All of

Bela carefully prepares an escaped criminal (Boris Karloff) for a "special" plastic-surgery job in *The Raven*.

the Poe-like torture devices are brought into sharp focus and used with near-lethal effect. But as in *King Kong* "it was beauty killed the beast," in *The Raven* there's a soft spot under Karloff's beastly grotesqueness; and as the deadly pendulum is a hairsbreadth from slicing the girl's father in two, Karloff shuts off the mechanism and saves his life. Lugosi shoots the "traitorous" Karloff and shoves his prisoners into a chamber. Now Bela is completely raving mad, and his laughter reverberates through his gallery of horror, as gradually, the chamber's walls threaten to crush the prisoners. But Karloff isn't quite dead, and in a last burst of strength he frees the victims. It is Lugosi instead who becomes the victim of his own instrument and is crushed to death.

In this film Lugosi is, of course, provided with one of his best roles, and Universal (like the rest of Hollywood) continued pandering to middle-class views by holding up intellectuality as hare-brained and as rich fodder for derision.

84

Personal misfortune and poor business sense began taking their toll, and Lugosi's status was now seriously on the wane. This was very evident in *The Invisible Ray* (1936), in which Karloff is the star and Bela one of the supporting players. Though Bela's role is much the smaller, it is quite important in that it quashes a canard and exposes the limitations of overrated critics and college-circuit journalists who, after seeing several Lugosi films (usually his poor Z-budget Monograms and PRCs on TV), label him a "limited" horror actor. Indeed, in his exquisitely polished and sympathetic role as Dr. Benet in *The Invisible Ray*, Lugosi complements his career and proves his great flexibility by never once conveying even a scintilla of "menace" or "overacting," as some have accused him of after seeing him in low, low budgeters—and, indeed, he *had* to overact in such films, for he was consciously aware that only this would redeem their pin-headed plots.

After a number of unimportant roles in unmemorable films (e.g., *The Best Man Wins*, 1935; *Postal Inspector*, 1936), Bela took off for England where, like Karloff, he

A special production shot of Bela for *The Invisible Ray* (Universal, 1936).

A particularly rare closeup head shot of Bela in *The Invisible Ray.*

Bela is being accused by an insane Karloff of having stolen his great discovery in *The Invisible Ray.*

Karloff, Bela, and Walter Kingsford in *The Invisible Ray.*

Bela is the epitome of the dangerous intriguer and espionage agent as he is accosted by Lawrence Grant in Republic's 12-chapter serial, *S.O.S. Coast Guard* (1937).

hoped his fortunes would improve and where he was to star in *Mystery of the Mary Celeste* (1936). Loosely based on the famous factual story of the nineteenth-century ghost ship discovered on the open sea completely intact but without a soul aboard, it starred Lugosi as the man responsible for getting rid of everyone. Unfortunately he wasn't very successful in the part, and the film was completed and released for the critics to chew up; for once they weren't entirely wrong.

Bela around 1938.

Virtually without work for two years and with his funds drying up, Bela was on the brink of selling everything he owned and applying for welfare relief. But even if fortune wasn't smiling broadly, at least it grinned enough to permit him an auspicious return, now that the "ban" on horror film-making was gradually lifting. Proving once more his ability to adapt to any part, he took on the very demanding role of Ygor the crazed shepherd in *Son of Frankenstein*. Hung by the neck by the local villagers and thought dead, Ygor survived with a crooked neck to continue a lonely and strange existence as the "friend" of the Monster (Karloff). When Baron von Frankenstein (Basil Rathbone) arrives to claim the estate he has inherited, Ygor uses him to revive the Monster so that the creature can murder those villagers who hanged him. As it finally dawns on Baron Frankenstein that Ygor has been up to foul play with the Monster, he shoots Ygor dead. Outraged and brokenhearted, the Monster kidnaps the Baron's wretched little son—a regular little Son of a Baron, and undoubtedly the film's only major flaw—but fumbles his chances for vengeance and seemingly dies in a sulphur pit.

It is generally conceded that Ygor was one of Lugosi's best performances; it was so well played—often in rich, graveyard-humor style—that he stole scene after scene.

The year 1939 was an interesting and profitable one for Bela. MGM grabbed him to appear in a small but outstanding role opposite Greta Garbo in Ernst Lubitsch's Award winner, *Ninotchka*—that of the "Comrade Commissar" who gives Party orders to Garbo to carry on their "glorious cause." Fox reunited him with Lionel Atwill in a remake of an old chestnut titled *The Gorilla*, a horror comedy starring the Ritz Brothers as zany detectives in the old "monster-loose-in-the-old-mansion" tradition.

England called Bela back to star in *The Human Monster* (1940), easily one of the most effective essays in Grand Guignol put on the screen—crude, bloodletting,

A revealing shot of the prop "pit" out of which Bela and Boris emerge on a cue from the director of *Son of Frankenstein* (Universal, 1939).

Bela, as the loyal creature's aide, guards the Karloffian Monster in *Son of Frankenstein*.

modern film escapades notwithstanding. Playing two roles, he runs an insurance racket under the name of Dr. Orloff and dons a disguise and changes his voice to become the elderly, kind, and blind Mr. Dearborn, director of a run-down home for the blind. After insuring his victims he disposes of them from his blind people's home which he uses as a front for his criminal practices. His usual method of murder is to lure his victims to a private attic in the sanitarium where, with the aid of Jake, a hideous blind giant, they are first drowned in a tank before being dropped from the attic into the River Thames. Unaware that Lugosi has murdered her father, Diana Stuart (Greta Gynt) goes to work as a secretary in his insurance office—Lugosi feels it's safer for her to be close enough where she can be watched. But Lew, a blind mute street violinist, knows too much:

"You have been very foolish, Lew," says Lugosi. ". . . You're blind and you can't speak, but you can hear, and that will never do."

The inhuman doctor places two wires, hooked onto an electrical machine in his evil loft, into Lew's ears and destroys his hearing, thus turning the blind cripple into a helpless invalid. Meanwhile, an autopsy reveals that one of the drowned victims has clear tap water in his lungs, not the dirty water of the Thames. Clues start piling up, and Diana can no longer be trusted. Lugosi sends Jake to her apartment with orders to take care of her (Jake has already been seen on one of his London field trips murdering a potential witness in his bathtub). Jake's attempt to murder Diana is foiled by detectives who spot him fleeing through a window. The next day at the sanitarium, Diana confronts Lugosi with incriminating evidence. He admits that he's killed her father, then drags her upstairs to his loft to dispose of her. As Jake, acting on Lugosi's instructions, lifts her bound form to drop into the water-filled tank, she screams out: "Jake—where's

Walt Disney hired Bela as a model for Satan's face in *Fantasia* (Walt Disney Productions, 1939).

Diabolical scientist Bela operates the hideous robot he created in the 12-chapter serial, *The Phantom Creeps* (Universal, 1939).

Patsy Kelly, the Ritz Brothers, and Bela (in *back*) starred in the horror-comedy, *The Gorilla* (20th Century-Fox, 1939).

Lew, Jake?" (The helpless Lew had been drowned in the tank and disposed of earlier by Orloff.) Diana realizes that yelling out Lew's name is her only hope of arousing the pathetic compassion that Jake had shown for the helpless man in the past. Diana says, "He's gone, Jake. Orloff got rid of him like he got rid of all the others. Out of this window into the river!" Searching for Lew, the brutish Jake proceeds to tear the room apart, bellowing in rage. Lugosi can no longer control him and fires a shot from his gun. He is about to finish off Diana himself, but she is saved when he hears the police below; failing to contain them, he retreats to the attic. As Lugosi flees up the stairs leading to the roof, his leg is grabbed by a hand—Jake is still alive and hell-bent on revenge. Swinging his great arms around trying

Bela (*background*) sermonizes from a lectern in his poorhouse for the blind in *The Human Monster* (Monogram, 1940).

Bela masquerading as the kindly blind poorhouse director in *The Human Monster*.

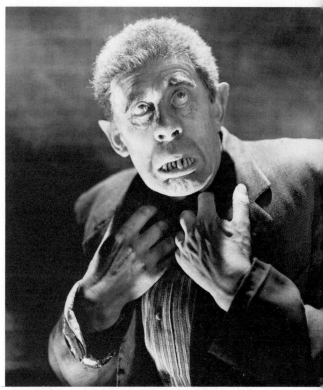

The blind monster, Jake (Wilfred Walters), in *The Human Monster*.

Bondage photos were considered taboo in magazines and books during the '40s and even during the early '50s, especially if they showed the victim being touched, as in this scene from *The Human Monster* with Bela, Wilfred Walters, and Greta Gynt.

Bela is a mad scientist raising monster bats for fun, profit, and . . . murder in *The Devil Bat* (PRC, 1940).

to trap the elusive Lugosi, and nearly being pushed into the Thames in one unguarded moment, Jake has his vengeance at last and shoves his evil master into the terrible mud flats below.

Human Monster was officially the last film of any stature that could be called a "Lugosi vehicle," even though shoestring companies would capitalize on his name as

the star of execrable films with comic-book plots, such as Monogram's *The Devil Bat* (1940), whose one-line plot starred Bela raising a giant bat that kills his enemies if they put his *special* shaving lotion on their necks. But it wasn't just Monogram that was grinding out bombs. Universal that year cast Bela in an awful gangster bit role in *Black Friday*. The film starred Karloff, even though it was mainly Stanley

The Devil Bat. Alan Baldwin doesn't realize that using Bela's special shaving lotion will not only make him popular with girls but will attract a monster bat.

Ann Nagel, Stanley Ridges, and Bela in *Black Friday* (Universal, 1940).

Ridges' film (he's a dear old professor who takes on Jekyll-Hyde tendencies after Dr. Karloff places part of dead racketeer Bela's brain in his head, etc.). It may be considered odd that Arthur Lubin was the director, since he went on to create the excellent *Phantom of the Opera* three years later—but maybe it's not so strange, since he reverted to potboilers like the *"Francis-the-talking-mule"* film series, the *" 'Mr. Ed'-talking-horse"* TV series, and *"The Incredible Mr. Limpet-talking-fish"* film that, fortunately, never became a series.

Bela fared somewhat better in *You'll Find Out* (1940), sharing the spotlight with Karloff and Lorre as one of three dangerous crooks masquerading as occult mediums; but Kay Kyser (and his madcap orchestra) was the comedy star, and he resembled Harold Lloyd enough to look adequately funny while getting scared by the three professional bogeymen.

But 1941 was a year of degradation for Bela. For the first time, he met the Bowery Boys in *Spooks Run Wild;* played a geek-like gardener bit in the cretinous *The Black Cat;* stood in attendance in a small butler role in *Night Monster,* saying "Yes, sir; no, sir"; and was reduced to playing a bit role in the film in which he had originally been slated to star—*The Wolf Man.* Ironically, in this he was cast in the role of

Bela, Maria Ouspenskaya's werewolf son who infects Lon Chaney, Jr. before getting clubbed to death by a silver cane.

The general acclaim accorded *Son of Frankenstein* (1939) inspired Universal to resurrect Lugosi's Ygor role and that of the Monster for *Ghost of Frankenstein.* Even if the public began wondering how much longer the Monster could endure its innumerable revivals, the studio had at least enough discretion to have Ygor admit he was pretty sick, battered, and could use a new body. He asks Dr. Frankenstein (Cedric Hardwicke) to put his brain into the Monster's head. Hardwicke is appalled at the idea—an intelligent, ruthless brain like Ygor's would make the Monster more formidable and terrifying than ever. He goes on with his original plan to transplant

Kay Kyser was a perfect Harold Lloyd-like foil for Bela in *You'll Find Out* (RKO, 1940).

Besides Bela, the most notable thing about *Spooks Run Wild* (Monogram, 1941) was that Carl Foreman (a famous director years later) wrote the script.

Universal's *The Black Cat* of 1941 bore no similarity to the 1934 classic; it featured Bela in a minor red-herring role.

Playing Ygor for the second time, Bela led the Monster (Lon Chaney, Jr.) on to new thrills and adventure in *The Ghost of Frankenstein* (Universal, 1942).

the brain of Dr. Kettering (a good friend killed earlier by the Monster) for the good of mankind, thus preserving Kettering's genius in the Monster's body. Of course, this never happens, though it would have been interesting, if not riotous, to find an intellectual Monster later having office hours and practicing medicine. Even the "true" Monster (Chaney, Jr.) has his own opinion; he would like the brain of a little girl he fancies. Apparently in a dispute over brains, the Monster crushes Ygor, and leaving the audience to deduce whatever can be drawn from his answer, Lugosi says, "Then Ygor die for you!" Under prearranged plans, a malcontent doctor (Lionel Atwill) will insert Ygor's instead of Kettering's brain in a last-minute switch, hoping later to achieve fame and power with an Ygor Monster behind him. While Atwill gloats, Hardwicke is horrified to hear Lugosi's voice coming out of Chaney's Monster body and wonders why Atwill *changed his mind.*

The Night Monster (Universal, 1942). *Left to right:* Frank Reicher, Lief Ericson, Ralph Morgan, Francis Pierlot, Lionel Atwill, Nils Asther, Don Porter, and Bela as a butler.

Neither Atwill nor Monster gloat too long; a fact overlooked when performing the brain transplant was that Ygor and the Monster were of different blood types, resulting in the Monster suddenly going completely blind, becoming berserk and bringing down the laboratory, and ending the film. Quite obviously the Frankenstein series was starting to go downhill.

One film worthy of attention that emerged from Lugosi's Z-films was *Bowery at Midnight* (1942), which was understandably though mistakenly avoided by even the hardiest buffs under the impression that Lugosi would be seen being bothered once more by the Bowery Boys. Much was accomplished on the tiny budget, including the hiring of some of the best B-film actors available: David O'Brien, Tom Neal, Wanda McKay, John Archer, and even former silent-comedy star Snub Pollard. The plot was a direct swipe from *Human Monster* but with new twists and embellishments. Lugosi's dual role has him appearing as a respected college professor by day; on the side, he operates a weird Bowery mission for the poor, getting rid of his victims in an even weirder basement. There was also a little borrowing from *Arsenic and Old Lace:* the mission's basement contains a growing group of burial plots in full view—though the dotty Brewster sisters in *Arsenic* only speak about their basement cemetery, which is never seen. An occasional camera shot in *Bowery* reveals that underneath the burial plots there is a delightfully mysterious sub-basement inhabited by ghoulish types—they seem to be either former occupants of the graves above or some "unnameable" obscenities from Lovecraft's Cthulhu mythos. The action and story move neatly, with an assortment of interesting characters—quaint mission derelicts, puzzled policemen, a hero and heroine, and many more. In the end, as Lugosi tries eluding justice, one of his own disenchanted henchmen, old "Doc," pushes him into the sub-basement among the ghouls, who start going to work on him.

For *Black Dragons* (1942), Monogram

94

Bowery at Midnight (Monogram, 1942). An unusually good low-budgeter, and not a "Bowery Boys" flick, as its title might suggest. The plot and Bela's dual role were similar to those in *The Human Monster.*

Nazi plastic surgeon Bela agrees to change Japanese into Caucasians for espionage work in America in a scene from *Black Dragons* (Monogram, 1942).

Bela is consoled by his understanding sister (Minerva Urecal) in *The Ape Man* (Monogram, 1943).

turned Bela into a Nazi plastic surgeon sent to Japan to change Oriental spies into Caucasians. The studio even carried Bela's alleged personal endorsement in its ad campaign: "I defy moviegoers not to gasp when they see *Black Dragons*. Never have I worked in a story so startling or so blood-chillingly shocking. See it if you dare!" Monogram's usual plywood-and-cardboard sets surrounded Bela in *The Ape Man*, in which he's an odd, brilliant scientist who lives so long with a pet gorilla used in blood and hormone experiments that he begins to look like the beast. To return temporarily to normal, Bela kills girls for their spinal fluid. The gorilla may have considered this a slur, for he kills Bela. Falling into the category of films that are so bad that they're good, *Ape Man* is sheer pleasure. It co-stars perennial loser-type Wallace Ford and that old hatchet-faced barnacle of the Z-films, Minerva Urecal.

Columbia Pictures tried an essay on vampirism starring Bela in *The Return of the Vampire* (1943)—a strained attempt to imitate *Dracula*, using war-torn London as a setting. Bela stars as Armand Tesla, a strange Continental who mingles in London's high society which little suspects his vampirical motivations. Aiding him is a reluctant stooge, Andreas (Matt Willis), who can only go about doing evil work when he turns into a werewolf under Bela's supernatural influence. Some good moments really accomplish little in overcoming long and drawn-out drawing-room scenes and dull dialogue.

Universal erred badly that year by casting Bela in the Monster role in *Frankenstein Meets the Wolf Man*. Personal problems and excesses had taken their toll of Bela and were now so evident that stunt-man Ed Parker was hired to double for scenes that would have been routine for Bela a few years before. Essentially, the film placed heavier emphasis on Chaney, Jr. as Larry Talbot, the Wolf Man, with the Monster reduced to almost a travesty.

The Ape Man. Bela is the one on the right, of course.

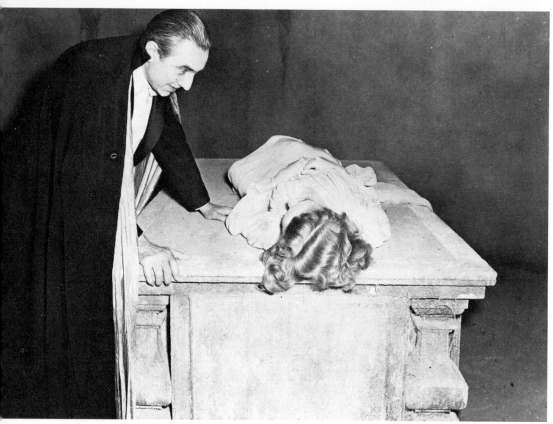

Bela assumes a Dracula-like stance in *The Return of the Vampire* (Columbia, 1943).

Publicity shot of Bela for *The Return of the Vampire*.

The Monster à la Lugosi in *Frankenstein Meets the Wolf Man* (Universal, 1943).

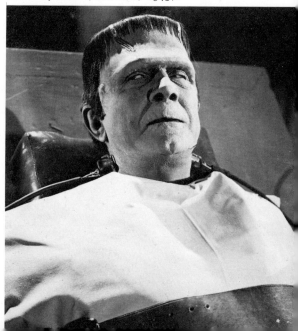

Ilona Massey, Lon Chaney, Jr., and Bela in *Frankenstein Meets the Wolf Man.*

United with John Carradine and George Zucco (one of the finest but most neglected actors of all time), Lugosi muttered, "Life unto life" a couple of times and did other things in *The Voodoo Man* (1944), which almost—but not quite—became a candidate for the "so bad it's good" Hall of Blame. Bela has literally recruited an organization dedicated to the sole purpose of kidnaping girls so that their "life force" can be transferred to his comatose wife, who has been in a trance more than twenty years. She can only be revived if Bela finds the "right" girl. But this experiment is a chronic failure; each female victim becomes a zombie and takes her place in a catacomb-like basement attended by John Carradine, who plays a geek and probably mumbles the best line while ushering in the newest arrival and stroking her hair: "H—mmm—you're a pretty one."

Odd and unusually mediocre films had practically all but claimed Lugosi by the

Huntz Hall and Leo Gorcey trussed up and undoubtedly getting their just desserts in *Ghosts on the Loose* (Monogram, 1943). Next to Bela (*right*) is Minerva Urecal; to her left is pudgy-faced Frank Moran.

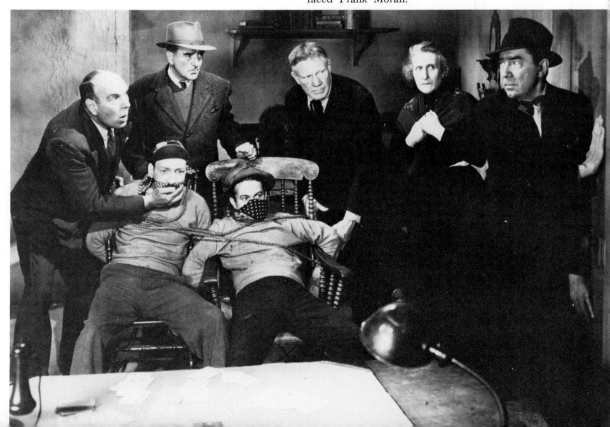

George Zucco and Bela are the dynamic duo in *Voodoo Man* (Monogram, 1944).

Bela keeps a B-budget bogey at bay with a blow-torch in *The Return of the Ape Man* (Monogram, 1944). Frank Moran is the bearded, not-so-jolly "scream" giant.

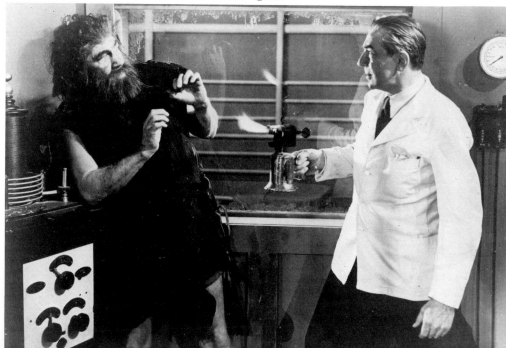

mid-fifties, though he fought valiantly against his inevitable decline even while appearing in things like *Zombies on Broadway* (1945); this featured Alan Carney and Wally Brown, RKO's shoestring answer to Universal's Abbott and Costello. And while even a great actor may look foolish in a bad film, Bela, under Robert Wise's excellent direction, shone well though briefly in the role of Joseph in *The Body Snatcher*, starring Boris Karloff. Working for eminent Edinburgh physician Henry Daniell, Bela cannot refrain from blackmailing Karloff into sharing with him his lucrative cadaver business. Bela's greed is his undoing when Karloff "demonstrates" his corpse-making technique.

Universal decided to gang up all its great monsters in 1948 for one last fling in *Abbott and Costello Meet Frankenstein* (by now everyone was referring to the Monster as "Frankenstein"). Bud and Lou, however, not only did *meet* old flat-top but also a mad female scientist (Lenore Aubert), Chaney, Jr. as the Wolf Man, and . . . Lugosi, appearing in a film as Dracula for the first time in seventeen years. The studio's makeup department did yeomanlike work in disguising Bela's years; once more it was like the good old days, as he stalked about hypnotizing Lou, and now possessed extra powers through a special ring capable of restoring the Monster's good health in order to carry out his orders. Count Dracula's objective is solidly to entrench himself for some kind of power-play that is shrouded in ambiguity and all but forgotten amid the delightful antics of Bud and Lou and the rest of the cast. The center of attraction, of course, is Lou Costello—nothing would please Dracula more than to have Lou's brain transferred to the Monster's skull; this is part of Dracula's master plan which is to be carried out with the scientific aid of Lenore Aubert, who has fallen under his spell. The total result is hilarious, well-planned horror-comedy satire, rarely ever created so well for the screen, and the best of all the Abbott and Costello films.

Abbott and Costello Meet Frankenstein (Universal 1948). An interesting study of Bela's face as Dracula, seventeen years after his star debut.

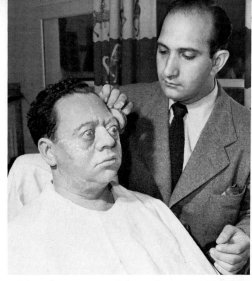

Bela's influence turned second-rate comic Wally Brown into a zombie for *Zombies on Broadway* (RKO, 1945). Here Brown gets made up for the role.

Bela (*center*), as Joseph, assistant to Henry Daniell (*right*), stands by as Daniell and an ominous Boris Karloff talk in *The Body Snatcher* (RKO, 1945).

An altercation between Glenn Strange (the Monster) and Lon Chaney, Jr. (the Wolf Man) is being refereed by Bela in this publicity shot for *Abbott and Costello Meet Frankenstein.*

Glenn Strange (also famous as the barkeeper on television's "Gunsmoke" series) as the Monster, Norman Abbott, and Bela take time out on the set between takes of *Abbott and Costello Meet Frankenstein.*

100

Bela on the set of Renown Pictures' *My Son the Vampire* (1951), also shown under the titles *Old Mother Riley Meets the Vampire* and *Vampires Over London*. The friendly visitor is horror-film producer Richard Gordon (*The Haunted Strangler, Corridors of Blood,* etc.).

Without doubt his role in *A & C Meet Frankenstein* was Lugosi's final blaze of glory, though for the next eight years he did appear in a few increasingly inferior films that were, if anything, tragic testimonials to the man's personal and professional ruination spanning twenty years.

Lugosi's career problems were well known for a long time throughout Hollywood. Bad management and the lack of sound promotion, combined with his own difficulty in swinging with the right circles, undoubtedly raised barriers. Some believed that his idiosyncratic ego invited professional ruination. But even if his bungled affairs and eccentricity could have been surmounted, there isn't the slightest doubt that the skeleton he had hidden for twenty years would have broken any professional's career—for Bela had a serious *drug problem.*

In 1955, while placing himself under official hospitalization for therapy, Lugosi revealed to the press how he had started suffering from physical complaints in 1935 during the filming of *Mark of the Vampire.* To alleviate the misery, which he described as "shooting pains in my legs," Lugosi underwent medical treatment that involved a series of morphine injections. When the treatment ended, he had become heir to a monkey on his back!

In a more enlightened generation Bela's problem wouldn't have been a stigma. In the late fifties, Alexander King—the renowned fantasy artist, author, and raconteur—explained to the millions who watched him on the Jack Paar show how medical malpractice could transform a once-normal man into a junkie. King revealed how he, at one time, suffered from severe pain stemming from a kidney ailment. Various doctors relieved the agony by giving him large doses of morphine. Later, with only part of one kidney left, he marvelled that he had survived. In his best-selling autobiography, *Mine Enemy Grows Older,* he also described his periods of sedation as the most blissful moments of his life. After ten years of uncontrollable addiction, King finally went in an out of Lexington several times to be cured.

Forty years ago drug addiction was a social nightmare and turned a man into a social leper. When his doctors were done with him, Lugosi, like King, had nowhere to turn; consequently, for three years he resorted to devious connections for his fix. Bela said, "I knew after a time it was getting out of control."

Methadone treatment, with its heinous side-effects, was virtually unknown throughout most of the world until the 1960s; but it had been developed in England during the late thirties, and something was known there of its effect in treating addiction. Bela had journeyed to England in 1938, anxious for a methadone cure. He later said, "I smuggled a box of it back. I guess I bought a pound." Treating himself under methadone and Demerol in the privacy of his home, Lugosi eventually realized to his despair that he had traded one drug problem for another. He said, "I didn't eat. I got sicker and sicker."

Since professional therapy for addiction was either taboo or unheard of at the time, Lillian, Bela's fourth wife, took full charge. She not only went through the Herculean

101

job of being his soul-mate but became his nurse and doctor as well. Her approach was extremely intelligent and sensitive, probably far better than any treatment center could provide today. Gradually she lessened his dosage, and at last he appeared to be cured. But Lillian's ordeals over the years became more than she could bear. To her, Bela seemed recovered. And, quite abruptly, now feeling unchained, she left him.

Though Bela seemed superficially recovered, Lillian's desertion had a traumatic effect; then, too, his addiction and drawn-out cure had exhausted him physically and spiritually, and he felt unfit to resume his career. As he explained in an interview: "She gave me the shots. And she weaned me. Finally, I got only the bare needle. A fake shot, that's all. I was done with it. Then she left me. She took our son. He was my flesh. I went back on the drugs. My heart was broken."

On April 21, 1955, two years after the court granted Lillian her divorce and full custody of their son, Bela voluntarily admitted himself to Los Angeles General Hospital as a self-declared drug addict; the next day, a judge granted him his request for professional care, and he was transferred to Metropolitan State Hospital in Norwalk, California. Typically unrestrained, bluntly and cruelly, the papers sensationalized the event: "Bela Lugosi Admits He's Used Narcotics for Twenty Years!" "Bela Commits Himself as Dope-Addict!" While in the streets the ignorant

said, "I always thought he was a bit too weird."

Bela was now so wasted away, he looked like a mere ghost of his once stately and aristocratic self; he stood over six feet tall in stockinged feet but weighed only 125 pounds.

Bela's recovery was indeed amazing, if not monumental. The doctors pronounced him cured fifteen weeks following his commitment. In view of what he had endured for twenty years, his release was a brilliant testimonial to the man's long-submerged inner strength—it was as though he were hurrying to make up for years of humiliation, of being sometimes all alone. Feeling bouyant and on the threshold of a new life, he spoke about his hospitalization in a *Newsweek* interview, exclaiming that his recovery "was the greatest thing that ever happened to me!"

To prove his fitness, Bela grabbed his first film assignment barely two weeks after leaving the hospital, and stood before the cameras for United Artists' *The Black Sleep*. Heading the stellar cast were Basil Rathbone, John Carradine, Akim Tamiroff, Lon Chaney, Jr., and Tor Johnson. But by any standards, Bela's part was a sad comedown; he appears as an old, mute butler working for mad-doctor Rathbone, who is engaged in scholarly but gruesome experiments upon humans. Bela was happy to be back in harness, though, among old friends again. His personal ordeals had also battered him enough so that he required scarcely any makeup. Old age had apparently taken him over at seventy-three; he was now deaf in one ear, arthritic, and easily fatigued; he had trouble following cues and remembering lines. When a friend remarked about his appearance, Bela agreed he didn't look well, but quickly retorted, "Yet I feel like a new and better man inside. Give me a few months. I'll be back in shape; I'll look better."

True to his word, Bela did indeed seem to improve. Furthermore, a week after he

Bela, reduced to playing a mute butler, faces Basil Rathbone in *The Black Sleep* (UA, 1956).

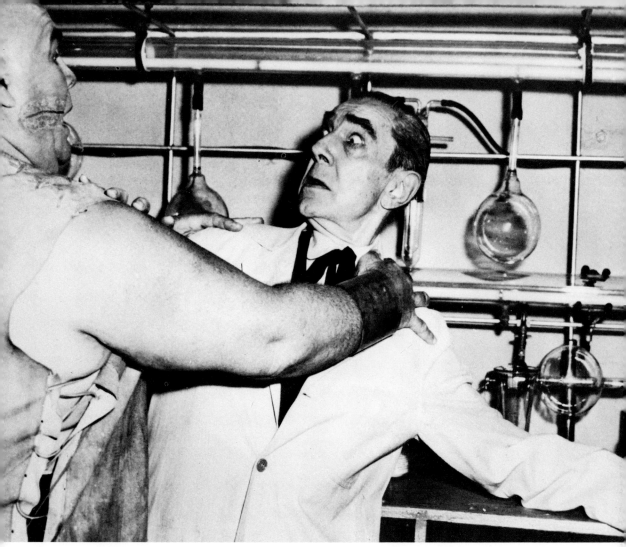

Tor Johnson turns against his master, Bela, in *Bride of the Monster* (Edward D. Wood, Jr. Productions, 1954; released 1956). Alternate title: *Bride of the Atom*.

he started work in *The Black Sleep*, Bela married his fifth wife, Hope Linninger, a clerk in a film-studio editing department who had been a fan-correspondent of his since the thirties.

In his next film, as the lead in *Bride of the Monster*, he looked as if he had shed many years. Lacking substance as well as quality, the film was yet another reprise of Bela as a mad scientist, futilely attempting to create supermen. Co-starring were veteran stuntman, Ed Parker, and former wrestling ham, Tor Johnson. Execrable but most droll, *Bride* should interest anyone

Bride of the Monster. Bela is probably informing his female victim that low-budget film-making also includes a low-budget lunch.

Plan Nine from Outer Space (D.C.A., 1956). Bela's last film appearance.

Bela as he looked while hospitalized for drug addiction in 1955.

searching for gigantic production flaws, such as laughably obvious painted "stone walls." Sadly, it was also Bela's last *true* film.

Calling *Plan Nine from Outer Space* Bela's "last" film is seriously open to challenge, since it's questionable whether he ever officially acted "in" the film. Approximately two vague minutes of his presence can hardly justify star billing; what little is evident shows Bela fumbling around the doorway of his actual residence, and then strolling outside down a walk. The sequence bears no relationship to anything in the film and actually looks like low-quality amateur test footage. By far one of the worst films ever concocted, it's a "winner," nevertheless, because of innumerable unintentionally hilarious errors. Because it was completed posthumously, all key scenes implying Bela's presence used a Chris Lee-like double, discreetly holding the folds of a cape across his face.

The Lugosis had been occupants of a neat garden apartment at 5620 Harold Way in Hollywood for over a year. Early on the fateful evening in August 16, 1956, Hope left Bela resting comfortably and headed for a local food market. Though tired, he had seemed in good spirits throughout the day; thus it never occurred to Hope that

One of the last photos ever taken of Bela Lugosi— while he was recovering and planning a comeback in 1956.

104

in less than two hours after returning she would be interviewed by the press and say: "He didn't answer me when I spoke, so I went to him. I could feel no pulse! Apparently he must have died a short time before I arrived. He was just terrified of death. Towards the end he was very weary, but he was still afraid of death. He told me he was. I did my best to comfort him, but you might as well save your breath with people like that. They're still going to be afraid of death."

Death had come to Lugosi at around 6:45 P.M. and was officially diagnosed as a massive heart attack. Even at his own wake he seemed forlorn; only several relatives, a few friends, and sprinkling of fans came to pay their last respects. Two days later, Bela was interred in Lot 120 in the Grotto Section of Holy Cross Cemetery. He was laid to rest according to his wishes, wearing the cherished cape he had worn in *Dracula*.

Castle of Frankenstein contributor and Lugosiphile, Barry Brown (recently a star in his own right in Bogdanovich's *Daisy Miller*), said in a touching tribute to the star:

"Lugosi's career was filled with ephemeral film plots that all sprang from his one ethereal characterization: Dracula. He died without achieving his greatest wish: to be acknowledged and revered for his dramatic talent. Like the suicide of Marilyn Monroe, Lugosi's tragic pilgrimage through the dreary drugworld once again demonstrated the consequences of Hollywood's misuse of true talent."

Bela's final resting place.

Mr. and Mrs. Brian Donlevy (the former Lillian Lugosi) shortly after their wedding in 1965.

Bela Lugosi, Jr., who is today a corporation lawyer and a partner in the Los Angeles firm of Hanna and Morton.

The apartment house where Bela died: 5620 Harold Way, Hollywood, California.

Boris Karloff

1887-1969

For good reasons Boris Karloff (born William Henry Pratt in 1887) has been acclaimed one of the greatest performers who ever lived, even though his fame and fortune came from being typecast as a horror star for more than thirty-seven years. A number of years ago, in a book of humorous sketches about film stars, noted author and screenwriter Wolf Mankowitz wrote: "K is for KARLOFF, or the monster who was made good by the Frankenstein of television. . . . The Shirley Temple of the horror-film business, he acquired in twenty years of filming a mythological reputation sufficiently sinister to be used for scaring refractory children."

Yet if others showed worry or concern over Karloff's typecasting, certainly Karloff wasn't bothered. He had already appeared in hundreds of rolling stock-company productions from the boondocks of Canada (where his dramatic career first began in late 1910) to small towns and whistle-stops in the United States. A stock company he was in finally landed in California, after touring a number of midwestern and western states. Finding himself suddenly without steady employment after the company unexpectedly disbanded, Karloff quickly discovered the young and bustling Hollywood of 1917 as a source of modest but steady income. Until fortune would smile upon his Frankenstein Monster head nearly fifteen years later, he was to appear in

106

more than ninety films, most of them lost forever, or even forgotten, involving so many varied roles and titles that even Karloff himself was unable to remember them all. So, by the time he was in his forties and still unrecognized, Karloff had easily paid his dues twice over.

Typecasting? "No problem," Karloff said in his homage to the genre and to *Frankenstein*, the film that made a man into a professional "monster."

"The monster was indeed the best friend I could ever have. I was already well past forty and not getting any younger, and worried," Karloff said. "They tell me I'm typecast. Well, I've been fortunate. Actors are extremely lucky to be typecast, like any tradesman who is known for specialization. It is a trademark, a means by which the public recognizes you."

He once said: "I didn't begin my stage or screen career with the idea of becoming a horror character, but the chance which led me into that type of role has brought me the things I want and lifted me out of the rut. It is the most difficult thing in the world to play straight parts in which an actor has to be himself."

Karloff had said that ability must mark time for the "lucky break"; if one can agree, then it does indeed appear that chance played a part in turning a hitherto unknown, if experienced, actor into the world's most famous monster overnight.

But the Karloff facade and *presence* had much to do with his success, too. His face had a mystic quality that is unique; the dark, intense eyes, compressed line of mouth, and strongly sculpted planes of cheek and jaw were solid bases upon which to build the dozens of astounding masks—with or without makeup—he was capable of assuming. It was a face molded by the cruelest elements of life, by a hundred challenges met and conquered. It was said that his face mirrored the long struggle for success. The pain was there, but the gentleness and wise acceptance of life were there also, and without this inner spiritual beauty

there never would have been a face at all. These were part of the qualities that not only formed his rich, gentle character but served to make him the world's best-loved and most respected horror star.

When he was once interviewed, he impressed everyone by his warmth and characteristic sincerity. Without fear of others' opinion, he expressed himself with directness, and in a simple and unaffected manner:

"On November twenty-third, 1887, I was born at Forest Hill Road, Dulwich, England. Here we lived until I was about five years old. I was the youngest of a fairly large family of eight sons and one daughter. As you can imagine, my brothers were always keeping me in my place, or what they considered was my place. I knew very little of my father, James Pratt, who had spent his life in the Indian Civil Service.

Boris Karloff (1914) in his barnstorming stock-company days.

As I was the youngest, Mother rather spoiled me. We moved to Enfield when I was about seven. From that time on, I began to see less and less of my brothers. They seemed always to be abroad, either in India or China.

"There was always one or another of them home on leave. Each saw me at various stages of boyhood and adolescence. Each would try to reform me during his six months on leave. There was always the general comment that I was going to the dogs and someone would have to do something about it. This brotherly benevolence became a trifle annoying. In time, I got used to it and recognized that their intentions were sound. But I feel that I owe much to that interest. All men of substance and standing, they impressed me with a sense of rightness and the need for doing the right thing.

"It was intended that I also would go into the consular service. My schooling began at the Merchant Taylors' School, followed by Uppingham and, finally, King's College. At no time was I keen on this idea of a diplomatic career.

"An elder brother had been on the stage under the name of George Marlowe, when I was about eight years old. He was the one I knew best when the others were abroad. He played with Fanny Ward at the old Strand Theatre in *The Royal Divorce*. Giving up this stage life, he went into the city as a partner in a Swedish firm of paper-pulp merchants. Still, the theater interested him deeply. He coached clubs, assisted at the Enfield Amateur Dramatic Society, and each year put on a show at the Enfield Cricket Club.

"His dramatic experience was really no encouragement for me. Despite the fact that George was an extraordinarily handsome man, he never went very far on the stage, which was the reason he gave it up for a city job. But I tried to emulate him. There was a church play each Christmas at Saint Mary Magdalene's for the parishioners' children. Then the Band of Hope

put on an entertainment and I was always in those things, giving everything in me, acting lustily and loudly. Curiously enough, my first part was the Demon King in *Cinderella*.

"While at Uppingham, from 1902 to 1906, I played the usual games. I was the enthusiastic rabbit, you know, at cricket and rugger. One thing I regret is that I did not satisfy my love of music. I sang in the choir and did two years of piano practice under pressure. If I had decided to work a little more at music, I should have had a great opportunity. The music master was a brilliant man. If any boy had any music in his soul, he would have brought it out."

Laughing, Karloff added reflectively:

"Yes, I made a great mistake, then, apart from no particular aptitude for music, in not taking advantage of that man's knowledge and patience. When I was nineteen I matriculated and went to King's to read for the consular service. Frankly, I didn't have enough brains to do the job, and certainly I was not in the least interested. Although my brother George had been dead for a few years the stage was my only interest. On every possible occasion, I went to the theater, read plays, and did everything I could to satisfy these dramatic yearnings. My brother's experience was held up to me by the elders of my family as the horrible example of what happens when you try to get on the stage. Forming a tribunal they pronounced:

"That I could not possibly succeed because I did not have George's looks or his talents.

'That it would be complete folly for me to try it.

"Finally, they would not countenance it!

"They urged me to see that the dignity and stability of a consular career was vastly to be preferred to the insecurity and uncertainty of the stage. They were right. From 1910 to 1930 I really had a very thin time. Then Luck stepped in and, in prankish fashion, smiled on me.

"The seventh of May, 1909, I sailed

from Liverpool, second class. The family had been informed that I intended to leave home. I felt I had to get away and work things out on my own. Fortunately, there were no brothers at home at the actual time of my departure. I don't remember that any obstacles were placed in my way or that I had to overcome any great difficulties. I imagine that when I got on the ship brotherly sighs of relief could be heard in various farflung British outposts. There was no weeping and no distress. I was on my way. To what, I didn't exactly know.

"I chose Canada because just about that time the Canadian government was sending out an appeal for immigrants. I had no idea what Canada was like. It was all a fantastic and frightfully exciting adventure. There were some plans to go on a farm in Ontario to learn farming, then to buy some virgin land and develop it by myself.

"How six weeks with an Irish farmer, the son of a retired country gentleman who had come over to Canada on a windjammer, could fit me for a life on the soil, I don't know. Still, that was the idea.

"I had one hundred and fifty English pounds when I left home. From Ontario, where I lasted six months, I went on to Banff. The rugged beauty and impressive grandeur of the Rockies will always remain a deep memory. Banff appealed to me, but it was no use as a place to find a job. So I went on to Vancouver. With exactly a pound to my name, I arrived in this delightfully situated metropolis of the West and began to look for employment. There wasn't a hope of stage work. There was little doing in the theater at that time and, in any case, managers were not interested in gangling youths with no experience. The dire necessity of eating was soon apparent. Men were wanted to dig a racetrack and a fairground, and the pay was one and three-pence an hour.

"I reported for work without having had any breakfast, as I didn't have the money to buy it. The first day was a long, dreary ten hours of pick-and-shovel work. My hands were blistered at the end of that day. By the end of the week, they were merely calloused. For three days I lived on threepence a day because the arrangement, made by an astute foreman, was that we were to be paid on Saturday. The steak that I bought that Saturday night was the finest meal I had ever tasted.

"But I was convinced that ditch-digging was not much fun. Walking on the street one day, Hugh Arthur, a friend of a brother of mine in China, spotted me. There was a boom in land at that time. He suggested that I become a real-estate salesman. Little better than a glorified office boy, I made some money and gave Hugh two pounds occasionally toward buying a lot for me. This did not work so successfully and, when there were no immediate returns, I shoveled coal and did some more ditch-digging. It was less of a hardship this time. Youth soon gets used to work, no matter how rigorous it may be.

"Late in December 1910, I called at the Hotel Vancouver for some reason. A man passed through the lobby. His face seemed distinctly familiar to me. Upon inquiry, I found he was my brother John, on his way from China to London. Sportingly he loaned me twenty pounds, enough to keep me going for awhile in my planned attempts to get on the stage.

"Incidentally, I have never repaid that loan, nor have I the slightest intention of doing so!

"For months I made overtures to three Vancouver stock companies. There didn't seem a chance, not even a faint hope of becoming an assistant to the assistant stage manager. In a rather despondent mood one evening, I glanced at a newspaper and saw an advertisement for a character actor for the Ray Brandon Players of Kamloops, British Columbia. I applied for the job using the name of Boris Karloff, which happened to be my mother's family name. Some time previously I had written to an agent in Seattle, pitching him the yarn that I was an experienced actor out in

Canada for my health. I told him of the parts I'd played, actually parts in plays I had *seen*. He must have had a good laugh at my expense. A letter from him arrived when I was out on a survey party, telling me that I had been engaged to join the company at Kamloops at the princely salary of six pounds a week. To Kamloops I went, feeling no slight trepidation at the prospect of my first professional stage work. I hadn't the foggiest idea of how to take stage direction. Rehearsal routine and makeup were both completely foreign to me.

"My first part was an old man of sixty—Hoffman, the banker husband, in *The Devil* by Molnar. At the end of the performance, as I was slinking away to some dark corner, the manager came toward me with a malevolent gleam in his eye. 'Karloff, you know darn well you've never acted before. Still, we like you and you'll stay with us at four pounds a week.'

"For over a year we toured western Canada. Strange as it seems, I became fairly popular as a villain. Early in 1912 we were stranded in Regina. Everyone in the company, including myself, of course, was absolutely flat broke. The situation was rotten and prospects were dismal. Maybe the finger of Fate was pointing at me. The day after the manager announced our complete lack of funds and inability to proceed, there was a terrific storm in Regina and I got a job as a laborer cleaning up the mess. A haulage concern, called the Dominion Express Company, needed men. Being fairly husky, I got temporary employment.

"Again, a stroke of luck. The company sent me to the railway station to collect some crates of goods. As I crossed the tracks to the warehouse, someone threw an old copy of the *Billboard*, a theatrical journal, from a train window. Casually I picked it up and glanced at it. I saw an announcement that the Harry St. Clair Players, a repertory company at Prince Albert, wanted a young leading man. I dashed off a letter of application posthaste and, to my surprise, I received a reply a few days later asking me to join them in Prince Albert.

"We played in Prince Albert for nearly two years. Thanks to Harry St. Clair, who held back a certain proportion of my salary each week, I managed to save fifty pounds. This was enough to keep me going for a little while, and I decided that I now had sufficient experience to try one of the bigger theatrical centers, and I chose Chicago, arriving there on October thirteenth, 1914. There was a frightful slump in the theater business at the time and I just couldn't get an engagement. Rather discouraged. I went to the Brinkham Theatre in Minnesota. This was very dull, and I was very happy to rejoin Harry St. Clair."

At this time Karloff tried very hard to get into the British army as World War One began. He was rejected because they thought he had a heart murmur.

"Probably the finest experience you can get in the theater is to be with one of these repertory companies. We did one hundred and six different shows in fifty-three weeks. At last I was beginning to know something of my job. Realizing that success would come only by playing the large cities, once more I went to Chicago. And once more I failed. Billie Bennett's *The Virginian* company was going on tour. They took me with them, and we toured through Minnesota, Iowa, Kansas, Colorado, and Nevada, finally arriving in Los Angeles in December of 1917.

"Movies were in full swing then. I had no thought of getting into pictures. All my ideas were centered on a stage success. *The Virginian* tour did not last very long. The San Pedro Stock Company had a series of engagements in Southern California for about six weeks. Through them I enjoyed my first wanderings in this part of the world. Then another repertory company went on a tour through the San Joaquin Valley and ended at San Francisco. Life became one stock company after another until

110

an influenza epidemic ruined theatrical business in the West. My early training on the land stood me well. For two months I managed to earn a living pulling sacks of flour and loading lorries.

"My top salary on the stage up to now had never been more than ten pounds a week. Somehow, I managed to keep intact a tiny capital of twelve pounds, enabling me to have a little security and to venture afield in search of engagements. There was a vaudeville act arranged by Alfred Aldrich, a friend of mine, at San Jose. Its existence was brief indeed, and when Aldrich tried to get a booking in Los Angeles, he had no success. Yet he sent for me to join him there. Wondering what it was all about, I joined him. He must have had some belief in me, for he loaned me sufficient money for food and lodging until I made the rounds of the only possible outlet, the film studios.

"I appeared before the camera for the first time in a crowd scene being directed by Frank Borzage at Universal City. Certainly no one there thought anything at all about me. Similarly, I didn't think very much of prospects in pictures. This was well proved, for that was the only day's work I managed to obtain. In despair, I gave up calling at the studio casting offices and went to San Francisco to the Bob Lawrence Company at the Majestic Theatre for a three-months' session.

"Alfred Aldrich remained in Los Angeles. He scouted round, looking for possible opportunities for me. Reports from him were hopeful. Returning to Los Angeles, I was introduced by him to Al MacQuarrie, an agent. Through him I worked a few days in Douglas Fairbanks' *His Majesty, the American*, as a guinea extra. The film magnates of those days did not wax enthusiastic about my particular type. But, while I was in the vicinity, I thought I might as well expose myself to any opening. I made the rounds of all the agencies. Late one afternoon I was entering the office of Mabel Condon. She saw me and enthused at

once about my type. Thanks to her good offices, I obtained small bits and little parts in independent film productions.

"William Desmond and Blanche Sweet were the stars in the Jesse Hampton picture in which I played. I can't remember the name of it. Then followed a part in *The Deadlier Sex* with Blanche Sweet. This time it was quite a decent role.

"Working in several pictures encouraged me to forget the stage for awhile and remain working as long as I could in Hollywood. The typing system was used even in those days. Casting directors regarded me as a French-Canadian type, and I worked in a number of pictures in that category. Richard Tully's *Omar the Tentmaker* featured me prominently. Prospects were encouraging, when there came a ghastly slump in production. I carried on as long as I could until my small capital was exhausted.

"Spring of 1923. I was flat broke. The future very doubtful, I was told I could get a job driving a truck for a concrete and cement firm in Los Angeles. The first thing to do was to learn to drive. I spent Sunday with a friend learning to drive his car. Monday morning I applied for the job and got it. It was one of those simple tasks entailing the handling of a seventeen-ton truck. After learning the little idiosyncrasies and whimsicalities of this, they told me to take out a speed lorry delivering three hundred casks of putty. All I had to do—very simple when looking back—was to carry those three hundred casks from the warehouse to the lorry, drive about twenty-seven miles and then unload them. For this I received about five dollars a day. It wasn't really so bad except that I was a little older and, for the first few days, I ached in every muscle.

"The foreman, a kindly man named Charles Curtis, was very decent. He arranged matters so that I could take an occasional day to work in pictures and, at the same time, get a little relaxation. We carried on this way for over a year. Bert

Dynamite Dan (1924) starred Karloff as a rough-neck.

Lytell was starring in *Never the Twain Shall Meet* and I went to San Francisco on location. Apparently I couldn't have my cake and eat it, for this stay on location lost me my job handling putty.

"So I just had to stay in pictures. People were very kind, as I think they always have been to me. Through Robert Florey, who later became a director at Universal, I got a job in an Elaine Hammerstein film at the old FBO studios. Here I worked in four pictures, culminating with a featured role in *Forbidden Cargo* with Evelyn Brent.

"The stage still enthralled me. A brilliant English actor and producer, Reginald Pole, gave me a good part in *The Idiot*. He must have had astounding faith in my acting ability, as I had not read a line for almost seven years. Further opportunities to demonstrate my power as an actor came in San Francisco. In Los Angeles at the old Egan Theatre, I had an important part in *Window Panes*."

One of Karloff's most interesting experiences was his acquaintance with Lon Chaney. It was only natural that Karloff would be equated with the veteran "Man of a Thousand Faces" and called a "second Chaney."

"Lon Chaney was an individual," Kar-

112

loff emphasized, "and there will never be another man to take his place. I hope that I, too, may make a place for myself, without being called Lon's successor, imitator, or *second*."

Hollywood began recognizing Karloff's uniqueness after the success of *Frankenstein* (which, by the mid-fifties had already grossed more than twelve million dollars!). In producers' eyes, Karloff was every bit as great as Chaney, but with a completely different personality and style. Karloff learned the priceless importance of individuality directly from Chaney, at a time when the Karloff name was still only another of the hundreds listed on studio rosters.

One day Bill Taylor, a veteran character actor, introduced the bit-part player and yet unknown Karloff to Chaney. From then on the great Chaney would meet Karloff especially around sports events, and greet him warmly on a first-name basis. Chaney was particularly fond of boxing matches and Karloff could be seen standing outside the box offices of one event or another, hoping to glimpse a celebrity in the throng of sports fans. He couldn't afford to pay the admission price since the studios weren't very liberal with wages even for their better supporting players.

Reflecting on this period, Karloff said: "Then, one day, just as I was leaving the studio, pretty discouraged at the way my 'career' was going, I heard a car honk behind me—and Lon Chaney gave me a ride home. We talked for over an hour about the picture business and my own chances of getting somewhere. He said to me:

"'The secret of success in Hollywood lies in being different from anyone else.' He cited his own career, his own unusual parts, as an example: 'Find something no one else can or will do—and they'll begin to take notice of you. Hollywood is full of competent actors. What the screen needs is individuality.'

"The most successful screen actors and actresses I've noticed," Karloff continued, "are limited to certain types. And after all, that's perfectly natural. A man can hope to do one certain thing better than anyone else; but he can't expect to do *everything* better than others. And pictures, as they are made today, demand the tops."

Encouraged by Chaney's advice, Karloff persevered and was soon rewarded by an important role, the part of Galloway, in a Los Angeles stage version of *The Criminal Code*. Los Angeles stage roles were always coveted by aspiring stars—on any given night important talent scouts and studio personnel would be found in the audience. To the acclaim of enthusiastic press reviews, *Code* became a success and was adapted for the screen, with Karloff in the original role and Walter Huston and Constance Cummings starring.

The studio brass were impressed by Karloff's interpretation of the sadistic prison trusty in *Code* and were now giving him important supporting heavy parts in a number of important 1931 films.

"When I made *The Walking Dead*, directed by that grand fellow, Michael Curtiz," Karloff said, describing the great director whom many said *made* Warner Brothers, "I discovered that it was my name and not so much my ability that helped me get my early chance in pictures. A few months before Mervyn LeRoy chose me for a double-faced newspaper reporter in *Five Star Final*, I was called in for an interview by Michael Curtiz. Seeing me, he at once hesitated, and then said: 'Well, I called you over, so I suppose I shall have to use you.' I didn't understand what he meant. He gave me the role of a Russian, however, in *The Mad Genius*, the John Barrymore picture he was directing for Warners.

"The other day I was talking to Mike and he asked me if I remembered working for him previously. 'The reason I called you in was because I thought you actually were a Russian. Your name is Karloff—it certainly sounds Russian. When you came in, you seemed so anxious to get the job that I decided to let you have it.'

"Mervyn LeRoy saw my work in *The Mad Genius*. Even though he was im-

pressed, I think it took great courage on his part to give me that fairly important role in *Five Star Final*. George E. Stone, one of my oldest friends, had a lot to do with my getting it. He literally worked for me, talked about me, made sure that the producers would not miss knowing about me."

And now came the moment that Karloff, that any actor, waits for all his life. *The* part and role that will establish him; that will mark him with, as Chaney stressed, that dynamic *individuality* necessary to turn him into a Star.

Karloff said, "When I was offered the part of the Monster in *Frankenstein* I knew that I'd found it at last. The part was what we call a *natural*. Any actor who played it was destined for success."

How did he get the part? What made Universal Pictures cast him in Mary Shelley's horror classic, in a role that catapulted him to fame? Different people give varying accounts of the event. Karloff himself said that his portrayal of Galloway in *Criminal Code* impressed a Hollywood executive enough to prompt him to consider Karloff for the Monster role.

Carl Laemmle, founder and then head of Universal, talked of Karloff's eyes. "They mirrored the sufferings of the poor dumb creature, in contrast to his frightful appearance and hideous strength."

They also mirrored the personal trials and tribulations of a man who had often gone weeks without a decent meal or a dollar in his pockets.

But perhaps the real story was told by Bela Lugosi, in an interview with the press in 1935. The Hungarian-born actor had turned down the role because it had no dialogue, and then called up Karloff to tell him that the part was "nothing" but might mean some money for him.

Karloff gave this account:

"I was working at Universal at the time, and James Whale was in the commissary having lunch. He asked me over to his table to have a cup of coffee and said he wanted me to take a test for the Monster.

I can only assume that he had seen *The Criminal Code*—either the play or the film. I didn't ask him, and he didn't tell me."

Karloff was asked if he had seen the very first version of the 1910 *Frankenstein* made by Thomas Edison: "No, I never did. I didn't know it had been made; it's news to me, though I knew it had been done as a play—in London, I believe."

Karloff then tried to clarify the controversy surrounding Lugosi, who had been first considered for the Monster role; he was asked if the Hungarian's original screen tests had been seen by him:

"No, but I was once told that he insisted on doing his makeup himself—and did this awful hairy creature, not at all like our Monster."

Creation of the Monster's makeup has been cited as a masterpiece. Many have wondered how much of it was master makeup-artist Jack Pierce's work.

"All of it," Karloff said, "except for one very tiny detail. It was effective because he experimented and tried all sorts of things. Finally, when we were in the last stages and getting it down to what it would be, my eyes seemed too normal and alive and natural for a *thing* that had only just been put together and not born, so to speak. I said, 'Let's put some putty on the lids.' He put some putty on and shaped it so that the lids were the same . . . and that was it."

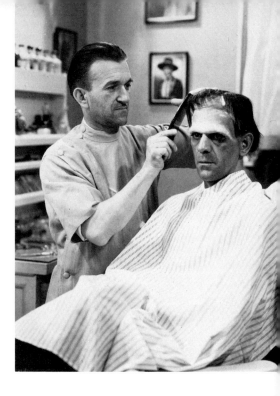

Karloff being made up by makeup master Jack Pierce for *Frankenstein* (Universal, 1931).

Karloff was quick to praise director James Whale's abilities, saying he was "a very, very fine director indeed." Then he clarified a puzzle—the cut scene when the Monster throws the little girl into the lake.

"Well, that was the only time I didn't like Jimmy Whale's direction. We were on our knees opposite each other when the moment came that there were no more flowers. My conception of the scene was that the Monster would look up at the little girl in bewilderment and, in his mind, she would become a flower. Without moving, he would pick her up gently and put her in the water exactly as he had done to

114

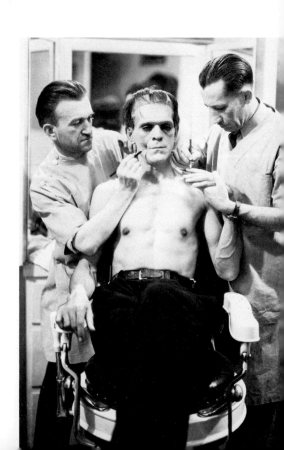

the flowers—and, to his horror, she would sink. Well, Jimmy made me pick her up and do *that*," Karloff motioned violently over his head with both hands, "over my head, which became a brutal and deliberate act. By no stretch of the imagination could you make that innocent. The whole pathos of the scene, to my mind, should have been —and I'm sure that's the way it was written —completely innocent and unaware. But the

moment you do *that*," he motioned again with his arms, "it's a deliberate thing; and I insisted on that part being removed."

Though he donned the Monster's garb briefly in 1962 in a horror-spoof for the TV series "Route 66," Karloff played the part seriously a total of three times. After *Son of Frankenstein*, Karloff said, "I refused to play him anymore. He was going downhill. We had exhausted his possibilities. He was beginning to become a clown."

Of the three Monster films (1931's *Frankenstein*, 1935's *Bride of Frankenstein*, and 1939's *Son of Frankenstein*), Karloff spoke about his favorite:

"It was the first. In the second they made a great mistake about which I also complained, but, you know, you don't have much to say concerning decisions. The speech—stupid!" he said commenting on the '35 sequel. "My argument was that if the Monster had any impact or charm, it was because he was inarticulate. This great lumbering inarticulate creature. The moment he spoke you might as well take the

Edward Van Sloan futilely trying to overcome Karloff the Monster in *Frankenstein*.

The Monster (Karloff) carrying off his creator, Dr. Frankenstein (Colin Clive) . . .

. . . about to toss Clive from the windmill in *Frankenstein*'s climactic scene.

mick or play it straight. In the third one I didn't like it because they changed his clothes completely, wrapping him up in furs and muck, and he just became nothing. I mean the makeup, like the clothes, had become part of him. If you accepted the convention that he lived or came to live, as it were, at the end of the film—after practically being destroyed—you could accept that he wore the same clothes to meet the script. So the first one I enjoyed, which was the best of the three."

Shortly after *Frankenstein* was released, an article appeared in April 1932, describing Karloff's makeup ordeal each time he arrived at the studio for the Monster's next scene and the amount of preparatory study it had entailed:

Jack Pierce . . . had to do a little researching on his own. He read all sorts of medical books—he talked with physicians and surgeons, sketching with them his ideas. What would the *complete and original human transplant look like?*

The color of the skin was particularly difficult to get just right. Something that would screen like the pallor of a dead man—gray-white, which would have served the purpose on the stage, did not give the right effect under the Klieg lights. Neither did the yellowish tones. A dead, greenish-gray finally passed the test —the seventh one. The impression of "dead" fingertips was given by the use of black makeup.

Each time the monster was created, Karloff had to sit in the makeup chair for three and a half hours. First his eyes had to be given that heavy, half-dead, insane look—a matter of applying coats and coats of wax to his eyelids to weight them down. Next, invisible wire clamps were fixed over his lips to pull the corners of his mouth out and down. Then, the overhanging brow and high, square-shaped crown of the head, supposedly "grafted" from the head of another man. These, as well as his face and neck, were shaped and built up by means of thin layers of cotton, applied with a special liquid preparation so that it went on smoothly like so many thin layers of flesh. Then the grayish makeup on top of all. Boltlike plugs were placed on the side of the neck and held there by means of more layers of cotton and adhesive liquids. For a long time afterwards Karloff bore two small scars on his neck, where the bolts had been fastened.

An assistant who helped apply the Monster's features stood by every moment the picture was being filmed, for emergency repair work on the makeup. Sometimes it was an eyelid that came loose; another time the wig would slip in a fight, or one of the heavy bolts would work loose in a particularly frenzied scene.

Removing the makeup was not much simpler than putting it on, and certainly more painful. It required an hour and a half of prying, pulling, and coaxing, plus special oils and acids—"plus a great deal of bad language!" adds Karloff.

First, the eyelids came off; most painful, to say the least, and enough to inspire any quantity of questionable language! The deep scar on the Monster's forehead was then pried into as a good starting point, and from then it was just one pry and push and acid soaking after another until Boris was himself again. . . .

Seven years later, the Monster's creator himself, Jack Pierce, revealed some of the "secrets" of his success:

"I didn't depend on imagination. Before I did any designing I did some research in anatomy, surgery, criminology, ancient and modern burial customs, and electrodynamics. I discovered that there are six ways a surgeon can cut the skull and I figured Dr. Frankenstein, who was not a practicing surgeon, would take the easiest. That is, he would cut the top of the skull off straight across like a pot lid, hinge it, pop the brain in, and clamp it tight. That's the reason I decided to make the Monster's head square and flat like a box and dig that big scar across his forehead and have metal clamps hold it together. The two metal studs that stuck out of the sides of the neck were inlets for electricity; plugs, not bolts. Don't forget the Monster was an electrical gadget and that lightning was his life force.

"Also I had read that the Egyptians used to bind some criminals hand and foot and bury them alive. When their blood turned to water after their death, it flowed into their extremities and stretched their arms to gorilla length and swelled their hands and feet and faces to abnormal proportions. I thought this would make a nice touch for the Monster, since he was supposed to be made from the corpses of executed felons. So I fixed Karloff up that way. The lizard eyes were made of rubber, as was his false head. I made his arms look longer by shortening the sleeves of his coat. His legs were stiffened by steel struts and two pairs of trousers. His large feet were the boots asphalt-spreaders wear. His fingernails were blackened with shoe polish."

Had the movies not helped, along with radio, to ruin American stock companies, in all likelihood Karloff would have remained with his first love, the stage. He probably would have become famous and prospered as a stage actor; but the world would have been deprived of his great macabre presence upon the screen.

Before *Frankenstein*, Karloff did appear in a rather chunky horror role—five years earlier—which many film fans of today do not know or have overlooked: the role of the mesmerist in *The Bells*, directed by James Young (formerly married to actress Clara Kimball Young, whom he divorced in 1919). He had already directed Karloff in three previous films and was deeply fascinated by Karloff's mystical facial qualities and manner. Lionel Barrymore starred as a guilt-ridden inn proprietor who murders one of his guests for his gold. Karloff played a carnival mesmerist who impresses the town's elders so much that they hire him to solve the murder via hypnotism and ESP. About this experience, much influenced by *The Cabinet of Dr. Caligari* (as were so many other films), Karloff said:

"Lionel was a stimulating man—a marvelous, a great man. Because my makeup for this part was a conventional Svengali-like job, Lionel sat down and on an envelope sketched an idea for Young and the makeup person. What he sketched was Caligari!"

With *Frankenstein* wrapped up, better studio offers were now coming to him. However, officially, he was not yet of "star" magnitude, because when Universal first released the film they had purposely left Karloff's name off the screen credits and publicity. The part was simply listed as: "The Monster: ?"

The idea was perhaps a little sensational but designed to endow the film with an added sense of mystery and awe. In any case, it was a good publicity stunt, though Karloff, long imbued with patience, had to wait out almost another year for general recognition and fame.

For his next eerie junket, Karloff appeared for Universal in a totally different concept: as the inscrutable and ageless Im-Ho-Tep in *The Mummy* (1932). Unlike Frankenstein's Monster, who grunted and growled but never spoke, the eternal Egyptian had many lines of dialogue. A stately, strange, and commanding figure, with wrinkled parchmentlike skin and burning eyes, he was on screen for most of the film, glaring hypnotically into space or involved in ancient occult rituals.

Written by John Balderstone, author of the stage *Dracula*, the story depicted the survival of an ancient Egyptian prince who had been buried alive for having stolen the sacred scroll of Thoth. Remaining undead for thousands of years, he finally sees daylight when his ancient sarcophagus is uncovered by an archaeological expedition. (The scene showing Karloff's mummified form coming to life is in itself a masterpiece of sustained, mounting fear.) The expedition ends in tragedy when one of the archaeologists goes insane from witnessing Karloff's horrific mummified presence walking away from his ancestral tomb. Years later, a second expedition to the same area is visited by a mysterious Egyptian, Ardath Bey, who offers to guide the group to the

Karloff in 1932.

by the greater power of the goddess Isis in answer to Helen's prayer.

Unquestionably, *The Mummy* withstands the test of time with amazing durability and easily ranks alongside the top dozen or so "best" horror classics. Even those who have maintained traditional snob attitudes against the genre have capitulated before the power of *The Mummy*. As is the case with many artistic triumphs the star and all others connected with a production share in its glory. Film, however, is largely a director's medium, and on him alone (barring interference) rests the final outcome. And who else could do *The Mummy* but a director like Karl Freund? It would be hard but not impossible to imagine added subtleties in *Frankenstein*, if Freund had been the director. His film credits read like a listing in a Film Hall of Fame: he was the cinematographer of such immortal film classics in the twenties as

lost tomb of an ancient princess. Bey is none other than Im-Ho-Tep, freed of his mummy wrappings and, though strange in appearance, looking more human and possessing the magical knowledge and wisdom of the ages. When the princess' mummy has been found, Im-Ho-Tep tries restoring her to life through an incantation, but fails. Her soul has been reincarnated down through the ages and now resides in the body of Helen Grosvenor (Zita Johann), a modern living woman of Egyptian descent. Having loved his princess when she had lived thousands of years ago, Im-Ho-Tep is now determined that she shall share his fate and remain alive forever. But first, she must die, to live again. From then on it becomes a constant occult duel between Im-Ho-Tep and the scientists and friends of Helen. Chief opponents of the Mummy are David Manners and Edward Van Sloan, in a reprise of his psychic detective role in *Dracula*. Appearing to be winning at every turn, the Mummy is destroyed in the end

118

Karloff being made up for *The Mummy* (Universal, 1932).

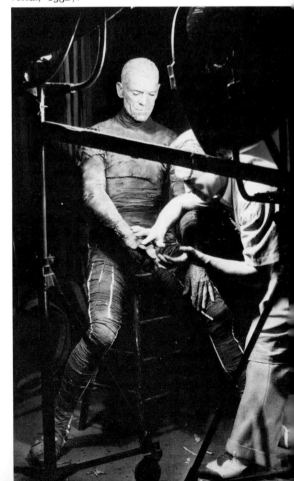

The Mummy. Bramwell Fletcher, Edward Van Sloan, and Arthur Byron open Im-Ho-Tep's sarcophagus for the first time.

The Last Laugh, Metropolis, Variety, and *Berlin,* and of future greats such as *Mad Love, Camille,* and *The Good Earth.*

Always a trouper, Karloff also was to star in films which, unfortunately, did not have the guidance of men like Whale or Freund. But even routine thriller programmers take on an indefinable quality and are even rescued from oblivion by a single magnetic presence like Karloff's, as would be proven in the years ahead.

In the same year, 1932, Karloff made a total of ten films—a very busy period! Two were comparatively good crime adventures in which he had fine supporting roles: *Scarface* and *Behind the Mask.* In *Scarface* (starring Paul Muni) Karloff, as a member of a rival mob, is knocked off in a bowling alley; even as he drops dead, his ball rolls on, scoring a strike. In *Behind the Mask,* he is the callous head of a dope syndicate who is foiled by ace government agent Jack Holt (parenthetically, it might be noted that Holt became such a cliché cop and government man in numerous B- and C-budget programmers of the '30s that he inspired in later years Al Capp's scathing comic-strip character Fearless Fosdick in "Li'l Abner"; though essentially satirizing Dick Tracy, the cartoon face was Holt's).

Karloff's next important film marked another radical change of pace. It was as the sinister Oriental, Dr. Fu Manchu, in *The*

Mask of Fu Manchu. Karloff doubly benefited from being its main star (with an excellent cast: Lewis Stone, Myrna Loy, Charles Starrett, and Jean Hersholt) and from the competent direction of Charles Brabin, who shortly afterward directed all three Barrymores in the excellent *Rasputin and the Empress.*

Fu was a very demanding and uncomfortable job for Karloff. It was decided to have him wear thin shell teeth over his own, specially built shoes to raise his height to six feet nine inches, and two small celluloid clips to slant his eyebrows. The usual method for slanting eyebrows was to use a strip of thin membrane, attached to the skin and painted; but Karloff felt this would hinder the movements of his facial muscles.

The film's script required him to inflict a variety of tortures on his helpless victims. At one point, he injects one with a mixture of rattlesnake and tarantula venoms and gloats: "You are now helpless and completely in my power!"

After *Fu,* Karloff found himself, in the same year, crouching by chimney flues in *The Old Dark House,* playing the role of a lurching "butler" à la Dr. Frankenstein's

Karloff as Im-Ho-Tep, the mummy, ready to come to life and go "for a little walk."

Karloff's love scene with his Egyptian princess (Zita Johann) was deleted when *The Mummy* underwent general release.

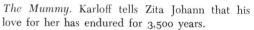

The Mummy. Karloff tells Zita Johann that his love for her has endured for 3,500 years.

The Mummy. Karloff being condemned to death for daring to steal the sacred Scroll of Thoth.

Under Karloff's hypnotic power, Zita Johann is told that she must first die and then be made into a living mummy to join him in immortality.

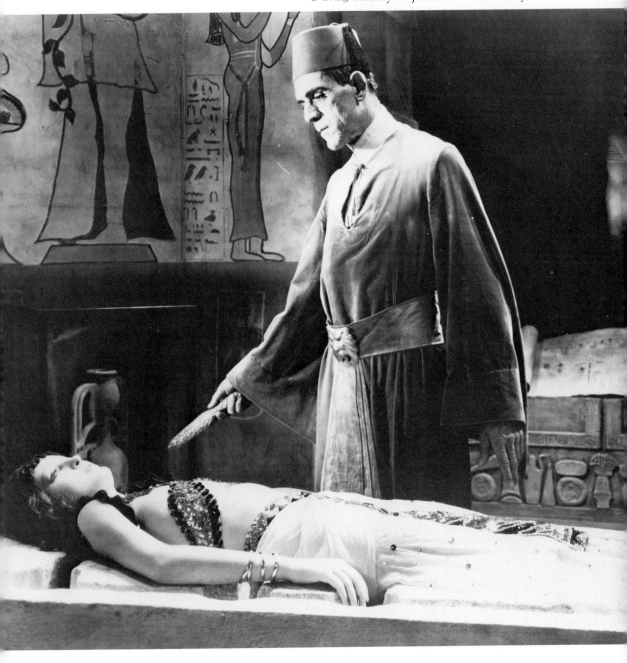

The Mummy. Among the most significant of a number of scenes deleted from this production prior to its general release in 1932 were several elaborate sequences (here and on opposite page), depicting the reincarnation of the Egyptian princess (Zita Johann) as various women in history. These four rare stills show Zita in two scenes as an early Christian about to be martyred, in another as a tragic Viking maiden about to take her life, and in the fourth as a noblewoman during the time of the Crusades. The soldier standing to her right in both Roman scenes is Henry Victor, who played heavies in films throughout the forties, and who was famous as Olga Baclanova's villainous consort in *Freaks.*

Monster. Until very recently this movie had been assumed by many to be another addition to the "lost-film-classics" department. But to the gratification of fans and buffs galore, the jewel was retrieved to be reset in its proper diadem for festival screenings and showings in other filmic temples of worship.

Dark House, adapted from J. B. Priestley's novel, relates the story of a group traveling by car through a remote English countryside. Cut off by a storm and floods, they take refuge in a large old house high in the hills. It turns out to be occupied by a family of madmen: a weird brother and sister; a father in an attic bedroom, aged 102; a second brother, kept under lock and key because of his little trick of starting fires; and a butler (Karloff) who can't speak but, with a few drinks under his belt, becomes hell-bent on murder. Some time ago, in his notes for a special screening of *The Old Dark House*, film historian William K. Everson described why this is one of the most important films in the genre:

It is a film that almost invariably disappoints on the first viewing. From the second viewing on, it gains tremendously, and is the kind of film that one wants to see again. Its scenario is carefully balanced, pitting the house's five inhabitants against the five guests. Roughly, each has an opposing counterpart, and the night of terror brings out the best—or worst—in all, solving their problems just as dawn breaks, banishing the insoluble fears and dangers of a nightmare. (Although, admittedly, it is a little difficult to consider oneself free of problems with Karloff still lumbering around.)

The Old Dark House is more than just a delightful example of its genre; it is also a kind of prototype in reverse—a belated

123

Karloff as the insidious Dr. Fu Manchu in *The Mask of Fu Manchu* (MGM, 1932).

An imaginative poster design created by Universal for *The Mummy*, showing David Manners, Zita Johann, and an Op Pop-art depiction of Karloff.

The Mask of Fu Manchu. Charles Starrett, who later became a famous cowboy star, is the unconscious hero being menaced by Karloff as Dr. Fu Manchu and his equally evil daughter, Fah Lo See (Myrna Loy).

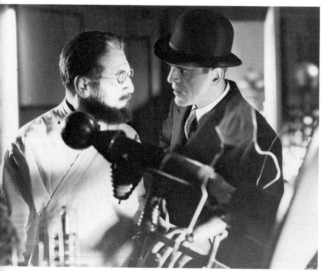

With Edward Van Sloan, Karloff was involved in illegal drug trafficking and the underworld in *Behind the Mask* (Columbia, 1932).

The Mask of Fu Manchu. Karloff as Fu Manchu experimenting happily in a great mad-lab scene.

Lawrence Grant is being exquisitely tortured by Karloff under a huge bell in *The Mask of Fu Manchu.*

Lewis Stone (years before becoming the venerable Judge Hardy in the Mickey Rooney–*Andy Hardy* series) is next in line for one of Karloff's numerous torture treatments in *The Mask of Fu Manchu.*

Karloff's missing, but this shot establishes the typical mood of *The Old Dark House* (Universal, 1932). *Left to right:* Eva Moore, Ernest Thesiger, Gloria Stuart (back to camera), Raymond Massey, Charles Laughton, and Lillian Bond.

By 1933 Karloff gets top billing in *The Old Dark House*, even though he did not have more than a strong supporting role.

blueprint and summing-up of what had gone before in *The Bat, The Cat and the Canary*, and so many others, distilling the best from these earlier works and adding so much that was uniquely James Whale's. Despite its many colorful ingredients, it works best when it eschews the grim exterior set and fearsome Karloff figure. There's really no plot, merely a basic situation, and the highlights bear little relation to what plot it does have. James Whale's always sardonic sense of humor is very cunningly employed. A "shock" closeup of the principal menace in his initial introduction was always an unwritten law in this kind of film, and Whale dutifully supplies it—but then immediately follows it up with a comedy line dialogue which quite squashes the Karloffian menace, suggesting that a tongue-in-cheek approach is under way. To an extent it is, and the audience is nicely lulled into a false sense of security, heightened by a deliberate anticlimax *near* the end, only to be outsmarted when Whale directs his final act completely straight.

Unlike *Dracula* and many early horror films, *Dark House* does not suffer from a lack of music. There is no music, but the constant sounds of wind, rain, lightning, flapping shutters, and billowing curtains form their own kind of symphony. Moreover, the film is so tightly paced that there are none of those awkward pauses where one becomes aware of the absence of music.

Photographically it is superb and represents some of the late Arthur Edeson's finest work. The first glimpse of the old house, through the mud and lightning flashes, is one of the most effective establishing shots ever created, and as good as or better than anything of a like nature in the great German fantasies of the '20s. Though the sets are splendid, they still needed a man of Whale's taste. Universal later rented the same sets to smaller companies such as Mascot for cheap thrillers, and they were almost unrecognizable since so little was done to exploit them in terms of camera placement and lighting. A few scenes are beautifully constructed miniatures, and Whale wisely never gives us a good look at the exterior of the house in the daylight; even though the individual menaces are explained away, the house itself, as a kind of baleful embodiment of evil, can remain undiluted in our memories. *The Old Dark House* is one of the real masterpieces of its genre.

Others in the notable cast included Melvyn Douglas, Charles Laughton, Raymond Massey, and Ernest Thesiger. Dominating much of the film was a character actress of the British stage, Eva Moore, as a dotty old lady; already in her sixties, she continued acting almost till the time of her death in 1955. Though not centrally the main star, Karloff's name was now prominent enough as the "new Chaney" for Universal's advertising department to make it seem that he was in virtually every sequence instead of in only a few scenes. There is no connection and only a fleeting resemblance to the *Dark House* remake of a few years ago—apart from being perhaps William Castle's worst film, it was further debilitated by Pat Boone's presence as the *star*, no less!

Karloff's next role in *The Ghoul* is a special curiosity in that after ten films in 1932 this was his only one for 1933 and probably the rarest Karloff vehicle. It was shown *only* during its original release and it disappeared completely within five years. In theory, then, it may be considered "lost," although a rather fair duplicate copy (perhaps the only one in existence) was mysteriously unearthed and screened several years ago through the good graces of its finder. *Ghoul* signified Karloff's *first* British film, and also marked Ralph Richardson's *first* screen appearance. Its director was T. Hayes Hunter, an American who had made some unimportant films in Hollywood and continued pursuing an unremarkable career in England. *Ghoul* proved an exception to Hunter's dull career purely by virtue of having a good, weird plot and outstanding actors. As an occult antiquarian of strange repute, Karloff possesses an unusual ring endowed with the power of granting ever-lasting life if its owner follows an unusual ancient Egyptian ritual. Ernest Thesiger connivingly arrives at Karloff's deathbed; instead of fulfilling his expiring friend's instructions, he steals the jewel. Returning from the dead, Karloff revenges himself on those standing in his path.

Notwithstanding a great cast, which included Cedric Hardwicke, and a rich plot, director Hunter's plodding technique is too often visible; sequences that should be great are only adequate; powerfully dark haunting scenes and fine exchanges of dialogue are overcome by static, lethargic camerawork, apparently mitigated only by potluck and the cast's sensible awareness. Yet *Ghoul* does have Karloff in one of his very best performances and it comes through as a charming and important horror film.

Elements of devil-worshiping, science fiction, and unadulterated horror combined in 1934 to bring Karloff and Bela Lugosi together for the first time in *The Black Cat*. Characteristic of great performers is their ability to convey new moods and create different hues with each new role. Makeup trickery aside, Karloff was one of the few who rarely repeated himself in a new role. But even more paradoxical is that in each characterization he actually did appear to be *physically different*, more so than any of his horror colleagues! This ability, evident in *The Black Cat*, would become increasingly apparent in years to come. Accordingly Karloff is seen in yet another completely *different* form as the complex and insidious intellectual, Hjalmar Poelzig, an engineer who lives in an outré gadget-filled mansion of his own design, built upon the ruins of the Austrian fort he had betrayed to the enemy in World War One. As the leader of a devil cult, he keeps the bodies of beautiful women—one of whom is the late wife of Vitus Verdegast (Lugosi) —preserved in glass crypts. Lugosi comes to the mansion to try to unravel the cause of his wife's death. With him is a young couple (David Manners and Jacqueline

Karloff and his wife en route to New York to take a trip to London. Purpose of the trip: to make *The Ghoul* (Gaumont, 1933).

Karloff with Mrs. Karloff and their Bedlington terrier, Silver, aboard ship on the way to London for *The Ghoul*.

Wells) whom he had befriended on the train and who had become sidetracked later by a bus wreck. Lugosi is meanwhile content to await his moment, unaware that his young daughter lives and is now Karloff's new wife. The hour of reckoning approaches. Karloff has called about him the dark minions of his devil cult. As they are about to sacrifice Miss Wells, Lugosi and his husky major domo disrupt the ritual, and Karloff retreats to the former fortification's sub-basement, a Stygian nether region. After a hot pursuit, Karloff is subdued by Lugosi and his burly servant, stretched out on a rack and . . . flayed alive! As the young couple barely escape, the great chateau is blown sky high by long-hidden explosives, detonated by the dying Lugosi who, though a hero, was mistaken for a villain and shot while trying to save the girl.

Among Universal's last great horror epics of the early thirties, *The Black Cat* has a timeless quality missing even in some of the all-time "classics." An aural, dramatic, and visual delight, it benefited by John Mescall's imaginative photography (which was more obvious later in *The Bride of Frankenstein*) and is Edgar G. Ulmer's best directorial effort, though afterward he made more than a few highly competent films (for example, *Bluebeard*, 1944). Having worked under F. W. Murnau (*Nosferatu*) and in various German studios, Ulmer's *Black Cat* is infused by the experience and mystical sense that permeated German film culture in the twenties, recalling the Fritz Lang worlds of *Metropolis* and the *Mabuse* films. Indeed, Karloff himself seems like a physical synthesis of the archetypal twisted mastermind personified by the German Chaney, Rudolf Klein-Rogge, the star of most early Lang films. Though Hollywood musical scoring was still in its early stages and used haphazardly, it plays a vital part in elevating *Black Cat* to its classical level, at times endowing the principal players' movements with a lyrical opera-ballet rhythm under-

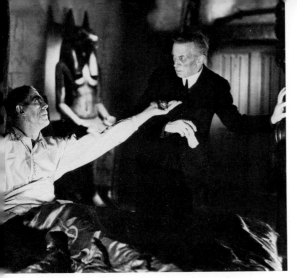

Karloff and Ernest Thesiger in *The Ghoul*.

scored by variations from Brahms, Liszt, Tchaikovsky, and others. Classical music in films has rarely been used with such grand effect and understanding, anticipating Kubrick's successful use of it in *2001* and *A Clockwork Orange*—two generations later.

The same year, Karloff played two non-horror roles, one as a religious-fanatic soldier who eventually goes mad in the desert in *The Lost Patrol*; the other, as the corrupt anti-Semite, Baron Ledrantz, Chancellor of Prussia, besieged by Napoleon's armies and forced to ask Rothschild's financial aid in *The House of Rothschild*. He and Lugosi also guest-starred in a semi-cameo inside-joke sequence in *The Gift of Gab* in which they played themselves.

More than two decades of hardship and struggle were now way in the past. Audiences, critics, and the studios regarded Karloff as a star. Some great stars, however, are imbued with enough quiet dignity and humility to express sincere amazement at their own fame. Perhaps Karloff's greatest drawback was that, having suffered too long, he was too grateful for what success he had achieved and continued to chronically underestimate his international importance. In one of his most relaxed and expansive moods, Karloff revealed much of his own true nature, reminiscing about his

family's first reunion in almost quarter of a century. It was just after he had arrived in England to star in *The Ghoul*. Present were three of his brothers who had distinguished themselves in the British government service: Sir John Pratt, originally with the Diplomatic Corps in China, and now head of the London Foreign Office's Chinese affairs; Justice E. M. Pratt, retired, formerly Judge of the High Court of Bombay, India; and F. G. Pratt, retired, formerly of the Indian Civil Service's Executive Branch, a member of the viceroy's staff and, for a long time, governor of an Indian province. Gathered at this London reception to honor Karloff were also many other notables, including a photographer for an important national magazine who wanted to take photos of the star with his brothers.

Said Karloff: "This was the moment I had been dreading. I felt that they would consider it beneath their dignity and I expected to be told in no uncertain terms that such a thing was impossible. But I hunted them up and put the proposition to them. 'I realize,' I said apologetically, 'that I make my living in rather a queer fashion,

Karloff and Bela Lugosi in *The Black Cat* (Universal, 1934).

and I only bring this to your notice because the man is so insistent. I assure you that it is not an idea of my own, but—well, there is a photographer here who wants to take our picture together.'

" 'Where is he?' asked Sir John excitedly. 'Bring him in here and let's be photographed in front of this fireplace!' They were as pleased as three boys, and when the photographer had come in from the other room, they began to argue as to where each should stand. Finally, it was decided that we should line up according to age, with my brother John on one end and myself on the other. No sooner was the picture taken than all three brothers began to inquire how soon they could secure prints; and by this time I was in a positive glow of relief. A film actor had been received in the British diplomatic circles and had made good!"

The year 1935 rolled in and proved a very good Karloff year, highlighted by the monumental *Bride of Frankenstein,* exceptionally unusual because sequels (especially Universal's) are rarely as good as their predecessors. *Bride* was not only as good, but better, than *Frankenstein!*

One reason for this is that sound films were not quite out of the "novelty" stage in 1931, though they had been around, in one form or another, more than three years. Even if some audiences were averaging three different shows a week (a common practice in early pre-TV days when neighborhood theaters were many, changed their bills every other day, and charged fifteen to twenty-five cents for admission), the 1931 *Frankenstein* was for them an entirely unique experience. Mad scientists and monsters had come and gone before, but mostly in thinly distributed German films of the 1920s and *silent* Chaney vehicles. And there lies the rub: *silent.* Certainly no one had ever before witnessed the hissing, crackling, zapping *sounds* of a mad lab during the process of creating a Monster, counterpointed by Dr. Frankenstein's ecstatic screams of "It's alive! It's alive! Oh, it's alive!" And then, already nearly one-fourth into the film, the Monster—the *creature* that

audiences knew was created from dead bodies—gradually came into view, ready for an unveiling by Dr. Frankenstein (Colin Clive) before his skeptical friend, Dr. Waldmann (Edward Van Sloan). Tension mounted, the tower door slowly opened and the creature appeared; but even the most squeamish weren't frightened, because the Monster wasn't in full view just yet. One couldn't quite make him out. Then it became obvious why this was so— he makes his entrance walking backwards. As he moves away from the doorway shadows into the light, be begins to turn. The audience was psychologically steeling itself, but no shock or jolt was necessary. As the Monster's face finally came into full view, his presence transfixed everyone' as they witnessed the masterpiece created by Jack Pierce and Boris Karloff. A masterpiece of terror.

Practically everyone in *Frankenstein*, including the minor players, has a juicy scene; but even Edward Van Sloan's craftsmanship and all the colorful histrionics of Dwight Frye (the sadistic little hunchback who torments the Monster) and Colin ·Clive couldn't measure up to Karloff's artistry; once he appears, all others take a back seat—the audience's only thought is about Karloff's next appearance.

Dominating the film proved entirely to Karloff's advantage and to everyone's delight for more than forty years. Speculation of what others would have done with the Monster role is practically useless. Suffice it to say that Karloff's knowledge of theater evinces itself in every stance and gesture. The Monster's inarticulateness is grandly compensated for by Karloff's rich, booming guttural groans and deep basso rumbles, of course; but it is his pantomime artistry and interpretation of the Monster's anguish, based on his own understanding of suffering, that has immortalized Karloff and the film.

Undeniably assured of its proper niche, *Frankenstein* is, nonetheless, a flawed masterpiece. There are several stage-bound scenes which a musical background would have at least mellowed—notably, those of Frederick Kerr, badly miscast as Baron Frankenstein (the young Frankenstein's father), a wheezing, hammy buffoon who seemed old enough to be the grandfather. And one could conjecture at the outcome had James Whale abstained from anachronisms and the cheerful, sunny atmosphere of the villagers that, in retrospect, appear more in keeping with the films of Laurel and Hardy or of Ruritanian exploits.

But *Frankenstein* remains a classic, flaws and all; and what it lacked was more than compensated for by *The Bride of Frankenstein*, ranked by some as *the best* in the genre. It succeeds by not only investing Karloff with an equally powerful, if not better, role as the Monster, but also raises the supporting players to in-depth prominence. As William K. Everson analyzed it (in his notes for a special screening):

> By far the best of Universal's eight Frankenstein films (the Monster's activities dwindled after the first four, and in the eighth he was merely a stooge for Abbott and Costello), it is probably the best of the "manmade monster" genre from any period. If one judges a horror film only by the genuine fright that it inspires, then *Bride* perhaps might have to take a secondary position; but in terms of style, visual design, literate scripting, performance, music and nearly every other individual ingredient, it is practically unexcelled. As an essay in Gothic Grand Guignol, it far surpasses its predecessor which, good though it was, lacked pace and especially the dynamics of a good musical score.
>
> Just as the original *Frankenstein* derived a great deal from *The Golem*, so does *Bride* (originally made and publicized as *The Return of Frankenstein*) also draw a great deal from some of the silent German fantasies. Elsa Lanchester's head movements, and the framing of her close-ups, are quite clearly patterned on those of Brigitte Helm as the robot in *Metropolis*. Indeed, Brigitte Helm was among the

The Lost Patrol (RKO, 1934). *Left to right:* J. M. Kerrigan, Victor McLaglen (hat in hand), Karloff (kneeling), Alan Hale (behind Karloff), Brandon Hurst, Reginald Denny, Billy Bevan, and Douglas Walton.

131

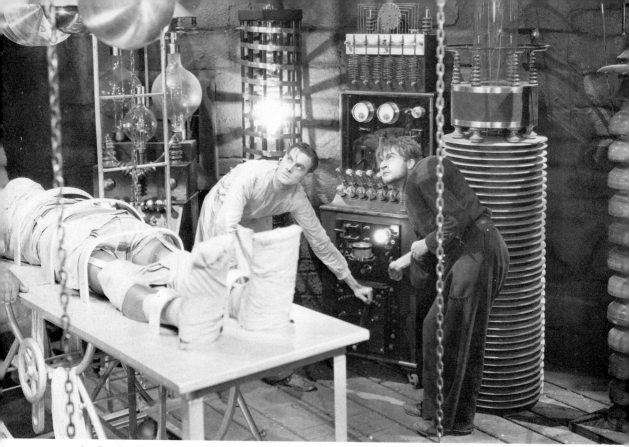

The local village may have suffered a blackout when Colin Clive and Dwight Frye sent thousands of volts into the Karloff Monster in *Frankenstein* (1931).

players Whale considered for the role of the Monster's mate.

The film shows occasional signs of having been reshaped, with sequences transposed, after completion; and a cut that has always been there (after the monster has kidnapped Dr. Frankenstein's bride) renders inexplicable one of Thesiger's lines. The period is somewhat in doubt, too, with Thesiger beating Alexander Graham Bell to the invention of the telephone (herein referred to as just "an electrical device") yet using a great deal of post-Bell equipment in his laboratory work. The post-code moralities of the 1930s are also evident in the burgermaster's admonition that "it is high time every man and *wife* was home in bed!"

But it seems churlish to quibble over such a lavish and enjoyable fairytale, which offers such genuine pathos along with all its thrills and Karloff's excellent

performance. Thesiger, of course, steals the whole show with a marvelously written and played bravura performance, though Dwight Frye also gets the best and juiciest lines of his career.

Entirely studio-made—unlike *Frankenstein*, which used some actual exteriors—*Bride* interiors aren't always convincing; but since they are *consistent* they work.

The special effects work—especially involving Thesiger's miniature people—is ingenious, and the laboratory scenes are the best and most elaborate ever created for this kind of film. Franz Waxman's score, ranging from the march as the dim-witted villagers take to their torches to the pealing of church bells when the Bride is presented, is likewise superb. The interior sets, making good use of painted shadows, and also of such standing sets as the crypt where Thesiger first meets Karloff (also used in *Dracula* and *The*

132

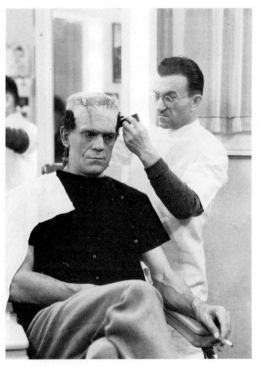

Karloff being made up by Jack Pierce for *The Bride of Frankenstein* (Universal, 1935).

Closeup of Karloff as the Monster in *The Bride of Frankenstein*.

Karloff "greets" his prop dummy on the set of *The Bride of Frankenstein*.

Karloff the Monster.

133

The Bride of Frankenstein. Publicity shot taken during the sequence in which the Monster breaks out of the village prison. *Left to right:* Karloff, E. E. Clive, Tempe Piggot, Gunnis Davis, Dwight Frye.

The Bride of Frankenstein. Valerie Hobson is about to be kidnapped by Karloff.

Mystery of Edwin Drood) are all beautifully designed. One wonders, though, what kind of oversized delinquents ran wild through the countryside with such regularity as to justify the local jail's huge stone throne and chains, conveniently *just* the Monster's size!

The Bride of Frankenstein marked the peak of the 1930s' horror cycle, but not quite the end of important Karloff films. *The Raven* was also, in many respects, an oddity because Bela Lugosi was cast in an important leading role in a *quality* film for almost the last time and Karloff—though now a top star—in a powerful but nonetheless almost secondary part. Lugosi is in top form (as detailed in the Lugosi chapter), mad as a hatter, as Dr. Vollin, who forcibly recruits escaped criminal Karloff to assist him by horribly mutilating one side of Karloff's face, but promising to restore it if he helps carry out Lugosi's evil plans. From wild heavy, Karloff turns into sympathetic hero, dying in the end but not before foiling Lugosi and killing him.

Perhaps Edgar Ulmer's and James Whale's services were more costly now than what Universal wished to pay. There were also rumors of censorship against horror films that became grim reality within a year, causing a critical financial setback for the genre, when Great Britain created an official boycott of most foreign horror films, thus instituting "X for Horror" for the first time. Whatever the reason, Lambert Hillyer was assigned to direct *The Invisible Ray*. Though this was his first film in the genre, Hillyer had established himself as writer and director of many famous William S. Hart, Tom Mix, and Buck Jones westerns; also in 1936, he directed with great virtuosity the quite-underrated *Dracula's Daughter*. Recognized as one of the industry's more competent workhorses, with innumerable B's and other low-budgeters to his credit, Hillyer, in *Invisible Ray*, achieves a charming serial-

On the set of *The Bride of Frankenstein:* even a great Monster had to take time out for a smoke and a cup of tea.

Another candid shot—lunchtime for Karloff on the set of *The Bride of Frankenstein.*

The Bride of Frankenstein. The Monster returns to "negotiate a deal" with Dr. Frankenstein.

Between takes on the set of *The Bride of Franken-stein*, Karloff admires a neo-realistic portrait of the face that launched a thousand shocks.

Frankenstein Monster-maker Jack Pierce and director James Whale on the set of *The Bride of Frankenstein*. A dummy might have been cheaper to use, but they seem convinced it would never replace Boris.

adventure quality not hard to fathom considering the fact that four years later Hillyer directed the popular and outrageous *Batman* serial. For some odd reason, *Invisible Ray* appears to be one of the least appreciated and most neglected of its class, having nothing to do with rarity, since it appeared frequently on TV. Anticipating by at least fourteen years popular science-fiction-horror themes which have been recurring ever since 1950, it grows in stature next to others in the genre as the years go by. High in production standards, with Franz Waxman's fine musical score and a well-conceived, literate script—and Karloff and Lugosi in excellent form—everything is in its favor. But, sadly, it was also the end of an era.

In the film Karloff appears for the first time as a doctor-scientist, in one of his oddest roles—that of a radioactive man who can kill with a mere touch. Co-starring is Lugosi in one of his most sympathetic and best roles. Opening with Karloff's laboratory and observatory in the Carpathians, he discourses with visiting colleagues on the importance of "Radium X" from outer space. Through his invention—a kind of television that projects the past—he demonstrates the radium's existence by showing how it fell to earth ages ago.

They journey to Africa to locate the

An exquisite scene that exemplifies some of *The Bride of Frankenstein*'s expressionistic atmosphere. Shown here are Ernest Thesiger (*left*) and Dwight Frye.

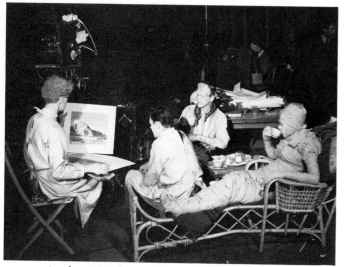

Another rare shot: coffee/tea break time for the cast of *The Bride of Frankenstein*. Backs turned: Ernest Thesiger and Colin Clive; Karloff and Elsa Lanchester sipping tea.

Poster used in the colorful publicity campaign launched when two of Universal's horror films were released together.

The famous village set, used for a number of Universal's mystery and horror shockers, including *The Bride of Frankenstein*.

Escaped criminal Karloff is deformed by the sinister and aberrated Bela Lugosi in *The Raven* (Universal, 1935).

element; but on finding it, Karloff becomes contaminated. He glows in the dark, and anything he touches dies. Lugosi manages to create an antidote for him, and they return to Paris. But Karloff, going insane from contact with the element, imagines his discovery has been stolen, determines to take revenge, and sets out to kill each member of the expedition. But he must take the antidote at intervals at all times or else the radiation will get out of control. Just as he is about to complete his plans, his aged mother strikes the vial of antidote from his hands, destroying it. "It is better this way," cries Karloff, and jumps from a window. But the radiation is too strong, and in a bright flare his body is turned to ashes before it touches ground.

Columbia called on Karloff in 1935 to star in *The Black Room,* an unusual turn of events, since until that time this company had long been notorious for low-budget productions of inferior caliber. In this instance, however, Columbia surprised critics, and perhaps even amazed itself, by creating this very fine film that is considered one of Karloff's "top-ten" best. In an unusual dual role, Karloff plays twin brothers, one good, the other evil. The good child, afflicted by a paralyzed right arm, is taken away in his youth to be educated abroad. The evil Karloff is left to reign over the baronial estates and the local village, to the growing regret of its inhabitants who find his lecherous ways and cruelties increasing with the passage of time. Much to their relief, the good Karloff, now a grown man, returns home to share in the estate responsibilities. Hostility against the evil brother is strong and bitter, and rather than gamble with a lynching party, the bad Karloff notifies the villagers that he is leaving and allowing his good brother to take over. All cheer—but not for long. Giving up all his keys to the castle, he takes his good twin on a tour and shows him . . . the black room! A long-hidden, secret torture chamber. Opening a trapdoor, he hurls his good brother into a pit, where he dies.

Assuming his brother's identity and imitating his paralyzed arm ("I must never use it again!"), his next plan is to enrich himself by marrying the daughter of a very wealthy neighboring count. When the prospective father-in-law celebrates the forthcoming marriage with a toast, Karloff accidentally reveals himself by signing a document with the "paralyzed" hand. To protect his secret, he kills the count, whose death is thought to have been caused by someone else, and Karloff proceeds with the marriage plans. At the church the next day, about to conclude the marriage vows, the evil Karloff is unmasked: his brother's great mastiff hound rushes in for the attack, filled with hate for his beloved master's murderer. Exposed before all those who are assembled, Karloff darts from the church in a panic, the large dog at his heels in hot pursuit. With nowhere else to hide, Karloff opens the secret panel to the black room and enters. Mystified, the villagers do not know where he's vanished to, until the dog shows them. Breaking through the secret panel, the beleaguered Karloff is caught off-balance, falls into the deadly pit upon a dagger, and expires next to his brother's corpse.

In his analytical notes for a screening of *The Black Room,* William K. Everson says:

> Much in the Wilkie Collins and *The Woman in White* tradition, it is a curious one-shot horror film for Columbia. Superficially at least, it is almost as stylish as the James Whale's for Universal, and Columbia never again did anything quite like it. Certainly their series of horror films with Karloff in the 40s, though interesting, did not approach this much earlier film. With its traditionally Victorian story of prophecy, curses, sealed rooms, and an effectively Gothic pictorial veneer in the castle, cemetery, and church scenes, it is the kind of melodrama that just isn't being made at all anymore. Many of the exteriors, with their painted brooding skies and distorted trees are deliberately nonrealistic, as were the woods and rocky

Karloff as Grigor, the evil twin brother, in *The Black Room* (Columbia, 1935).

Boris as the radium-infected scientist plotting revenge in *The Invisible Ray* (Universal, 1935; released in 1936).

141

hills in Universal's first three *Franken-stein* films. Backed by a cast of good solid reliables, Karloff turns in an excellent performance and the editing in his dual-role scenes is particularly neat. The musical themes throughout are first-rate, interestingly speeded up in the climactic reel, and thus transformed from macabre mysterioso into all-out agitato music. In this speeded-up form, the themes were later used as standard fast-action music in *The Secret of Treasure Island* and other serials and westerns.

But the honeymoon of horror could not last indefinitely. In the first place, not many good scripts could be found; in the second, each succeeding movie, psychologically speaking, *had* to be more horrifying than the last or it might not be "box office." Suddenly, in 1936, horror films were unofficially banned. However, Karloff's name was a guarantee to sell tickets, though the luster and magnitude of his future films—but for remote exceptions—would never again quite attain the classical dimensions achieved by the Universals that starred him until *The Invisible Ray.*

As horror films quickly withered away, Karloff was quick to answer another call from England (which still tolerated its domestic shockers, even if rated "X") to play in two films which had very poor subsequent American distribution and are now, presumably, lost. In both he played doctors, slightly mad as usual: *Juggernaut* starred him as Dr. Sartorius who poisons himself once his crimes are discovered, then delivers a lecture on his dying symptoms. As Dr. Laurience in *The Man Who Lived Again*, Karloff scares audiences by wielding a scalpel to transfer the brains of cripples into the heads of his "enemies."

Back in America, when Warner Brothers wanted to make *The Walking Dead*, they knew whose name would be best in the role and on theater marquees. As a pianist unjustly sentenced to death and executed, Karloff is brought back to life by a doctor friend, and proceeds to revenge himself on

Karloff in the process of murdering Katherine De Mille in *The Black Room.*

those who conspired to put him in his grave—by scaring them all to death. While the above two British titles and this production would be Karloff's prototypes for a spate of many similar ones far beneath him, *Walking Dead* is a good and underestimated little shocker, well paced and stylishly directed by Warner's ace, Michael Curtiz.

Universal then announced that Karloff's next role would be "a big surprise" to all his fans—a *sympathetic* role. Rather extensive publicity was created and released to humanize Karloff for the curious public. During this brief holiday, movie fans enjoyed widespread photos and interviews of Karloff at play on his three-acre Hollywood estate, surrounded by his Scotch terriers, ducks, and Violet, his pet pig.

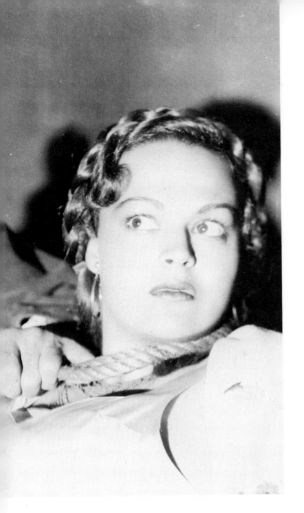

had achieved the pantheon of shock entertainment, was an institution. With the horror-film "ban" still in effect, Karloff was in danger of becoming a star without a place. Warily, he slipped back into character again as a lovable Chinese bandit general in *West of Shanghai* (also released as *War Lord*), though he was tragically executed at the end by a rival.

Amid a plethora of hackneyed low-budgeters surrounding him in the late thirties, *Mr. Wong, Detective* creeped in. This was the first in a series of five imitation Charlie Chan films, with Karloff in the lead, produced by Monogram, a studio renowned for cheapness and poor quality. Averaging two films each year, the series terminated in 1940 with *Doomed to Die*. The Wong plots were all of routine pulp-thriller standards, replete with third-rate clichés and cardboard characterizations, but worthy of examination if only for Karloff's gracious presence and for hearing him speak in his distinguished dulcet tones (he refused the director's suggestion that he affect a stilted Oriental accent).

Appearing quite at ease and content on the surface at this time, he showed some trepidation when he asked one reporter: "Shall I try a really straight role? Do you think they will let me change and like me just as well?"

Indeed his fans did! They had been pouring in letters on the subject for a long time. "Give Karloff a chance to act!" they pleaded. They considered producers blind and indifferent to his other potentialities and felt he should be allowed to be more *himself*.

But in 1937 *Night Key*, whch all had hoped would provide Karloff with new directions, was a failure, and a drearily directed little B-film at that. Karloff, as a gentle, friendly old man, was totally out of his element. Karloff, as a symbol who

Publicity shot of Karloff for *The Man Who Lived Again* (Gainsborough, 1936).

Karloff, Marguerite Churchill, and Warren Hull in *The Walking Dead* (First National/Warners, 1936).

(ABOVE AND BELOW) As Karloff looked when brought back to life in *The Walking Dead*.

Antipathy against horror was now beginning to cool, and in 1939 Universal returned to the genre with renewed vigor and *The Son of Frankenstein*, uniting Karloff and Basil Rathbone, with marvelous menaces Lionel Atwill and Bela Lugosi in strong supporting roles. Deemed by some as the most elaborate of the series, officially it was also Karloff's last time as the Monster. Following is William K. Everson's program-note analysis:

Director Rowland V. Lee was quite expert at imitating the style of others, and the best of *Son* is the best of James Whale. However, Lee's own style was plodding and Germanic, and *Son* is somewhat overlong for sustaining feelings of terror or genuine excitement—especially since an obnoxious brat of a child (Donnie Dunagan) has no fear of the Monster, and thus we, the audience, aren't supposed to be too concerned either. Moreover, in its attempts at *class*, the film downplays physical action: the Monster's first appearance comes very late in the day, and scenes of violence—murders, the laboratory scenes, etc.—are quite cursory. But it's a fascinating production and, if only on the level of art direction, sets, lighting, and overall visual elegance, it must certainly rank as the second best in the series.

Via constant rain, thunder, and gloom, *Son* creates its own nightmarish world. We never see the sun or sense the fresh air, and the only trees we see are all dead. The little town is as unreal as Fairbanks' in *Thief of Bagdad*, but as convincing, since Lee, like Doug, never shows it to

1937. Karloff enjoying the company of his Bedlington terriers on the grounds of his Cold Water Canyon home above Beverly Hills.

Another candid shot of Karloff relaxing in his Cold
Water Canyon home.

Karloff as kindly old Dr. Mallory in *Night Key*
(Universal, 1937). *Left to right:* Warren Hull,
Jean Rogers, Karloff, and Alan Baxter.

Night Key. Karloff (*center*) bullied by gangsters (Ward Bond and Alan Baxter on the right).

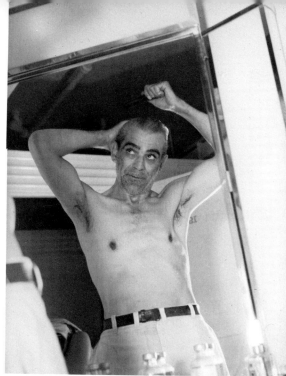

Preparing himself in a hot dressing room for his role in *The Invisible Menace*.

The Invisible Menace (Warners, 1937). Karloff received top billing in this interesting though routine crime thriller, playing a heavy murder suspect who turns out to be a red herring.

Karloff as Mr. Wong in *Doomed to Die* (Monogram, 1940).

Manacled to famed criminologist, Edward L. Lawes, warden of Sing Sing Prison, in a spoof publicity shot in 1938 for "Lights Out."

Karloff (1938) in his early radio days in the first of his five appearances on "Lights Out," the acclaimed horror program series.

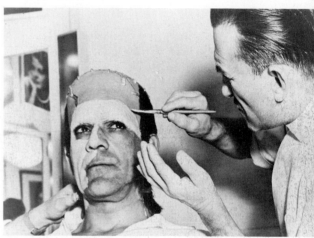

Jack Pierce makes Karloff up as the Monster for the last time for *Son of Frankenstein* (Universal, 1939).

Even the Karloff Monster probably found Dr. Frankenstein's precocious son (Donnie Dunagan) too trying in *Son of Frankenstein.*

Karloff in *Son of Frankenstein*.

us in juxtaposition with things that *are* real. Everything, from the rain to the doorknocker to the distorted stairs, is magnified to giant macabre proportions. It's one of the most exciting, and certainly one of the most Germanic, visual moods to be created by any Hollywood film, especially in that rather prosaic period.

Mentally, the Monster continues to be somewhat inconsistent from film to film. The voice and humanity he had acquired in *Bride* are now forgotten. In the next one, *Ghost of Frankenstein*, he acquires Lugosi's brain and voice, but goes blind. #5 (*Frankenstein Meets the Wolf Man*) restored his eyesight, but took away his voice again. The villagers however retain their own fickle reliabilty: unreasonably hostile at the beginning of *Son*, they are all smiles and devotion as they bid Baron Frankenstein farewell at the railway station . . . unaware of course that Sir Cedric Hardwicke is due in on the 4:10.

Son's melodrama is a little more logical without one of those convenient all-purpose switches that blew up everything in *Bride*. Performances are, generally, restrained, Lugosi being especially good and touching as Ygor (one of his most underrated performances), though Rathbone, sad to say, is decidedly hammy, even allowing for the hysterical note on which his role is written. The dialogue is a joy, albeit the best lines are unintentionally funny, as opposed to *Bride*'s rich fruity theatrics. "Strange country," mutters Rathbone, looking at the forest of dead trees and dry-ice mist through the train window. Examining the Monster, he also diagnoses that "no human heart could beat like that," quite forgetting that it's the very heart that Colin Clive obtained from another body in the first film. The maid's solemn little verse, "When the house is filled with dread, place the beds head to head," is a piece of Transylvaniana worth remembering, as is Lugosi's ambiguous, "He does things for me," referring to his chumminess with the Monster.

Atwill has one marvelous lapse of tact when he is describing a victim's mutila-

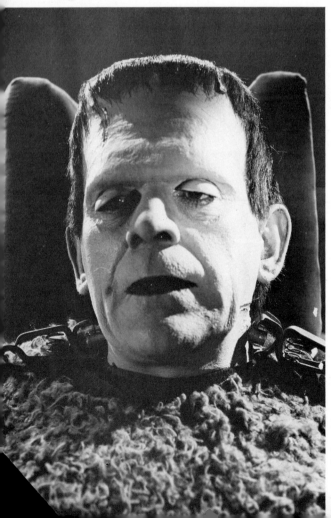

A fine closeup of Mr. K. as the Monster in *Son of Frankenstein*.

Droll publicity shot: lunchtime—between takes of killing the butler (Edgar Norton) in *Son of Frankenstein*.

tion: "The cart passed over his chest . . . his heart burst," and Atwill raises the blanket just in time to give the corpse's grief-stricken widow a good eyeful. But perhaps the best line comes when poor Edgar Norton (the doctor's assistant also in March's *Jekyll and Hyde*) has vanished, and a helpful servant offers the information: "We sent him up to the nursery for the baby's supper tray, and we haven't seen him since!" Lines like this quite seem to fit in the surrealist-nightmare framework of the whole, in which a man-eating tot would seem not at all out of place.

Karloff at the time revealed himself as a practical joker, and along with his colleagues and old friends Lugosi, Atwill, and Rathbone, turned the elaborate sets into a playground and had each other rolling with laughter much of the time. "In the scene where Bela slowly tells Basil," said Karloff, "'He—does things for me'—and there I am, all stretched out on this dais—well, we all just doubled up, including everyone else on the set—the entire crew, cast, and even Rowland, who said he didn't mind the extra takes for the chuckles it gave everyone."

That year audiences were also treated to *Tower of London* and the sight of a bald Karloff, grinning malevolently while he sharpened a huge axe. He was playing Mord, Richard III's lord high executioner, henchman, and torturer of the Tower. More Grand Guignol than straight history and loosely based on Shakespeare's play, it starred Basil Rathbone as the evil Richard "Crookback" who systematically goes about bumping off one member of the royal family after another to become king. Director Rowland V. Lee managed to pull off a minor miracle since, essentially, it's every bit a B-film but with an A-budget

In *The Man They Could Not Hang* (Columbia, 1939), Karloff is a misunderstood scientist, and thanks to his mechanical-heart invention, returns once more from the dead, assisted by Byron Foulger (*left*).

quality appearance. Vincent Price (in a supporting role) is also murdered by Karloff and Rathbone, but had his revenge by appearing in an overblown remake as Richard III himself in the 1963 version.

By this time Karloff, despite the higher standards of Rowland V. Lee's films, was growing leery of various parts handed out to him, and was reappraising an earlier statement he once made when success was still a novelty: "Should my employers insist that I submit to amputation of my limbs in order to portray a character that will advance me in my profession, I am ready! Only death will bring about my surrender now!" What Karloff suspected, by 1941, was that he might have already surrendered without realizing it. Some of his films by now were marred by bad taste and without class.

Re-echoing in his mind was his hopeful statement: "Between horror characteriza-

Karloff has an axe to grind as Mord, the head executioner, in *The Tower of London* (Universal, 1939).

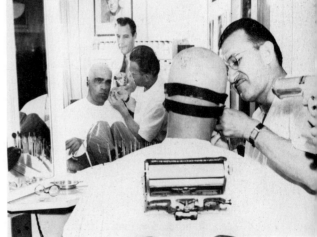

Jack Pierce making up Boris for *The Tower of London.*

Karloff in full swing as Mord in *The Tower of London.*

151

tions I should like to be more of a human being. After all, you know, I am human and I would like the public to think of me in that light occasionally, instead of always picturing me as a supernatural monster."

Security and the opportunity to study and perfect his skill as a performer had removed the necessity of acting behind a face not his own. Anonymity was comfortable, but it made for a pallid and uninteresting existence. And whether they admit it or not, most actors need the stimulus of public interest in themselves as well as in their craft. If, during the decade of success, Karloff had become a more polished actor, he had also evolved emotionally and desired recognition of himself as an individual. The quiet rebel was rebelling once more.

During those years, he had become more than just a country gentleman. As a man of diversified interests, he raised prize-winning roses, bred Bedlington terriers, played cricket, and enjoyed entertaining his expanding list of friends. His extensive reading habits took him deep into the field of scholarly research; a devout musicologist, he also tried his hand at composing. Evenings he would gather around his fireplace friends with whom he could discourse on the profoundest aspects of humanity, often delving into a discussion of the supernatural and metaphysical ideas. Having attained full growth as a man, Karloff the artist was being condemned to professional sterility.

At a most appropriate time in 1940, the New York stage rescued him. Howard Lindsay and Russell Crouse were producing Joseph Kesselring's *Arsenic and Old Lace* and wanted Karloff for the lead! The role was like hand in glove for the star; he played the part of Jonathan Brewster, an escaped maniac who has been made to look like a "famous" movie star by plastic surgery in order to escape detection. And the star he is made to look like *is* Boris Karloff! A clever mixture of adventure-comedy and gallows' humor, the

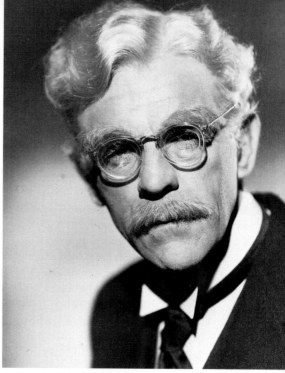

Before I Hang (Columbia, 1940). Karloff means well as a kindly old scientist who, again, returns from the dead. He has perfected a plasma-serum technique that restores life. Though he grows younger, a murderer's blood in his veins has a disastrous effect on his personality.

play opened in New York in January 1941, and was a huge success.

Although a well-known star, he still had some doubt about appearing on Broadway. "I was scared stiff about how they'd like me," he said. "After all, I was just a provincial actor. I'd never played in New York before, and I certainly wasn't going to use my screen reputation," he added with characteristic modesty. Exulting over being back on the stage again, he said: "There is really nothing quite like the theater, if you love acting, of course. A live audience is wonderful after a cold camera."

Though he never admitted to being especially superstitious, Karloff always carried a 1928 silver dollar during the play's run. He had gotten it several years before in Hollywood while courting Mrs. Karloff

152

and said, "You wouldn't find me playing without it." He once lost it when someone used it to pay for a newspaper, but a quiet search through neighborhood newsstands recovered the lucky piece. One time, also, he was careful, while posing for a certain publicity photo, to *appear* as if he were standing under a ladder. To justify such beliefs, he reported that a black cat he had once posed with had clawed a piece out of his suit.

At this point the entire course of his life was altered. The plunge back into the theater's congenial and creative atmosphere, combined with the stimulating effect of New York, succeeded in jarring Karloff loose from sterile producers. With fresh perspective he saw Hollywood for what it had become—bound up in useless tradition, wasting away the careers of talented people, and in an inflexible position where narrow provincialism was policy, and intelligent creativity the exception.

Already a veteran of over a hundred radio programs, Karloff now broke all ties and threw himself into a new career of more radio, theater, and, eventually, television. He could afford to be choosier about his films, and appeared in only two in 1941 and 1942; none in 1943, and just one in 1944. The best of them was *The Devil Commands* (1941), with Karloff as a devoted scientist attempting to contact his dead wife through weird machinery of his own creation; though succeeding at least in hearing his dear departed's voice coming in from "somewhere way out there," his experiment backfires as machinery, house, and all blow up. The most stylish film of this period, *The Climax*, starred Karloff in a thinly disguised but hackneyed imitation of Universal's resoundingly successful *Phantom of the Opera*, released the year before (1943).

Universal called Karloff back in late 1944 to surround him with every known monster from its roster (except the Mummy) for *The House of Frankenstein;* several cute little twists were tossed into

Black Friday (Universal, 1940). Karloff dabbles in brain surgery, and turns a kindly professor friend into a killer in a marvelous example of filmic medical malpractice.

Devil's Island (Warners, 1940) attempted to depict the cruelties of France's penal system. Karloff starred in the role of a well-meaning doctor unjustly sentenced to the horrors of the notorious prison colony.

The Devil Commands (Columbia, 1941). With Anne Revere's aid, Karloff communicates with the supernatural through scientific wizardry of his own making.

Karloff, Susannah Foster, and Turhan Bey in *The Climax* (Universal, 1944).

House of Frankenstein (Universal, 1944). Karloff, as a sinister mad scientist, exhibiting Dracula's skeleton (which later turns into John Carradine) at a carnival, with J. Carrol Naish as Daniel the hunchback.

the pot: J. Carrol Naish, stealing some scenes as Daniel the hunchback; poor, underrated George Zucco briefly seen as Prof. Bruno Lampini whose traveling carnival of horrors is taken away from him after Karloff orders Naish to break his neck; John Carradine in his interesting portrayal as Count Dracula; Glenn Strange creating an impressive but now second-rate Monster; and Lon Chaney, Jr. dominating much of the show as a worried-looking Larry Talbot, alias the Wolf Man. After breaking out of prison with fellow inmate Naish (Daniel), Karloff and the hunchback head toward the Castle of Frankenstein, not for back issues, but to look for Dr. Frankenstein's secrets-of-life-and-death, traveling incognito in the deceased Lampini's horror-show caravan. With a gypsy camp, a med-

One of a number of colorful exploitation posters used for *House of Frankenstein.*

dlesome vampire, and a werewolf put out of the way, Dr. Karloff then rolls up a few more hundred thousand volts of electricity to liven up the Monster; but the typical villagers get scent of this activity and march in to break it up. Karloff is hoisted by the loyal Monster and carried away from the debacle; but the Monster, now dumber than ever, heeds not his master's voice, warning, "Quicksand . . . quicksand!" and they both sink out of sight in studio Wheatena.

At a time when the genre—now in its "second cycle"—appeared to be heading nowhere, there arose from seemingly out of the unknown a former script writer and minor RKO executive called Val Lewton. Within several brief years he went down in history as the producer of undoubtedly the best American horror-mood films of the forties. Astute and selective as Karloff had now become concerning his roles, neither he nor anyone else could have predicted the success of these films, which have become part of film language and referred to as "Lewton classics." Appearing in lead roles in half of these Lewtons, Karloff vigorously rebounded into the limelight in some of the finest films in his career. *The Body Snatcher* (made in late 1943 but released in 1945) is set in nineteenth-century Scotland and tells of a dedicated doctor (Henry Daniell) who is unable to obtain cadavers for needed research due to the archaic laws of the time. He is forced to cooperate with the cold-blooded Gray (Karloff) who drives a hansom by day and disinters corpses at night. He had formerly worked for the infamous team of Burke and Hare, of whom the following rhyme was written and chanted in the streets:

> Up the close an' down the stair
> But an' ben wi' Burke an' Hare;
> Burke's the butcher, Hare's the thief,
> An' Knox the boy who buys the beef.

The Knox referred to was a doctor to whom they sold cadavers. Finding corpses

Karloff and Russell Wade in *The Body Snatcher* (RKO, 1943; released 1945).

in short supply, Karloff, unknown to Daniell, decides to make his own; but the doctor's servant (Lugosi) learns about this racket and wants to be cut in. Karloff obligingly demonstrates "How we Burke them," but Lugosi doesn't survive the demonstration. Discovering what Gray has been up to, Daniell kills him. And in one of the best-filmed horror climaxes ever made, Daniell carries off an old woman's body in a wagon through thunder and pouring rain; as lightning shatters the night's inky blackness, the corpse seems to turn into that of Karloff. Terrified by the sight and the elements, Daniell loses control of the horse, the wagon careens into a gully, and Daniell joins Karloff in eternity.

Except for period costumes, Karloff broke away from makeup men for the first time in years for the Lewton films. Younger and older audiences were pleased to discover an even greater actor who proved more than ever his abilities—and surprised skeptical critics—without resorting to the masks that lesser actors relied on.

In Lewton's *Isle of the Dead*, Karloff is General Pherides who finds himself marooned on a Greek island by a deadly plague. Haunted by a dead woman who isn't truly dead, Karloff's faculties begin to deteriorate. The Lewton technique of *suggesting* terror through continual sustained *mood*, instead of the more direct and commercial jolting-shock approach, is especially overpowering in *Isle*. Audiences and critics beheld something quite unique in the genre; and because it was uniquely inventive, most of the jaded and hack critics were caught off balance, some panning it (because of its deliberately slow construction) as dull and boring. But James Agee, one of the only two or three decent critics of the forties, said about it: "Tedious, overloaded, diffuse, and at moments arty, yet in many ways to be respected, up to its last half hour or so; then it becomes as brutally frightening and gratifying a horror movie as I can remember."

Based on some factual incidents and inspired by Hogarth's illustration of the lamentable conditions of asylum patients in eighteenth-century England, *Bedlam* was the last of Karloff's films for Lewton and, in a sense, the most enjoyable even if not the best one. A fat, lecherous aristocrat and governor of Bedlam (played by Billie House, unforgettable as the checker-playing store owner in Orson Welles' *The Stranger*) conspires with the asylum's distorted director, Karloff, to make Anna Lee, his mistress, one of the inmates. She's seen enough of the dreadful place in the past, has turned humanitarian, and poses a threat to Karloff's position by knowing too much. Karloff reigns supreme as master of Bedlam, terrorizing the helpless patients

Rare publicity shot of Karloff in *The Body Snatcher*.

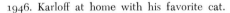

1946. Karloff at home with his favorite cat.

Karloff as a Greek general, with Ellen Drew, in Val Lewton's heralded *Isle of the Dead* (RKO, 1945).

Anna Lee and Karloff in *Bedlam* (RKO, 1946).

Bedlam. Karloff is being put on trial by the asylum inmates for his cruelties. Robert Clark (*right*) went on to appear in minor adventure and several SFantasy films, and is now married to one of the King Family girls.

158

and gloating over their misery; but Anna Lee's warmth and understanding dispel chaos and fear, and a few of the milder patients help her to achieve order in the place. In an eerie climax they seize Karloff and put him on "trial." After he has been struck down by a blade, they wall him up, thinking he's dead; as the last bricks are placed, Karloff returns to consciousness, realizing to his horror he is being entombed alive.

Karloff's versatility by this time was more evident than ever, and he began appearing in all media in a variety of work. In 1947 he was a droll villain in RKO's comedy-mystery *The Secret Life of Walter Mitty* (based on the James Thurber story), starring Danny Kaye in his usual one-note comedy style, a style lifted bodily from the long established and much funnier Ritz Brothers. Next came Karloff's first jaunt in a comic-strip adaptation—*Dick Tracy Meets Gruesome*—with Karloff dignifying the burlesque as Gruesome, who gives the famous 1½-dimensional cop a hard time. As an Indian chief in Cecil Blount De Mille's spectacular, *Unconquered*, he showed that years of cricket

Karloff as Gruesome in *Dick Tracy Meets Gruesome* (RKO, 1947). Wearing milk-bottle-thick glasses is Skelton Knaggs (*center*), the underrated British-born character actor who specialized in weirdo supporting roles in the '40s and '50s.

and physical fitness programs had kept him in good condition, and everyone wondered why he didn't play Indians more often.

In 1948 he returned to Broadway for Maurice Evans' production of J. B. Priestley's *The Linden Tree,* a sentimental work in the Mr. Chips tradition, with Karloff as an aging professor facing retirement. When notified that Karloff was to star, Priestley's immediate reaction was, "Good God! Not Karloff! Put his name on the marquee and people will think *The Linden Tree* is about an axe murderer!"

Karloff commented some time afterwards on Priestley's remark: "Perfectly asinine. Why, it's this sort of thing, even said as a joke, that holds back so many fine artists."

Fans who liked Karloff on the warpath in the De Mille film got their wish to see him again as an Indian in *Tap Roots* (opposite Susan Hayward and Van Heflin), set on a Mississippi plantation during the Civil War.

Probably Priestley was right—the same year Karloff was back on the stage again in the American production of *The Shop at Sly Corner,* a successful British thriller (not unlike *Arsenic and Old Lace*) and a little reminiscent of Tod Slaughter's material of the '30s. Karloff tried his best as a kindly shopkeeper—with murder in his heart; but the critics were harsh, and the play closed after a short run. Shortly before the play opened, Karloff's name appeared everywhere for the first time in an unusual way—this time as part of a film title: *Abbott and Costello Meet the Killer: Boris Karloff.* "Bud and Lou are wonderful chaps to work with," commented Karloff, "but we've all got to work, don't we; so the less said about this film the better."

But his next stage assignment was a definite hit, and an entirely new departure for him: the role of Captain Hook in *Peter Pan.* Jean Arthur played the title role in this new production of James M. Barrie's children's classic, which had music by no

Karloff reads his script for the Broadway play, *The Linden Tree* (1948), while director Maurice Evans looks on.

Karloff having a good time at a party around 1948.

Karloff stars on a children's radio special on New York's WNEW in 1949.

Karloff as Captain Hook in the stage presentation of *Peter Pan*. Jean Arthur played the title role.

less a figure than Leonard Bernstein. It ran for 321 successful performances.

Karloff was delightfully wicked as the one-handed pirate captain, alternately threatening Peter and the children, and quaking in terror before the approach of his nemesis, the crocodile. He also made the public aware for the first time of yet another facet of his talents by singing and doing a little dancing. In most glowing terms, Brooks Atkinson of *The New York Times* wrote: "There is something of the grand master in the latitude of his style and the roll of his declamations; and there is withal an abundance of warmth and gentleness in his attitude toward the audience."

That year (1950) marked yet another new phase for him—that of a children's entertainer. Not only did he play Hook, but he also served as narrator for the Czech puppet film *The Emperor's Nightingale*, based on the Andersen fairytale. The voice that had snarled and threatened had been nothing but an act all these years. Now, here was the ever-sentimental, tender, loving family man at home at last and displaying his fondness for children. Reflecting on this, Karloff said:

"Perhaps the best possible audience for a horror film is a child audience. The vivid imagination with which a child is gifted is far more receptive to the ingredients in these pictures than the adult imagination, which merely finds them artificial. Because they have vivid imaginations we must not underestimate children; they know far more than we think they do.

"Children choose what they want to see in an entertainment. This was brought home to me during the record run of Barrie's *Peter Pan* at the Imperial Theatre in New York. I played Captain Hook and, being interested in the children's reaction to the play, I invited a horde of them to come along to the theater. *Peter Pan*, as everyone knows, is a mixture of romanticism and adventure. The somewhat frightening exploits of Captain Hook are offset by the whimsy of Tinker Bell. The frightening element would possibly, one would think, stay in a child's mind far longer than the fairy element. After the final curtain I took them backstage and introduced them to the cast. Almost all the children would first want to meet Wendy and Tinker Bell and then they would want to put on the Captain's hook. Their first reaction when they looked at themselves in the mirror was to grunt and scowl and make the same type of lurching gestures as does Frankenstein's Monster."

Obviously, his role as a children's entertainer wasn't too far removed from the old. As he said: "There is more horror and violence in nursery rhymes than in TV or films. Forget *Frankenstein*. Take 'A Frog He Would A-Wooing Go.' By golly, a cat kills a mouse and a rat, and a frog is eaten by a duck. Awfully cruel and savage. As for Grimm's *Fairy Tales* . . . well, for heaven's sake!" But Karloff added reassuringly, "We were all brought up on fairytales and none of us turned out to be monsters—except maybe me."

As his screen work lessened, his radio and TV commitments increased in the early fifties; he often received proportionately more pay for a "gag" guest shot (averaging several thousand dollars) than for the time and trouble required for certain screen parts. Although by this time science-fantasy and horror films were now in full swing in their "third cycle," the movie companies tried economizing by using young or lesser-known players if they could get away with it; in other cases, Karloff was wisely turning down certain offers after just one look at a script, remembering too well some of the turkeys he had been in, thanking his stars that he had survived them, and recalling poor Lugosi's humiliation.

Only two films appeared with Karloff between 1950 and 1952. In *The Strange Door* (1951), loosely adapted from Stevenson's "The Sire de Malétroit's Door," Charles Laughton was curiously cast as a

Boris and Evelyn Karloff are interviewed in a New York theater lobby (1950).

Despite appearances here, Karloff played a heroic role in *The Strange Door* (Universal, 1951); Charles Laughton was the menace.

madman playing his villainy to the hilt, and Karloff had a sympathetic part as his patient major domo who knows the Gothic castle's rightful owner has been rotting below in a dungeon for ages. One of the best scenes: Laughton, unaware that his imprisoned brother (Paul Cavanaugh)

hasn't degenerated into a gibbering idiot, has tossed his brother's daughter and her lover into the same cell; then he proceeds to set an ancient waterwheel in motion that starts the cell's walls moving, threatening to crush its occupants. Several bullet holes and a few stabbings on his person don't deter Karloff from dealing with all malefactors, tossing Laughton into the waterwheel to get squashed—on screen in full view!—and saving the innocents' lives . . . before dying for this worthy cause. Considerably better than what might be expected and imaginatively directed by Joseph Pevney (director of *Man of a Thousand Faces,* starring James Cagney, 1957), it borrowed a little of *The Black Cat's* ideas and Grand Guignol style from which American International would capitalize with Karloff, Price, and Lorre ten years or so later.

The Black Castle (1952), with a more famous director, had Karloff in a subordinate and quieter role. Having scooped up the Academy Award as Best Director in 1941 for *How Green Was My Valley* (and director of the eye-popping *Seventh Voyage of Sinbad* in 1958), Nathan Juran's first essay in horror is spirited and vigorous but hampered by a formula-ridden script. Clichés clash, growl, and thunder in the night with Stephen McNally, wearing an eye-patch, as the mad baron of an eighteenth-century castle who tyrannizes those who have become his pawns and unwilling "guests." Held in thrall and also victimized to obsequiousness, undaunted by alligators in the moat or by the castle's dreaded torture chambers, kindly old doctor Karloff retaliates by assisting hero Richard Greene to destroy evil McNally.

Karloff had a heavy overseas workload in 1953, after the release of *Abbott and Costello Meet Dr. Jekyll and Mr. Hyde,* in which he plays the strange Doctor and Mr. H. as Robert Louis Stevenson never imagined. Jekyll is more werewolf-like in this version and infects Costello (A & C are American "detectives" in London),

162

turning him into . . . a comedy monster! The usual A & C slapstick is abundant, Karloff faring better in a meatier part than in his last tour with the boys. In the finale, after Karloff meets a typical snide, Hyde-like death, A & C end up in a local jail. Lou starts biting all the bobbies, and they in turn become monsters, too!

In England Karloff returned to the stage in George Bernard Shaw's *Don Juan in Hell*, in an enormous revival on both continents (see also the Vincent Price chapter). Karloff played the part of a statue, the same role undertaken by Sir Cedric Hardwicke in the Broadway version. Then he was off to India on location for *Sabaka*, co-starring Reginald Denny and Victor Jory, with Karloff as a local rajah's military chief, a cutesy-poo Sabu-like elephant boy, and troubles with an evil cult of Fire Demon worshipers. Karloff's several scenes were of little help to this poorly directed 1953 film (unreleased in America until 1955). But still stranger was his appearance in an Italian film called *Il Mostro Dell Isola* (*The Monster of the Island*), surrounded by an outstanding cast of Italy's most unknown actors. Karloff played a

Karloff looks sinister, mostly for the benefit of the publicity department, but is really a sympathetic doctor in *The Black Castle* (Universal, 1952).

Karloff as Dr. Jekyll in *Abbott and Costello Meet Dr. Jekyll and Mr. Hyde* (Universal, 1953).

A and C Meet Dr. Jekyll and Mr. Hyde. Two monsters for the price of one? Standing by Boris in monster costume is Ed Parker, popular Universal stuntman who bore the brunt of the more strenuous Mr. Hyde feats.

Lou Krugman (*left*), Karloff, and Nino Marcel in *Sabaka* (UA, 1953; released 1954).

terrifying and sanguinary leader of a band of smugglers who terrorize their victims, much to the worry of the inhabitants of the island of Ischia—where the story takes place—and to the amazement of audiences seeing Karloff speaking dubbed Italian. For various reasons, some quite logical, the film has never been released in America, though according to what Karloff had to say, it might appear if it *escaped:*

"I haven't the least idea what it was like," Karloff said. "Incredible! Dreadful! No one in the outfit spoke English. And I don't speak Italian. Just hopeless. I had a very good time, though; but that's beside the point."

It continued being a busy year, especially in England where he recorded a prize-winning radio play, *The Hanging Judge*, written by actor Raymond Massey. An absorbing essay on the fallacies of crime and punishment, Karloff plays Justice Sir Francis Brittain, a hardened man who believes in upholding the law to the letter, though he has misgivings when he sentences to death a man who seems innocent. As the story unfolds, it is revealed that the judge isn't a paragon of morality at all but has led a weird double life for more than thirty years.

As Colonel March of Scotland Yard, and wearing an eye-patch, Karloff appeared in *Colonel March Investigates* (1953–1954), a feature film consisting of

three separate stories drawn from the "Colonel March of Scotland Yard" series. The series was highly praised when seen on American TV and in England, and re-run in prime time through the 1957 season.

It was in 1955, however, that theater audiences saw Karloff again in a very fine part in an acclaimed play: Lillian Hellman's adaptation of Jean Anouilh's *The Lark*. Most critics thought he was superb as Bishop Cauchon opposite Julie Harris as Joan of Arc. Less than a year and a half later, in 1957, he repeated his performance with Julie Harris for a nationwide TV audience.

Between 1953 and 1957, in England and the United States, Karloff had racked up more than sixty profitable TV appearances, not including the successful "Colonel March" (containing twenty-six separate segments), several plays, radio, and recordings.

Movie screens were without Karloff for nearly four years, except for *Voodoo Island* (1957), in which he appears as the skeptical head of an expedition investigating the possibility of the undead and supernatural. Karloff's disbelief quickly vanishes when he finds terrible-looking papier-mâché "man-eating" plants and that the most deadening element seemed to be the low-budget quality. But, as with most of his films for ten years, his salary was excellent.

In *Frankenstein 1970*—also distinguished by being made in 1958 and almost unseen until general TV release in the mid-sixties— a film group journeys to an old German castle to make a horror movie, unaware that its owner is Karloff, a descendant of the original Frankenstein family who is also carrying on the Monster resuscitation business in secret. The group is not even sensible enough to realize something eerie may be afoot when they meet Karloff wearing a scar long enough to vie with the San Andreas fault. The Monster, completely swathed in bandages like a mummy, wreaks havoc and other unpleasantness;

166

NBC-TV's version of *The Lark* (February 10, 1957) starred Karloff, repeating the role of Bishop Cauchon which he had originated in the 1955 Broadway production.

TV time. Jeanne Mahoney, Donald O'Connor, and Karloff singing, dancing, and joking on "The Donald O'Connor Show" (February 19, 1955).

Julie Harris as Joan of Arc and Karloff in *The Lark*.

Karloff starred as a skilled organist who exalts himself above others in *The Man Who Played God*. Losing his hearing and the woman he loves, he develops an uncanny ability to read lips which gives him a powerful advantage over others. The play was colorcast on NBC's "Lux Video Theatre" (April 25, 1957).

Singing and gagging things up, Boris guested on "The Rosemary Clooney Show" (October 31, 1957) for a Halloween special.

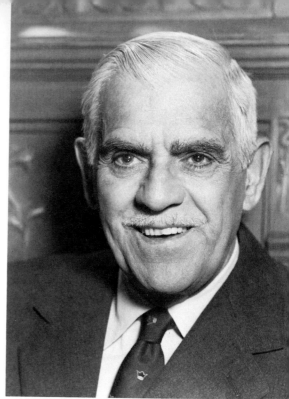

Publicity shot of Karloff sans makeup for *Frankenstein 1970* (Allied, 1958).

Murvyn Vye, Elisha Cook, Jr., and Karloff in *Voodoo Island* (UA, 1957).

and Karloff perishes in the end, but not before unveiling the Monster's cherished and hidden features: it is Karloff's own face from a twenty-five-year-old photo, pasted in position on the Monster's bandaged "body" for a cheap stop-action camera shot.

"Actors aren't to be blamed, of course, for the outcome of a film," Karloff said. "You're contracted for good pay to appear in a film; and if you're an able and conscientious worker, you do your best. You can never tell in advance what the lads will do later in the cutting room, alas!"

His next appearance, in *The Haunted Strangler* (released as *The Grip of the Strangler* in England), was one of two British films in which he did better that year. In the film, set before the turn of the century, criminal researcher-author Karloff probes into an old Jack-the-Ripper-type mystery considered closed by Scotland Yard. Investigating further, and strangely

168

Frankenstein 1970. Karloff may have cornered
the scar market when made up for the role.

Director Howard W. Koch, Boris, and wife
Evelyn on the set of *Frankenstein 1970*.

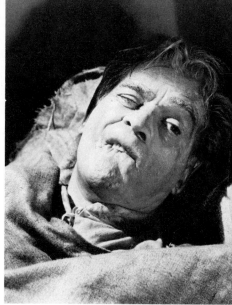

Karloff relied solely on his artistic ability to create
a horrific visage, and used no makeup for *The
Haunted Strangler* (MGM, 1958).

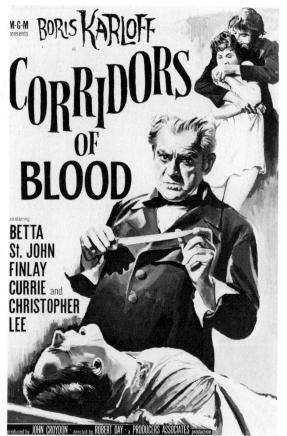

Poster used for *Corridors of Blood* (MGM, 1958;
first United States release, 1963).

fascinated, Karloff learns the wrong man
had been executed twenty years before.
Finally, coming into possession of the
original murder scalpel, Karloff's face is
transformed into a mask of deranged evil
—he was the mad killer all the time. A
well-paced, tightly directed Gothic thriller,
The Haunted Strangler offered the added
thrill of seeing Karloff proving his superb
ability of creating a face of horror without
the benefit of one drop of makeup!

In *Corridors of Blood*, almost a remake
of *The Body Snatcher*, Karloff fooled everyone again in a sympathetic part—as a kindly
Victorian doctor experimenting in anes-
thesia to relieve suffering. Unfortunately,
his good intentions are frustrated by a
Burke-and-Hare-like team who try coerc-
ing him into their insidious London back-
alley peregrinations. Also produced in 1958,

Francis Matthews and Karloff as father-and-son doctors in *Corridors of Blood*.

TV situation-comedy time: Boris menaces Gale Storm and Zasu Pitts on "The Gale Storm Show" (January 31, 1959).

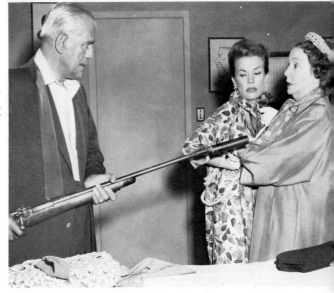

the film didn't find American release until mid-1963 under MGM.

TV and recording contracts continued to pile up in England and America for Karloff, involving more than one hundred appearances between 1959 and 1962 on TV and earning him well over a million dollars. Some of his most important TV work was as host, and sometimes actor, for sixty-six segments of the hour-long "Thriller." The series proved so successful in its 1960–1962 run on the NBC network that it became a syndicated favorite for the next five years. But it was conceded that its success rested largely upon Karloff's magnetic presence. And five years later, in 1972, "Thriller" went back into syndication throughout the entire country, but with a

notable title change—it was now highlighted as "BORIS KARLOFF Presents . . . Thriller!" Regretfully, greed took its toll, and station managers have sliced out many of the delightful Karloff vignettes to make room for more commercials, so Karloff usually shows up only in short prologues.

Barely out of his "Thriller" assignments, Karloff flew back to London in 1962 to host his own series, called "Out of This World,"

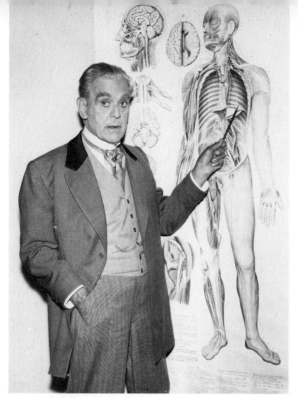

Karloff as Dr. Thorne in "The Premature Burial" on "Thriller" (October 2, 1961).

for British TV. Used to much quieter and sedate TV fare, British audiences responded with delight at seeing the old horror master hosting a number of excellent science-fiction-slanted thrillers, including stories by veterans such as Isaac Asimov, John Wyndham, and Philip K. Dick. Each week's program opened with an introduction by Karloff. White-haired and immaculate, and dressed like a theater first-nighter, he would stand against a futuristic background and philosophize on how little man really knows of the world he lives in. None of the shows has, unfortunately, ever been seen in the United States, except perhaps by those residing near enough to Canada to have received it when Canadian TV stations ran it for a short time.

Long past the age of retirement, Karloff maintained his oft-spoken resolution: "I'll never quit working so long as there's a breath still inside me. It's my whole life and everything I love," and adding with sublime modesty, "The greatest thing in life is to know that others still want you."

In a nostalgic and sentimental mood, shortly after appearing on NBC-TV in *The Paradine Case* (March 1962), he spoke of such homely details as redecorating the apartment he and his wife Evelyn kept in the Dakota in New York City and of the "flat" they kept in London as a home base:

"I lived so many years in Hollywood—we've lived in New York since 1951—I don't really know where my home is. When I'm here, I talk about going 'home' to London. When I'm in London, I talk about going 'home' to New York. The shocking truth is that I will probably spend more time in London because there I can indulge myself in my childish pleasures. All summer I can go to cricket matches every day. And when the cricket season is over, I watch rugby.

"You see, the trouble with baseball is the game is too short. It's all over in a couple of hours. In London, cricket is played at clubs. One goes to one's club in the morning and the game lasts all day.

Karloff hosting the British TV science-fiction series, "Out of This World" (1962).

Another rare shot of Karloff as host of "Out of This World."

There is a forty-minute break for lunch, and a twenty-minute break for tea; and if the action should get dull, one simply goes in the clubhouse and has a short nap, or writes some letters.

"It's a very pleasant way to spend a day, and I can't expect to go on working forever." He was now seventy-five and, as usual, underestimating himself. "The parts available to me are bound to diminish," he said wistfully. "I'm already a national scandal to have hung on this long."

Nothing could have been further from the truth. Horror films were now mushrooming in popularity as never before. For five years television had been showing earlier Karloff films to old fans and to a new generation of youngsters who were growing up to idolize him. At the age of seventy-six Karloff was more famous and greater than ever. In addition to more recording engagements and TV work, he was to appear in eighteen films within a five-year period.

Eager to take advantage of a walking gold mine, American International signed Karloff to a multiple-film contract that included at least three outstanding productions. The first of these was *The Raven* (1963), co-starring Vincent Price and Peter Lorre, a horror spoof pitting Karloff's evil black magic against Price's good white magic. Director Roger Corman's knack for whimsy, abetted by Richard Matheson's script, inspired Karloff and the others to render excellent performances. Special ef-

173

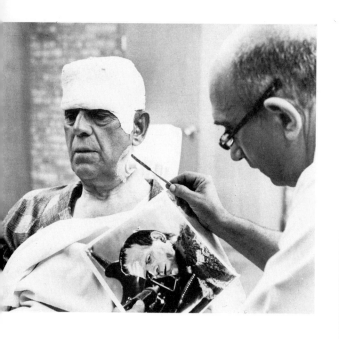

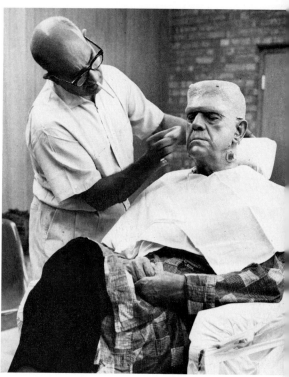

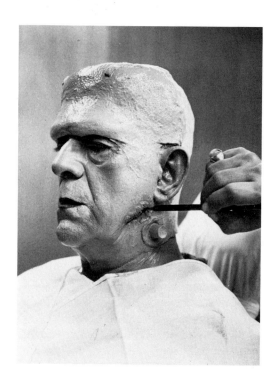

Here and on opposite page: Karloff steps unofficially into the famous Monster guise for a special Halloween segment of the TV series, "Route 66" (October 1962). His co-stars were Martita Hunt, Peter Lorre, Lon Chaney, Jr., and the series' regulars, George Maharis and Martin Milner.

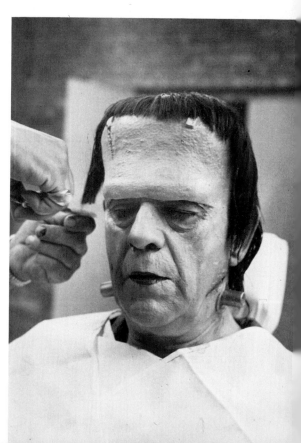

fects created for the scenes, showing Karloff and Price hurling magical powers at each other, were perfect additions to enhance the macabre hilarity. Succeeding finally in defeating his nemesis, Price departs from the shambles while Karloff emerges from beneath the castle's rubble; after dusting himself off, he sits with his sorceress friend, wondering how he could have slipped so badly and longing for the good old days.

Corman's renowned economy and fast production methods were evident, and *The Raven* was completed under the deadline with several days left to spare. As though Karloff hadn't already accomplished enough, he was reminded by Corman that he was bound to serve a few more days. Altering *Raven*'s sets only slightly, Corman produced a rushed script and, in *three days*, completed all major work on *The Terror*, starring Karloff. There's some notable incoherency and a smooth, rambling confusion in the film that, nevertheless, does little to detract from its amazing visual quality and mysterious fascination. It's all Karloff's vehicle from start to finish, as he is found residing in an isolated Spanish castle during Napoleon's time. When young hero-soldier Jack Nicholson arrives, he uncovers uncanny spells, sorcery, and a curse hanging over the place. There's also a witch, and a beautiful fey-like girl who appears to have the power to change into a hawk which descends on a man and claws out his eyes (this scene was cut for TV release, as are so many in other films, particularly several similar scenes in Hitchcock's *The Birds*). Karloff ends up in a battle royal with his long-dead wife-from-the-grave, thrashing it out in the flooded castle basement and finally disappearing in a watery grave. As though this weren't enough, Jack Nicholson rescues the beautiful-girl-in-the-plot, who was in reality "something else" and who decomposes to prove it in Corman's best butterscotch-topping tradition.

Comedy of Terrors (1964) cast Karloff

Boris as the mad magician in *The Raven* (AIP, 1963).

in a good but primarily subordinate role as Vincent Price's eccentric old father-in-law. The film was mostly a Price vehicle, but others in dominant roles included Basil Rathbone and Peter Lorre. All are more or less involved in a shady funeral business run by Price and Lorre. The accent is decidedly on black comedy and the story is virtually a spoof of Karloff's *The Body Snatcher* of a generation earlier.

Black Sabbath, produced by AIP, was shot entirely in Italy under the direction of Mario Bava, whose imagination and intelligent sense for horror film-making have earned him admiration and respect that have sometimes eclipsed even that accorded

Corman. Karloff hosted this 1963 (released in 1964) film's three terror tales and starred in the longest and best, *The Wurdulak*, based on Alexei Tolstoy's novelette of that name. Uniquely different and one of the sixties' most provocative tableaus of terror, it satisfied even the most demanding fans of the genre. A cold, remote section somewhere near Transylvania and a strange, lonely house provide the setting for a family ruled by Karloff and haunted by a terrible heritage—a heritage of unrelenting loneliness and vampirism that Karloff, the *wurdulak*, threatens to pass on to them. Against deep surrounding snows and a night that seems eternal, hovering fears deepen as

176

Vincent Price and Karloff as rival warlocks str ing to out-zap each other in *The Raven*.

Karloff's human exterior becomes more transparently a camouflage for the creature that he really is. Gradually, the family realizes the ultimate in terror, as some succumb as actual victims of Karloff, who is not only a vampire but a ghoul as well.

Karloff worked hard in *Black Sabbath* to create one of his best roles, which was complemented by the film's brilliant and moody Gothic power. Though suffering from arthritis and requiring a brace to enable him to work, his early physical training and amateur sports activity gave him an endurance many of his colleagues envied. What he least expected was that *Black Sabbath* would almost cost him his life:

January 26, 1963—Karloff on a publicity tour for *The Raven*.

Karloff in *Black Sabbath* (AIP, 1963).

Black Sabbath. Boris gloats over the head of a victim.

Karloff as Vincent Price's eccentric father-in-law
in *Comedy of Terrors* (AIP, 1964).

Black Sabbath. Karloff has evil designs on his grandson.

"It was brutally cold, and the hotel was a sort of marble palace. They don't warm up with one match being struck; and it was there that I got quite ill. I came back to England at the end of the film. I was able to complete it with a great deal of difficulty. I was desperately ill that summer and I had a very narrow squeak. It left my lungs, as you can hear, very short-winded. I had pneumonia."

His fans all over the world prayed for him when they learned of his serious ill-ness. He was on the critical list for many days, and his fight for life took a heavy toll of the gallant old trouper, leaving him with one weakened lung. For his remaining years he would keep a large oxygen tank in his quarters or, while traveling, a small one by his side; his wife was with him constantly wherever he went, acting as nurse, secretary, and a bulwark against routine pressure.

His illness had debilitated him so much that he played most of his scenes for the next several years from a sitting position; yet, heroically hiding his afflictions, he would take an upright stance when the director called "action" and he had to move about. Audiences saw him this way in *Die, Monster, Die* (1965) as Nahum Witley, an apparently paralytic old man, who practices strange rituals centered around a fearful object that's hidden away but that dominates his entire life and household. The object is revealed to be a weird meteorite, bearing a terrible power, that's been around a long while; the Witleys are affected by it and become hideous monsters, and Karloff realizes he's next in line. In a blind rage he goes to the secret chamber that houses the horrible stone and attempts to destroy it; but his nearness to it only accelerates its mutating effect, and he now changes into a terrifying monster, radiant with radioactivity and on the rampage for victims. In the end he falls dead, a heap of pulverized stone-like matter.

The next year Karloff appeared in the second and last of his two AIP teenage "beach party" films (he was in a brief cameo in 1964's *Bikini Beach*, uplifting the film and such supporting players as Frankie Avalon, Annette Funicello, and Harvey Lembeck, a sort of second-rate Don Rickles). In *Ghost in the Invisible Bikini*, Karloff mostly sat and enjoyed watching such wonderful supporting players as Francis X. Bushman, Patsy Kelly, and Basil Rathbone running about in this pleasant little time-waster of kooky haunted-house shenanigans.

With narrative work completed for *Mondo Bizarro* (a *Mondo Cane*-styled documentary), Karloff terminated his trying contract and ordeals under American International. *The Venetian Affair* showed him more relaxed and vigorous in a supporting role as Dr. Vaugiroud, a political scientist who possess information concerning a spy ring involved in bombings and heinous conspiracies. For all of Helen MacInnes' intriguing spy novel, on which the film was based, and Robert Vaughn, Elke Sommer, and Karloff's presence, the action in the film plodded under director Jerry Thorpe's unimaginative style, insistence on heavy dialogue, and overuse of interior sets.

The Sorcerers, a modest essay combining science fiction and horror, was a fascinating low-budgeter indicative of director Michael Reeve's high potentiality, considering that he was just twenty-three years old when he had completed this film. (A year or so later, shortly after finishing *The Conqueror Worm,* starring Vincent Price, a shocked film world learned of Reeve's tragic death.) In *The Sorcerers* Karloff starred as Professor Monserrat, ex-stage illusionist and mesmerist, who has perfected a machine that can monitor not only another's actions but also transfer all thoughts and feelings from afar. As an aged couple, Karloff and his wife, Catherine Lacey, envision what a divine benefit this might become to all the elderly who, though infirm, could still find happiness and escape through the experiences of younger "contacts." Eventually, Karloff's wife has other plans and starts exerting an evil influence over a selected subject who is ordered to go out and steal and, finally, to kill. Attempting to thwart her evil, the chairbound and semi-invalid Karloff is easily dominated and overcome by Catherine. Their victim, meanwhile, has met with a terrible accident in a car crash; as he burns alive in the wreck, his complete sensations are "transferred" to Catherine, incinerating her and Karloff as well in the spreading holocaust.

Always impressive in most of his TV appearances, Karloff created three especially memorable roles for the tube in 1966. One of them, in fact, has been so highly praised that it is now a classic and an annual Christmas event: "How the Grinch Stole Christmas," with Karloff narrating and doing the voice of the villainous Grinch, who reforms at the end and gives back the spirit of love and Christmas cheer to the friendly creatures from whom it

Here and on opposite page: *Die, Monster, Die!*
(AIP, 1965), based on H. P. Lovecraft's "The
Colour Out of Space," starred Karloff as the scion
of a family harboring a terrible secret.

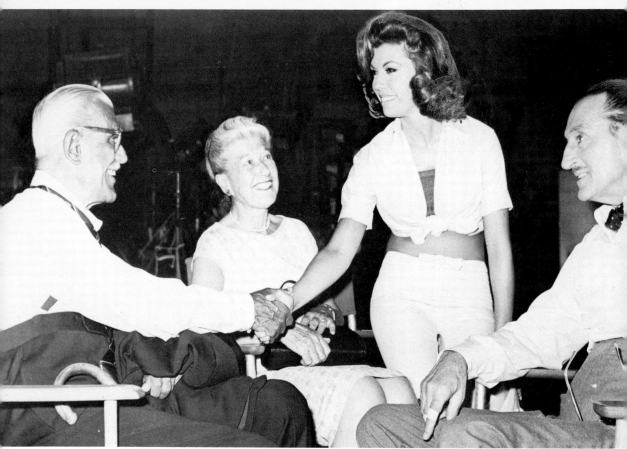

An informal moment on the set of *The Ghost in the Invisible Bikini* (AIP, 1966). *Left to right:* Karloff, wife Evelyn, Nancy Sinatra, and Basil Rathbone.

Boris on TV in "The Night of the Golden Cobra" segment of "Wild, Wild West" (April 1966).

was originally stolen. Based on Dr. Seuss' (Ted Geisel) illustrations and scripted by him, this excellent cartoon is the work of Oscar-winning Chuck Jones, animator of many of the best Looney Tunes, which have included Porky Pig, Daffy Duck, the inimitable and fabulous Road Runner, and innumerable others. It was Karloff's voice, though, that immortalized "Grinch."

Karloff astonished everyone when he donned female garb for the exquisitely unique role of "Mother Muffin" in "The Girl from U.N.C.L.E." In this obviously semihumorous spin-off program that developed from the successful "Man from U.N.C.L.E." series (inspired, in turn, by the James Bond films), Karloff starred for this segment as a notorious leader for T.H.R.U.S.H., a vast and ingenious network of international conspirators whose diaboli-

Karloff, at seventy-eight, looking at a scene from the 1931 *Frankenstein* shown on the back of his favorite magazine. "I can see that set now," he reminisced. (Photo taken in his London apartment during an interview by *Castle of Frankenstein* magazine.)

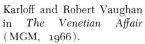

Karloff and Robert Vaughan in *The Venetian Affair* (MGM, 1966).

Karloff went in drag on TV as Mother Muffin for "The Mother Muffin Affair" segment of "The Girl from U.N.C.L.E. (June 1966).

cal services are either available to the highest bidder or employed in their own interest. Crime's goals on this show often seemed vague, as did Karloff's role; but in this case, it didn't matter. Karloff's completely different role, à la Margaret Rutherford, was the TV season's *pièce de résistance.*

In an "I Spy" segment ("Mainly on the Plains"), opposite Bill Cosby and Robert Culp, Karloff played another unusual but straighter role with significant poignancy. Karloff is an old Quixote-like, carefree Spanish professor whose life is in constant jeopardy because of his top-secret missile formula. Philosophically treating the human condition around him as a superficial passing parade, he refuses to take political sides. Almost too late he realizes the game he's been playing is one of life and death.

Praised for its qualities and Karloff's performance, the show was made on location in Spain, making it convenient for him to walk through briefly in *Cauldron of Blood* (originally titled *Blind Man's Bluff*) —a very routine horror exploiter that poorly attempted to capture certain elements of *House of Wax* and Corman's delightful *Bucket of Blood.* It co-starred Viveca Lindfors and Jean-Pierre Aumont, and was not released to the United States until late in 1971.

Though he was now almost eighty, and in the late winter days of his life, Karloff's zeal and dedication seemed to mock time and belie his years. Six more feature films and a number of TV appearances were yet ahead. But such were the amazing stamina and mental clarity of the man that many might have confidently bet he would reach the century mark.

In 1967 Karloff attained perhaps the most important milestone of his career by appearing in *Targets,* a film conceived through the inspiration of its director and producer, Peter Bogdanovich, not only as a tailor-made Karloff vehicle but with the intent of being a testimonial to the great old artist. Surpassing even its brilliant young director's expectations, it was more than even he intended: it is Karloff's legacy.

In effect, the film is an almost biographical account of Karloff's life, obliquely emphasizing his later years, and transmuted for screen linearity into semifictional adventure-allegory. Karloff plays Byron Orlock, a famous elderly horror-film actor who watches in frustration the changing world of the late sixties. No longer as romantic as he once knew it to be, the world has become a place where contemporary events and daily headlines seem more horrifying than his films ever were. Resigned to accepting retirement and eventual oblivion, he is unaware of a traumatic event that is about to unfold and affect his life. While Karloff is taking a walk, a young man, Tim

O'Kelly, is browsing inside a gun-supplies store; playfully he raises a rifle and aims it at the passing Karloff, little realizing how much they will soon have in common. O'Kelly purchases the rifle, adding it to a collection of other weapons hidden in the trunk of his car, and drives away.

In a sullen mood, Karloff quarrels with his secretary, producer, and Sammy (Peter Bogdanovich), and goes to his apartment with a bottle of whiskey to watch one of his old films on TV (*The Criminal Code*). Terror breaks out the next day when O'Kelly's latent violence erupts and he suffers a mental breakdown. After shooting his wife, his mother, and a grocery delivery boy to death in his house, he buys a huge supply of bullets and drives off. He then climbs to the top of a gas tank next to a highway and starts killing passing motorists; a gas-tank worker is also shot down while trying to investigate the snipings. O'Kelly escapes when he hears the sound of police-car sirens approaching. Karloff meanwhile has patched up his quarrel with his film-making associates and has agreed to begin a series of "farewell" appearances which his producer-

Karloff as a blind sculptor in *Cauldron of Blood* (Cannon, 1967). (Originally titled *Blind Man's Bluff* and made in 1967, but not released until 1972.)

Karloff as Byron Orlock, a fading old horror actor, who approaches a mad sniper and disarms him in this climactic scene in *Targets* (Paramount, 1968), directed by Peter Bogdanovich.

friend, Bogdanovich, hopes will renew the old star's interest in more productions. While Karloff is making a personal appearance at a drive-in which is showing one of his films (*The Terror*), O'Kelly hides himself among the hundreds of cars, then proceeds to enter the tower booth behind the screen, from where he can secretly see the entire audience. Like sitting ducks, people begin getting shot in their cars; the slaughter and horror mount as neighboring viewers in their cars are too buried in the darkness and engrossed by the film and its sounds to be aware of the carnage around them. The killer is caught off guard when he is stunned to see Karloff playing on the screen and confronting him in person at the same time. The weary but valiant old man, armed with only a cane, approaches O'Kelly and disarms him. The police then take O'Kelly away.

Targets marked Bogdanovich's directorial debut and impressed film buffs and critics so much that few were at all surprised when he emerged a short time later with *The Last Picture Show*, which won an Oscar for Cloris Leachman as Best Supporting Actress, and which was nominated for Best Director and Best Film awards among the films of 1971.

188

Had *Targets* appeared approximately ten years earlier, it would have still been a powerfully important film, but perhaps incongruous by being too much ahead of its time; but appearing as it did in the midst of the Vietnamese war, race riots, and in the wake of the assassinations of the Kennedy brothers, it is a dynamic synthesis of actual horrors ingeniously delineated to update the genre over which Karloff should rightfully reign as acknowledged king.

Boris Karloff's greatest "quirk" was his total loyalty and conscientiousness, more often far above and beyond the call of duty. But, then, he wouldn't be Karloff if he were not like that. In England, appearing in *Curse of the Crimson Altar* under unconscionable directorial working conditions, Karloff virtually ended his life. They were shooting his scenes in abominable weather and he caught a chill. When he went back to the small, drafty portable dressing room to warm up with a hot toddy, the director grumbled something to the effect that if everyone hurried up now it would be "all over" fast, and everyone could go home. Too much of a trouper to say, "Oh, go to hell! I'm eighty years old, not forty!" Karloff went back for the remaining takes. Shortly afterward he came down with a fever and was rushed semicomatose to the hospital with a case of double pneumonia.

Miraculously—but now looking a lot older and every bit of his years—the gallant actor recovered. Not long after, in April 1968, tired-looking and spent, but in his usual cheerful mood, he described the ordeal:

"I was making something called *The Crimson Altar*. And we started out shooting night scenes in freezing rain. It is a bit different in the States. There they have the sense to take you outside last of all and let you die in your own time. Much more sensible!"

He went into a humorous description of *Altar*'s stupid handling and how the staff had to continue shooting under practically flood conditions: "I performed from a bath chair," Karloff quipped, laughing out loud.

Even with Karloff and a fine supporting cast that included Christopher Lee, Michael Gough, and Barbara Steele, *Crimson Altar* was, predictably, everything it deserved to be: a disastrous film event.

That summer, after long delays and many difficulties created by his illness, Karloff was finally signed up by Mexican producer Luis Vergara to appear in *four* films. Doctors, however, advised Karloff that Mexico City's altitude might be harmful to his health. On the other hand, it was impossible for the producer to shoot all the films in England, where the star was staying, so all principals then arrived at what seemed the most sensible solution: the Mexican units would shoot certain sequences *around* Karloff, while Karloff scenes with some of the Mexican actors would be made in Hollywood.

The entire setup was an actor's dream. All four pictures were made in Mexico, and all of Karloff's scenes were created in a matter of a few days!

Some indication of Boris Karloff's important star status may be found in the fact that his salary from these Mexican films totaled over $300,000. The four films were titled *Fear Chamber, The Snake People, House of Evil,* and *Incredible Invasion.* Though shown throughout Mexico, they have been plagued by American distribution problems; in late 1972 they were sold in a special package-deal for television.

When TV producers learned he was back in the United States, the whole film capital started buzzing—*Karloff is back again!* Millions of fans never realized how ill and tired the kindly, devoted old veteran really was when he guest-starred September 1968 on "The Red Skelton Show," joking, spoofing horror, and making fun of himself. The same month he starred in *The Name of the Game,* a feature-length made-for-TV film, as Mikhail Orlo, a Czech author trying to protect his royalties to use for the cause of freedom fighters against the Russian invaders of his country.

For a Halloween special, on the "Jona-

The Crimson Altar (AIP, 1968; retitled *The Crimson Cult*). Making this film virtually terminated Karloff's life.

WHAT OBSCENE PRAYER or HUMAN SACRIFICE can SATISFY THE DEVIL-GOD?

The Master of Evil in his last and most shocking role!

BORIS KARLOFF
CHRISTOPHER LEE

The CRIMSON CULT

MARK EDEN · BARBARA STEELE · MICHAEL GOUGH
INTRODUCING VIRGINIA WETHERELL · GUEST STAR RUPERT DAVIES · GP COLOR

DIRECTED BY VERNON SEWELL · SCREENPLAY BY MERVYN HAISMAN AND HENRY LINCOLN · GERRY LEVY · TONY TENSER · LOUIS M. HEYWARD
A TIGON BRITISH AMERICAN INTERNATIONAL PRODUCTION AN AMERICAN INTERNATIONAL PICTURE

Poster exploitation for *The Crimson Cult.*

than Winters Show" in October 1968, carrying himself nobly, but very noticeably aged and requiring the aid of a walking stick, he stood before the cameras; then everyone, including himself, seemed to forget his infirmities as he began to steal one scene after another in a "monster," mad-scientist spoof. It was the grand Karloff of old. Nothing appeared to have changed after two fabulous Karloff-filled generations! And, finally, he got up and did a little dance with the rest of the cast and sang his last song, "It Was a Very Good Year." Inwardly we all knew and wept.

As previously mentioned, he never planned to retire. "If I did," he once said emphatically, "I'd be dead within a few months. I intend to die with my boots and my grease paint on!"

He was badly in need of rest, and something inside urged him to return home to his beloved England. There he was suddenly taken ill and rushed to King Edward VII Hospital, Midhurst, Sussex. As valiantly as he had fought against every trial and ordeal for sixty years, he fought for his life for three months against respiratory complications that would have defeated any number of men half his age. But for a man of eighty-one the battle was too much; he died on February 2, 1969. Surviving are his wife Evelyn Helmore, his daughter Sara Jane, and her two sons.

Famed for writing Hitchcock's *Psycho* and dozens of other fright stories for TV and the movies, veteran horror-story author Robert Bloch often had Karloff at his home and knew him well. In reminiscing about the great artist, Bloch said:

"My immediate thought was that I had lost a very close friend. The kind it's difficult to replace. Despite all those characters he played, he was a total skeptic. I remember once my wife and I were visiting his summer place and he took us for a drive through the English countryside. Along the way he pointed to a 'haunted house' and told some amusing stories about it, concluding with the comment: 'If it's haunted

by anything, it must be by insects.' Still, he had a great love for the literature of the macabre. He had a wide reading background and was acquainted with most of the classic writers. He compiled his own anthologies, you know," said Block, referring to some half dozen that included *Tales of Terror* and *And the Darkness Falls*. "A close examination of them will reveal those writers he thought the most of."

Bloch continued: "He had a tremendous sense of humor. On that same drive I was telling you about, Mrs. Karloff was pointing out tea *shoppes* and so on, when suddenly Boris leaned out the window and shouted, 'Oh, look—there's Ye Olde Woolworth's!' He didn't take himself pompously, he was always self-depreciating. One of the last funny stories told of Karloff concerns a science-fiction film he was making for a Mexican producer in Hollywood. Boris was portraying a scientist of some kind and had a lengthy speech in the final scene that went something like this:

" 'The aliens have left now, but where have they gone? Will they be back? I hope we've seen the last of them!'

"Then he turned to the camera and the crew and added:

" 'Because if they haven't, we'll have to do the whole damn picture over again!'

"His attitude about horror films was close to my own personal feelings. He felt horror and science fiction had been degraded by substitutes of shock and sensationalism. He often commented, 'There just isn't enough genuine feeling for the supernatural.' "

Bloch then revealed something very touching about the one goal Karloff had failed to reach:

"There was one unrealized ambition, though it had nothing to do with films. Karloff, as you know, started as a stock-company actor in Canada, and a long time after was in *Arsenic and Old Lace* for two years on Broadway. He co-starred with Jean Arthur in *Peter Pan*, and with Julie Harris in *Skylark*. But he always had wanted to appear in a West End production in London, which would be the equivalent to our Broadway. By the time it was possible, however, he was too well along in years and couldn't sustain the night-after-night pressures. But despite not achieving this goal, Karloff, in both thought and action, expressed the attitude that life had always been extra good to him."

The eulogies that poured in from film celebrities, dignitaries, and critics all over the world were of one accord: a kind, gracious man who, in or out of the genre, was among the greatest actors who had ever lived.

Peter Bogdanovich, who created *Targets* especially for Karloff, wrote in his most moving eulogy:

"What right did he have to retire? Actually he had plenty: a shattered knee that necessitated a leg brace at least and sometimes cane or crutches, together with a severe case of emphysema that badly constricted his breathing. It was extremely difficult for him to move about and speak both at once, but he never complained, was always prepared, and never held up shooting. One scene in *Targets* required him to tell a two-minute fable—a great many words to learn—and I wanted it done without cuts, which meant he would have to say it all straight through. Everybody was tired by the time we got to it—after midnight—but when the camera rolled, he did it in one take. Spontaneous applause broke out, which you could see moved him. I like to remember that moment. He had brought off a scene meant to be a tour de force—for he was a great storyteller and had a marvelous voice with which to do it—in a movie that could only have been conceived because there was a Boris Karloff."

Peter Lorre

1904-1964

Although Karloff and Lugosi would have been regarded as eminent SFantasy film stars even had they made only a baker's dozen in the genre, Peter Lorre seemed born and formed for the macabre more than any other film celebrity. Yet out of more than seventy-five films in his life, fewer than twenty-one are classifiably super-SFantasy or hair-raising shockers. Lorre's obvious status as an SFantasy superstar is primarily a synthesis of his unique personality and extraordinary talent which created bizarre, offbeat, Guignol-like moods that transcended even the most routine film situations. His prominent moon face; large, soulful, often sad eyes, atop his stocky five-

foot-three frame; and an outré, accentedly flexible but distinguished voice and style, made Lorre a living legend in his own time.

Offscreen and in private life, he possessed a razor-sharp, usually poker-faced sense of humor. Always a subject for impressionists, he satirized himself: "All you need to imitate me is a pair of soft-boiled eggs and a bedroom voice." Fully aware of his physical limitations from the very start of his career, Lorre was unhesitant in utilizing them to the fullest and creating millions of admirers for more than three decades.

The oldest of four children, Peter Lorre

was born "on location" in an area that would have been more than appropriate for many of his films. The date: June 26, 1904; the location: a small village in an isolated part of Hungary's Carpathian Mountains. Unhappily, he never knew his mother who died a few months after his birth. Six years later his family moved to Vienna where Lorre's father found employment with a car company and a stepmother for his brood.

Ill at ease with unaccustomed but growing discipline at home, and bored by the tedium of school, young Peter—inspired by glowing tales of theater life described by many of his drama-fan friends—yearned to become an actor. Vienna, international center of arts and sciences, had all the necessary advantages and stimuli that any young man could want, so unable to endure his family's old-fashioned ideas and objections, Lorre left home at seventeen.

Lacking background and experience, he was refused theatrical work wherever he went, and this resulted in a long, bleak period of near-starvation and sleeping in public parks, a state of affairs particularly aggravated by a terrible inflation and depression then afflicting all of Austria.

At long last, a small ray of hope: Lorre obtained a minor position in a bank to sustain himself and utilized what he could spare of his small salary to organize an amateur dramatic group consisting of acquaintances with theatrical aspirations. Unwittingly, Lorre's group pioneered the method of *improvisational* drama and acting; more recently, this style came into vogue with groups like Second City and The Premise. So absorbed was Lorre by his group's activity that, eventually, he couldn't get up for work on many mornings and was soon fired by his bank.

During this transitional period, he also studied under Alfred Adler and Sigmund Freud, pioneers in the yet-embryonic but controversial field of psychiatric research. Lorre reasoned that a career in psychiatry was not only intriguing but more than possible. But, basically, theater was his first love.

Finally, in 1924, his first theater job in a Breslau stock company—a mere walk-on part that later led Lorre to quip that he had acted in two plays before anyone in the audience knew of his presence. He was disappointed and expected more. But on the basis of this experience he secured membership in a Zurich stock company. Following a successful role as an old man in a German translation of Galsworthy's *Society*, he was called back to Vienna and remained there for the next two years playing a variety of parts.

In the German world of art and drama, though, the big time in the twenties was Berlin—where Lorre finally arrived . . . with only ten marks in his pocket. Fortunately, his good references and press notices obtained work for him almost immediately. After several hits he scored in *Die Pionere Von Ingolstadt* ("The Students of Ingolstadt") in 1928 . . . in the role of a sex fiend! The controversial play became the sensation of Berlin. At this time Lorre was approached by a number of film studios but he refused them because they offered what he thought were unsuitable parts. During a stage run Lorre became infatuated with a lovely member of the cast, Celia Lovsky, whom he was to marry several years later. Though her professional career was virtually curtailed and supplanted by the amount of work involved in managing her husband's career, Celia Lovsky has done many stints on stage and in film and on TV, and was particularly outstanding as a guest star in "Amok Time," the first program of "Star Trek's" second TV season in 1967.

While Lorre appeared in *Fruehlings Erwacken* ("Awakening of Spring"), in which he enacted a sexually frustrated student who commits suicide, the brilliant UFA director, Fritz Lang, visited Lorre in his dressing room following a performance and asked the actor if he would like to appear in a film for him some time in the future. Though Lorre had misgivings about a film career, since he was not a leading-man type, Lang's phenomenal international recognition and directorial genius charmed Lorre into agreement.

Two years later, in late 1930 while Lorre was rehearsing in a Bertolt Brecht play, he was visited again by Lang, who showed Lorre a completed shooting script and told him that he wanted him for the lead role. The screenplay was *M*, based on the factual case of a child-killer who cunningly eludes the police but is finally tracked down and captured by the underworld. The script was based on the Düsseldorf murders of 1929, and written by Lang's wife, Théa von Harbou, who also wrote *Metropolis*. Despite this film commitment, Lorre began rehearsing for a new play the night Brecht's play folded. Ironically, his stage role and the one for which he was under contract for *M* were complete opposites: a psychopathic murderer before the cameras by day: a humorous lead in a stage comedy at night.

Lorre once mentioned a generally unknown and bizarre incident that occurred during the filming of *M*. During the memorable kangaroo-trial sequence in a deserted warehouse cellar where Lorre is judged for his murders by a jury assembled from the Berlin underworld, Lang gave the film added realism by recruiting actual criminals for the roles. Lorre aided by accompanying Lang in dredging up a variety of criminals of the raunchiest kind from the shabby backwaters of the city. A police official, who was connected with the film, suddenly discovered many of the criminals he had been seeking for years; he immediately left the studio with secret exhilaration, shortly returning with nearly all the Berlin police force. Fortunately, Lang persuaded him to delay arresting six of the fugitives until after they had completed their scenes. "So we finished early," Lorre recalls, "let them off at four o'clock, and gave them a two-hour start on the police."

When *M* was finally released in 1931

194

it added more laurels to Lang's dynamic reputation and brought Lorre international renown. The critics generally agreed that *M* was not simply another screen shocker about lustful, hideous murder, but a humanistic drama of a pathological killer who is both villain and social victim—a film classic portraying tragedy and savage psychopathia.

Under Lang's skillful direction and innate sense for the macabre, the actual murders, while known, are not screened. The most frightening scene is when Lorre sees a little girl's reflection in a store window and the idea begins to jell in his sick mind that he is under a magnetic compulsion, a demonic psychopathic force, that is driving him to commit yet another child-killing. In the long run it is the underworld that entraps him, despite the entire Berlin police force's powerful but futile efforts. At this juncture the audiences are rooted to their seats as they watch the progression of Lorre's escape and his climactic "arrest." Encircled by leading underworld figures, ruthlessly cross-examined, Lorre is judged and almost executed by people who rank him too vile and barbarous to qualify even as one of their own kind.

Rated as one of the historically most important film sequences, Lorre—persecuted, examined, and brutally interrogated—screams out at his captors:

"You are all criminals because you want to be. But, I . . . I do what I do because I can't help it!"

Lorre's performance was terrifying not only because of the fiendish deeds he portrayed but because of his probing interpretation of a particular type of psychopathic personality. It would be almost redundant to bring up Lorre's psychiatric studies as the basis that inspired him with an insight far above that of most leading actors. As one of the screen's several greatest criminal characterizations, the role immortalized him and also permanently established his future career personality: that of one of filmdom's greatest villains.

As a result of his acclaimed success in

One of the original display posters used for *M*, distributed by Nero Films and released in 1931.

Peter Lorre as the psychotic child-killer on the run in *M*.

M, Lorre entered into a contract with UFA for several films which he alternated with stage work. His activity was suddenly terminated by the rise of Nazism, which was especially understood by the well-informed and half-Jewish Lorre, who was acutely aware of what untold evil would unfold once this political malignancy became entrenched.

Leaving Berlin, Lorre arrived in Vienna, which was still a gay, carefree, and art-loving center of European culture, and proceeded to resume his acting career in the film, *Schuss In Morgen Graven* ("Invisible Opponent"), co-starring Oscar Homolka. But the political climate was changing so rapidly and growing so dangerous,

Peter Lorre about to lure a child in *M*.

Lorre recalled that his first meeting with Hitchcock was one of the best "acting" jobs that he ever had to put over, since his English vocabulary was limited to either "yes" or "no." Lorre said, "A friend of mine tipped me off that Hitch loved telling funny stories. So when he talked to me, I'd watch him very closely and whenever I guessed that he'd come to the point of what I thought was a joke, I would laugh uproariously. This made Hitch figure that I knew enough of the language to play the part; and that's how I got the job."

While working by day in the Hitchcock production, Lorre was studying English at night; this resulted in re-takes of earlier scenes (much to Hitchcock's bewilderment but dignified patience) so that his two speech patterns would match. Celia Lovsky, who had emigrated from the Continent earlier, was also in the film, and it was after its completion that she and Lorre were married.

His first English-speaking role in *The Man Who Knew Too Much* was another important milestone. His performance, as the anarchist leader of a group of international saboteurs planning to murder a prominent European statesman, received accolades. One American critic remarked: "Lorre crowds his character with dark and terrifying emotions without disturbing his placid moon face." This version, unfortunately, will probably never again be seen by the general public; except for a rather battered, scratched-up copy rented by a few film societies and revival houses, all prints were reportedly destroyed when the 1956 version was made. This was not a unique or isolated incident but an endemic film-destruction problem that has existed until recently, largely abetted by the studios themselves which used to place a higher premium upon the square-foot value of storage space than on the historical and priceless value of a film "property." Except where television is concerned, this barbarism has been virtually ended, mostly be-

that Lorre was forced to go to France. In Paris he wound up sharing shabby quarters in a secondary boarding house with other future Hollywood luminaries such as Paul Lukas, Oscar Homolka, composer Franz Waxman, and many others. As a consequence of refugees coming in from all parts of Europe and a growing scarcity of work, Lorre could find only one job—voice-dubbing a minor French film, which was done in one day.

Penniless and desperate, Lorre went to England in early 1934, barely understanding a few words of English. At the British film-making center he was fortunate in being introduced to Alfred Hitchcock who was then planning and casting his first version of *The Man Who Knew Too Much* (the second version under Hitchcock's direction was made in 1956). Though he and Lorre had never met, by an odd coincidence, Hitchcock had also worked at UFA as an assistant director for awhile. Because German film-making in the twenties and early thirties proved to be such a monumental cornucopia of artistic and directorial talent, it must be cited as the most important phase of Hitchcock's development; for it was the unmatched inspiration of the UFA experience that established Hitchcock's sense of film grammar, style, and technique that would eventually garner for him the highest honors.

cause studios have become aware that old properties have unending commercial value —thanks entirely to a handful of professionals, dedicated film societies around the world, and the American Film Institute that created this awareness. But everlasting harm has been done and, as previously mentioned, thousands of films are gone forever. If a few films, hitherto thought lost, such as *The Old Dark House, The Mystery of the Wax Museum,* and Mamoulian's *Dr. Jekyll and Mr. Hyde* can be "found," as they were recently, it is not wholly improbable that the original *Man Who Knew Too Much* may show up intact someday.

Lorre's fortunes seemed to soar when, right after the Hitchcock film, Harry Cohn's representative from Columbia Pictures approached him with a Hollywood contract. Though he had received American offers

before, Lorre had rejected them for fear of "killer" typecasting. But knowing that a career in Europe seemed doubtful, and in view of Columbia's promise of a variety of roles, he shipped off to Hollywood in late 1934.

Although Harry Cohn gave him carte blanche to choose his own roles, Lorre soaked up the California sunshine for some time before a suitable role became available—and continued to improve his English; he was even loaned out to MGM as the star of *Mad Love* (a remake of *Hands of Orlac,* the German-made Conrad Veidt film of over a decade before), directed by Karl (*Dracula*) Freund. As a perfect macabre touch for his first American film, Lorre shaved his head to emphasize the sinister appearance of the brilliant but crazed international surgeon, Dr. Gogol.

In this acclaimed horror film Freund

Peter Lorre in 1935.

Lorre with his first wife, Celia Lovsky, in 1935.

wrested another outstanding performance from Lorre as the mad surgeon who lusts after the wife of the famous pianist, Orlac (Colin Clive), who survives a train wreck with mutilated hands. Motivated by a diabolical compulsion, Dr. Gogol grafts onto the unsuspecting patient the hands of an executed murderer—hands which seem to impart to the unfortunate pianist strange, uncontrollable impulses to kill. Gogol's further attempts to break Orlac fail in a most exciting climax: Gogol is about to attack Orlac's wife in a locked room; but Orlac, now in full possession of all his senses, arrives at the scene and, though unable to open the locked door, he unexpectedly but expertly throws a knife through a narrow slit, killing Gogol. Orlac's grafted hands had belonged to a man who was not only a murderer but a skillful knife-thrower as well!

Some of the eeriest scenes show Lorre playing the piano in his weird home and reading poetry to a wax image of Orlac's wife. In another, planning to drive Orlac insane, he impersonates a fictitious "former patient" of Gogol's, who had submitted to one of his horrible operations; for this, he wears a neckbrace, distorts his features, increases his height, and dons artificial steel hands—a characterization that would have been envied by Lon Chaney, Sr. The genius and incredible background of director Freund (he had been the photographer for such film classics as *Metropolis* and *The Last Laugh*), are apparent in the excellent Continental atmosphere and exquisite photography enriching *Mad Love*.

With his work in the Freund classic completed, Lorre returned to Columbia to appear in a version of Dostoevsky's novel, *Crime and Punishment* (Lorre also assisted writer S. K. Loren with the screenplay). Lorre underwent another physical ordeal before filming began when he had to reduce from 160 to 130 pounds for the complex role of Raskolnikov, the brilliant but impoverished student who, following the murder of an old haggish pawnbroker,

Mad Love. Lorre is a magnificent study of acting excellence as Dr. Gogol, an eccentric, affluent, and brilliant surgeon whose mind slowly disintegrates.

Mad Love. As Dr. Gogol, Lorre dons a special costume and pretends to be a monstrous body-transplant case in order to frighten Colin Clive out of his mind.

(LEFT) Lorre as the mad Dr. Gogol, in *Mad Love* (MGM, 1935), with Valerie Hobson.

Lorre in 1935.

enters into an intellectual struggle of wits with Porfiry (Edward Arnold), the prosecutor. Director Josef von Sternberg succeeded in limning his film with horror overtones in this brilliantly photographed version of the famous existential detective story, but the deletion of relevant psychiatric material from the script caused the finished film to suffer by comparison when a superior French version was released around the same time. Nevertheless, Lorre received good reviews for his second American film and anticipated working with von Sternberg again.

Unlike some of his fellow European actors, Lorre began enjoying life in Hollywood, and he started to collect story properties for future films. Among these was *The Good Soldier Schweik*, but nothing came of it. One of the properties, *Secret Agent*, interested Hitchcock, who also

One of a number of poster lobbycards, now quite rare, showing Lorre and Edward Arnold in *Crime and Punishment* (Columbia, 1935).

wanted Lorre for one of the top roles. Wishing to work with Hitchcock, because of fond memories of his former experience with the great director, and hoping to visit his family a bit, Lorre sailed with his wife to England in October 1935.

For the film, which starred John Gielgud and Madeleine Carroll, Lorre played a light and upbeat part for a change—a curly-haired and droll Mexican villain. Aside from a handsome profit made from selling the story, Lorre again enjoyed working with Hitchcock, but this spy melodrama, though a commercial success, was not one of Hitchcock's best.

Before leaving England, Lorre received a personal invitation from Adolf Hitler, who expressed admiration for Lorre's excellent delineation of screen murderers and who wanted the actor in his film industry. In neatly worded contempt, Lorre replied: "Thank you, but I think Germany has room for only one mass murderer of my ability and yours."

On his return to Hollywood in early 1936 he discussed with Universal the possibility of remaking *The Hunchback of Notre Dame;* but unfortunately this never materialized for Lorre, although it was produced in 1939, starring Charles Laughton. In the meantime, Lorre and his wife Celia took out their first papers for American citizenship. Another field opened during this time, as Lorre started to get involved in radio work; he was to alternate it with his film career through the years.

Meanwhile, Lorre's old friend Ferdinand Bruckner had completed a unique play based upon the life of Napoleon that deviated from the usual historical route by emphasizing the dictator's psychological traits. Lorre announced in a press conference in October that he would play the lead on Broadway. Arriving in New York to commence rehearsals, he was stunned to learn that producer Sidney Kingsley had cancelled the production without explanation.

Late in 1936 Lorre's morale was restored when 20th Century-Fox signed him up for an indefinite period. His initial role was in *Crackup,* a routine spy thriller; but his next part was an improvement, and he played a heavy in a rather stylized and taut kidnapping story, *Nancy Steele Is Missing,* starring Victor McLaglen. Illness forced Lorre to withdraw from a subsequent film, resulting in John Carradine's substituting for him. Next followed *The Lancer Spy,* in another routine role (as George Sanders' orderly) that was quite beneath Lorre.

Worried over his status and screen image, Lorre, impressed by the then-current success of Oriental detective series (such as *Mr. Wong,* with Boris Karloff and *Charlie Chan,* with Warner Oland), decided it might prove fortunate to do John P. Marquand's likable, shrewd Japanese detective, Mr. Moto, in a new film series. His Oriental makeup was surprisingly simple and consisted mainly of a special pair of prop eyeglasses. As shooting began on the first film, *Think Fast, Mr. Moto,* in October 1937, Lorre remarked, "Instead of committing murders, I'll be solving them."

Wearying of the B-budget *Moto* series, he completed one more film for Fox, *I Was an Adventuress,* before he left the company in 1939 to freelance. During production of his last Moto film, *Danger Island,* he created a waterproof rubber suit which he wore under his clothing for a swamp sequence. Its function, he explained, was to prevent colds which resulted in needless production delays.

His first assignment away from Fox was as the repulsive Cochon (Pig), who lechers after Joan Crawford in the MGM Clark Gable film, *Strange Cargo,* an offbeat allegorical semi-fantasy based on Richard Sale's splendid novel, *Not Too Narrow, Not Too Deep,* that dealt with escaped prisoners from Devil's Island. Each characterization bears a special symbolism

Lorre in *Mr. Moto on Danger Island* (20th Century-Fox, 1939).

Peter Lorre as Mr. Moto in Arab disguise in *Think Fast, Mr. Moto* (20th Century-Fox, 1937).

Iva Stewart, Lorre, and John King in *Mr. Moto Takes a Vacation* (20th Century-Fox, 1939).

A lobbycard scene of Lorre as Mr. Moto and Joseph Schildkraut in *Mysterious Mr. Moto* (20th Century-Fox, 1938).

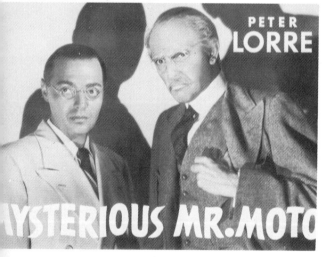

Lorre, around 1938.

involving premises too subtle and metaphysical for film producers in the late thirties, yet *Strange Cargo* still emerges as a well-developed and challenging production with excellent performances by everyone, even though it glosses over the poetry of feeling and impact that Sale created in his book. Today, Ingmar Bergman would be the natural director for a remake.

Nineteen thirty-nine was also the year when the film world's second horror cycle was beginning, offering an opportunity for the more bizarre side of Lorre's cinematic villainy to be put to use. In *Island of Doomed Men* he was a sadistic prison warden who loved classical music and relished whipping prisoners.

Stranger on the Third Floor (RKO), a great improvement over *Island of Doomed Men*, is an unusual, underrated, and overlooked little essay in psychological terror, with fascinating dream sequences. In this September 1940 release, Lorre successfully portrayed a homicidal maniac reminiscent of his earlier roles. Before leaving RKO, he appeared in an elaborate but banally plotted Kay Kyser horror-comedy filmusical, *You'll Find Out*, co-starring with the other two greats, Karloff and Lugosi, whose talents were also wasted. But many of these virtually plotless inanities were, as Lorre said, "Nice little thrown-together quickies that kept studios happy at the box office and paid off a lot of our bills."

He then returned to Columbia to do *The Face Behind the Mask* (originally based on a radio drama by Tom O'Connell) for director Robert Florey. In this gruesome shocker, Lorre is a Hungarian immigrant watchmaker who turns into a social outcast when his face is horribly disfigured in a rooming-house fire. Compensating for his bitterness, he becomes a master criminal, creates a special rubber mask to cover his scarred hideousness, and befriends a blind girl (Evelyn Keyes), who is ignorant of his criminal activities. During his accomplices' struggle for power, his beloved companion is accidentally killed. In a sym-

bolic climax, Lorre dies in the desert at the hands of his gang who, in turn, pay with their own lives by murdering each other later. Impossible to overlook is the powerful ending's similarity to von Stroheim's climax in the classic *Greed*.

To simulate a rubber mask for his role, Lorre wore two strips of adhesive tape to immobilize part of his face, patted on dead-white makeup and kept a restrained expression. Released in February 1941, *The Face Behind the Mask* was labeled a B-film by the critics, but it will nevertheless be remembered for some creative moments of horror and tension and a surprisingly

Three masters of the macabre: Lugosi, Karloff, and Lorre as three clever crooks spooking the hell out of guests Kay Kyser and his band in *You'll Find Out* (RKO, 1941).

As a new immigrant to America trying to make his way in strange surroundings, Lorre accosts Don Beddoe (playing a detective) and a patrolman in *The Face Behind the Mask* (Columbia, 1941).

204

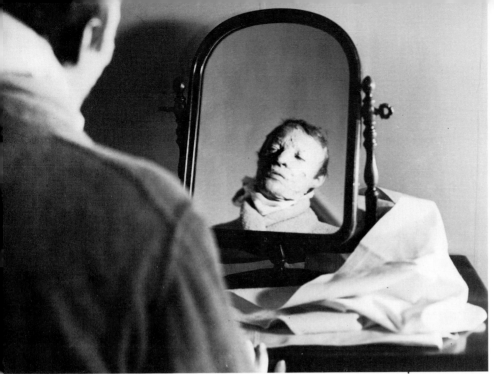

The Face Behind the Mask. Lorre studies his
scarred features in a mirror—the consequence of
a terrible roominghouse fire.

Lorre as Janos Szaby in *The Face Behind the
Mask.*

The Face Behind the Mask. Before turning into a master criminal, Lorre falls in love with a blind girl (Evelyn Keyes).

The Face Behind the Mask. Lorre gazes upon a bust used to create a mask to hide his scarred face. The mask looks a lot like Lorre.

Mary Astor, Humphrey Bogart, and Lorre in *The Maltese Falcon* (Warners, 1941).

high degree of character development. Despite the critics' categorization of it, it was a quality film in every sense, and Lorre's role in it was one of his best.

Another important change in Lorre's career took place when a young director, John Huston, gave him an interesting role in the Award-winning filmization of Dashiell Hammett's *The Maltese Falcon*, starring Humphrey Bogart, co-starring Mary Astor and Elisha Cook, and introducing a new menace upon the screen— Sidney Greenstreet as "the Fat Man." Not only did the film win a fine contract for Lorre with Warner's which would last for

The Maltese Falcon. Plotting to find a hidden fortune are (*left to right*): Humphrey Bogart, Lorre, Mary Astor, and Sidney Greenstreet.

Rare production shot of *The Maltese Falcon,* showing—*left to right*—young director John Huston,
Lorre, Mary Astor, and Humphrey Bogart.

many years of other fine roles, but it also
began an immediate and permanent friendship with Bogart.

Greenstreet's completely different and
remarkable personality, his bulk, and rum-
bling, booming laughter, compared with
Lorre's appearance and high nasal giggle,
proved such a resounding success from the
very start that they became a famous
Warner's team that endured through a
number of well-made box-office successes.

Warner's loaned out Lorre in 1942 for
Universal's *Invisible Agent.* In this routine
imitation of H. G. Wells' *The Invisible
Man,* he plays an insidious Japanese spy
who, failing to destroy Jon Hall, commits
hari-kari.

Columbia borrowed him and Karloff
(fresh from his stage success, *Arsenic and
Old Lace*) for the horror-comedy, *The
Boogie Man Will Get You* (1942). Lorre is
Dr. Lorentz, a sheriff-scientist who joins
another screwball scientist, Professor Nathaniel Billings (Karloff), in a ghoulish
experiment from which they anticipate
reaping ample personal profits. Cadavers
and comedy cops abound, all played with
a well-placed tongue-in-cheek from start
to finish.

Lorre went back to Warner's for a brief

part as an informer in *Casablanca,* now a standard film classic and famous for providing Bogart with one of his best roles. It was directed by Michael Curtiz, scripted by Howard Koch (formerly associated with Orson Welles' "Mercury Theater"), and co-starred Ingrid Bergman, Claude Rains, Paul Henreid, and Conrad Veidt, each of whom gave a stunning performance, ably assisted by a large and brilliantly directed supporting cast. An instantaneous smash hit, *Casablanca* became one of Warner's biggest winners; it contained some of the most memorable film characters and an unforgettable musical score.

Appearing in a few more Warner films of programmer quality, Lorre went on loan to MGM for a strong supporting role in *The Cross of Lorraine* in 1943. In this excellent though somewhat cruel depiction of French prisoners in a Nazi prison camp, Lorre effectively played the sadistic, cunning jailer, Sergeant Berger.

Reminiscing later, Lorre said that it was around this time that he started receiving quite a bit of unusual fan mail. People would write him, often detailing their personal masochistic and sadistic aberrations. A continual tide of correspondence from prison inmates and asylum patients filled his mailbox with troubled questions. One Lorre fan, who was a baroness, wrote:

"Dear Master: I would love to be tortured by you. . . ."

To which Lorre replied: "You have been tortured enough by going to see my pictures!"

Endowed with a rich sense of humor, Lorre was a compulsive clown and practical joker on movie sets, as all those familiar with him will testify. During the shooting of *The Mask of Dimitrios*—a very involved, top-quality, cloak-and-dagger thriller in which Lorre played a heroic "good guy"—he livened up between-takes coffee breaks and broke up the staff and visitors to the set by putting on a terrific

Lorre as the sinister Japanese agent Ikito, with Sir Cedric Hardwicke and J. Edward Bromberg, in *The Invisible Agent* (Universal, 1942).

Lorre as Berger, the sadistic Nazi commandant, in *The Cross of Lorraine* (MGM, 1943).

Playing a heroic author-investigator, Lorre was Cornelius Leyden, in *The Mask of Dimitrios* (Warners, 1944), with Faye Emerson.

act. He would begin by pacing up and down nervously, pretending to pull out his hair, shouting in reference to his usually absent producer-boss, Jack Warner, "Where is that creep? I sent him out for a bottle of beer a half-hour ago, and he isn't back yet!"

Maintaining an avid interest in collecting valuable story properties, Lorre had files which, by now, reached an estimated evaluation of more than $350,000.

In 1944 he varied his career with brief periods of stage work, starting off with a short vaudeville act called "The Man with a Head of Glass." The same year, Warner's started production on the stage hit, *Arsenic and Old Lace*, after the play

had ended a record three-and-a-half-year Broadway run. Lorre had the role of Dr. Einstein, a boozy plastic surgeon who operates on Raymond Massey's face to alter his appearance, but is interrupted by the police. Having to quit in the midst of the operation, he leaves Massey "looking like Boris Karloff" throughout the colorful black comedy.

Arsenic's central plot revolves around the activities of the aging Brewster sisters whose Good Samaritanship entails aiding lonely old men into the next world with poisoned elderberry wine. The setting around which most of the action centers is delightfully atmospheric: the Victorian Brewster manse and the Brooklyn grave-

210

yard of a Dutch Reformed Church, whose authentic location may still be on Church and Flatbush avenues. Others in this memorable and nostalgic production included Cary Grant, Priscilla Lane, Jack Carson, Josephine Hutchinson, and a grand supporting cast.

The following year Lorre married his second wife, Kaaren Verne, a German actress who subsequently gave up her career. Though enjoying a fine salary at Warner's, he was unhappy under such a restrictive contract and yearned for the freedom of choosing his own roles. Several films later, he went back to horror with a capital H under Robert Florey's direction in the outstanding chiller, *The Beast with Five Fingers*. However, Victor Francen almost stole the entire show with a master-

Lorre in *Three Strangers* (Warners, 1945).

Lorre in 1946.

Lorre and Sidney Greenstreet in *The Verdict* (Warners, 1946).

Lorre as the deranged Hilary Cummins, with Robert Alda and Andrea King, in *The Beast with Five Fingers* (Warners, 1946).

ful bravura performance. The excellent script by Curt (*Donovan's Brain*) Siodmak was based on William Fryer Harvey's modern classic short story of the same name. Horror, madness, brilliant pianists, and grand music had become worthy staples in the genre by this time. Not only did *Beast* prove that a new twist can be found in every old wrinkle, it went on to pull out all the stops:

A terrible stroke has crippled Victor Francen, a once-renowned pianist. Situated in a lonely Gothic chateau and surrounded by his memories and scheming houseguests, he is confined to his wheelchair; his main source of pleasure is still his piano, and though left with but one good arm he has learned to play brilliantly and with greater facility than most good pianists. Lodged permanently in the chateau under Francen's patronage is eccentric Peter Lorre, a dedicated but impoverished researcher and scholar. Apparently the only devoted person is Lorre who, to his horror, learns of Francen's violent death. Added to his terror is the fact that Francen's good strong hand has been severed.

In some of the eeriest scenes ever filmed, the hand is seen running wildly across the keys of the grand piano, playing doleful, macabre music; another time the hand crawls upon the floor, is ultimately caught and impaled by Lorre with

212

a huge spike upon a desk only to escape again, spreading terror.

Though *Beast* did handsomely at the box office and elicited excellent reviews lauding not only Francen's but Lorre's performance as one of his several best, Lorre left Warner's to freelance again.

His next assignment was as a routine heavy in UA's *The Chase*. Following this production, he began a brief run of stage readings of Poe's *The Tell-Tale Heart* in several major city bookings. Returning to Hollywood after his tour, he was cast for *My Favorite Brunette* (Paramount, 1947), starring Bob Hope. In this splendid satire of private-eye thrillers, Lorre and Lon Chaney, Jr. are droll heavies who cavort in the best Hope comedy-thriller tradition.

Next came *Casbah,* an elaborate musical remake of *Algiers* (originally starring Charles Boyer and Hedy Lamarr), starring Tony Martin, Marta Toren, and Yvonne De Carlo. Lorre plays a semi-heavy police in-

Publicity shot of Peter Lorre and Andrea King clowning around on the set of *The Beast with Five Fingers.*

spector who is sympathetic to Pepe Le Moko (Martin) but threatens to apprehend him should he ever leave the criminal sanctuary known as the Casbah. *Rope of Sand* (Paramount) followed, with Lorre cast in a similiar part.

Lorre went back to England the next year and received one of the finest accolades an actor could ever hope for when the BBC gave this testimonial, just moments before he was about to appear in a special TV dramatization of *The Tell-Tale Heart:*

"Mr. Lorre will be seen contorting his face in close-ups, and we feel that the experience of children watching this performance in a darkened room would be too alarming. We urge you to send· your children to bed early."

Then back to Hollywood as a blackmailing proprietor of a penny arcade in *Quicksand,* co-starring Mickey Rooney and Jeanne Cagney. Shot around a California resort town, *Quicksand* is an underrated small-budget actioner, successfully building up in suspense by gradual degrees and underscored by excellently photographed location scenes around a seaside amusement park and adjacent towns. Direction was by Irving Pichel, who starred in *Dracula's Daughter* and directed the Award-winning George Pal production, *Destination Moon* (1950).

In 1950 Lorre separated from his second wife; shortly after, in 1951, he made his first appearance on American TV. But, depressed by the usual Hollywood typecasting syndrome, he felt that an important change was badly needed. Returning to Germany for the first time in twenty years, he was so overwhelmed at witnessing the ravages of war and, ultimately, so inspired by a story by Egon Jacobson (based on an actual occurrence), that he planned to produce it as his own film. After completing the script, Lorre organized an independent film company and proceeded to direct himself in the lead role of a Nazi scientist who becomes deranged and turns into a cold

fiendish killer (the original *Dr. Strangelove?*). Titled *Der Verlorene* ("The Lost Ones"), its powerful anti-Nazi attack won high praise, awards, and made some money throughout Europe in 1951. Though Lorre controlled sixty percent of the film rights and felt it could gross handsomely in America, he remarked that his reason for refusing to release it here was because of the "cold war" climate that then prevailed.

Around this time he became seriously ill and, at one point, was on the hospital's critical list. As a consequence of his illness, his glands were affected, creating a metabolic change. His recuperation was followed by a weight increase, to the extent that he finally weighed nearly a hundred pounds more than he ever had. Aggravated by his illness was a dormant and heretofore mild blood-pressure problem that now necessitated permanent treatment.

After marrying Anna Marie Brenning, a pretty twenty-seven-year-old secretary who was doing film publicity for him, Lorre was called back to the States to work in the summer-theater production of *A Night at Madame Tussaud's,* which played five weeks at Norwich, Connecticut. Meanwhile, John Huston finalized plans for a new film, *Beat the Devil,* and wanted Lorre in the cast. Finally finished in Europe and released in 1954, the film was considered so sophisticated that it lost money the first time around, but was acclaimed by most cognoscenti as "ten years ahead of its time." Only after going into general re-release in 1964 did it begin making some money. In this very offbeat satirical adventure, Lorre plays O'Hara, a member of a band of international crooks. Co-starring in this film was his old friend, Humphrey Bogart, with whom he was reunited for the last time.

Commenting on *Beat the Devil,* Lorre said, "It was a flop in New York. Why shouldn't it be? It was a deliciously sardonic comedy, meant for art houses, and they opened it with a blood-and-thunder campaign. The people just didn't get it."

213

20,000 Leagues Under the Sea (Buena Vista, 1954). Lorre, somewhat miscast in this film, with his great co-stars James Mason (*left*) and Kirk Douglas (in background).

That year, when a girl was born to his wife, Lorre became a father for the first time; the child was named Catherine.

Lorre next finished work in Disney's *20,000 Leagues Under the Sea;* he appears miscast as a timid servant, but total production values, wonderful color, and special effects made the film into an overnight box-office winner and, to date, it ranks as one of the all-time top grossers.

Absent from the screen for a year, Lorre showed up in a cameo role as an Oriental ship servant in Mike Todd's *Around the World in 80 Days* in 1956. On TV he scored in a "Playhouse 90" production of "Seidman and Son," starring Eddie Cantor. His performance as a rebellious worker in the New York garment industry drew critical raves for him for the first time in years.

After being saddled by an ordinary clown role in *The Circus* with Victor Mature in 1959, he journeyed to Spain for a substantial supporting part in *Scent of Mystery*, a semidocumentary melodrama utilizing a highly touted and unpleasant gimmick called "Smell-O-Vision." During the filming, he collapsed from a sunstroke, and retired from the film for three days. Lorre's complaint that the press reports "exaggerated" the condition as a heart attack had a ring of integrity to it.

In an interview in 1960, he said: "Movies are no longer an *industry*. After all, who ever heard of an industry that offered no loyalty to its employees?" Pausing a moment to mix a drink and, in typical Lorre style, chain-smoking on a fresh cigarette, he went on: "You see, making movies used to be such great fun in the

214

Lorre as Colonel Arragas, in *Congo Crossing* (Universal, 1956).

old days. Of course, I suppose a lot of things in the old days were more fun." He sighed. "It isn't any longer. It's now a very cold-hearted business." He then began reminiscing about the old days—the times when he and Sidney Greenstreet were "menacing" each other, and when they, Bogart, Errol Flynn, Bette Davis, Claude Rains, and their ilk made Warner Brothers a really exciting place.

He said he found overseas work very profitable, but preferred making Hollywood his home. "I can't stand living in Europe. For that matter, New York isn't much better. But I like Hollywood; actually, it's the reverse of what most people think it is. It's not a crazy, nervous place. An actor is less bothered there than anywhere else. You can live your life as you please, and nobody cares."

Rounding out 1961, he played a quiet role as a marine biologist in *Voyage to the Bottom of the Sea*, based on the Jules Verne SFantasy novel. While some believed his career was now in a downward trend, 1962 marked an important turning point for Lorre. Badly neglected during most of the last sixteen years, his great talent for the macabre was now to be fully realized again. American International Pictures signed him up for one of the three Poe stories in *Tales of Terror*, filmed in glorious color, starring Basil Rathbone and Vincent Price. Even more remarkable, perhaps, was that AIP was the same studio that had started less than eight years before, filming quickie drag-racing, juvenile delinquency "adventure," and bad Z-films such as *I Was a Teenage Werewolf*, usually made in two to four days. Now, though, it had raised its

Voyage to the Bottom of the Sea (20th Century-Fox, 1961). *Left to right:* Frankie Avalon, Walter Pidgeon, Lorre, and Robert Sterling appeared in this Irwin Allen production. Later, under Allen's guidance, *Voyage* did well on TV as a regular series.

Lorre in "The Black Cat" segment of *Tales of Terror* (AIP, 1962).

Tales of Terror. "The Black Cat" segment also incorporated Poe's "A Cask of Amontillado," giving Lorre the opportunity to dispose of Vincent Price at tale's end.

standards considerably, having learned, after its box-office success with *The House of Usher,* that quality would outsell junk. Lorre appeared in "The Black Cat" segment of this three-part production, playing a crazed husband who walls up his wife alive when he discovers that she has a lover (Price). While not first-class horror, the While not first-class horror, the film restored Lorre to the top of the genre, to the great delight of many critics and all of his fans.

The role he seemed to be enjoying most, however, was that of fatherhood. Lorre stated that one of the finest tributes given to him was when he overheard his little Cathy, then age nine, remark to her friends, while watching one of her father's old thrillers on TV: "My father isn't a mean killer; he's a great actor!"

His next role that year was in another Verne adaptation, *Five Weeks in a Balloon,* for Fox. While on a publicity junket for this film, he guested on Groucho Marx's TV show, "You Bet Your Life." Groucho's ever-ready brand of barbed humor was immediately turned on. Referring to Lorre's now-famous rotund shape, Marx raised his eyebrows in inimitable Grouchian fashion and asked: "And are you playing the part of the balloon?"

Back in TV in October of that year, he did an episode in "Route 66" entitled "Lizard's Leg and Owlet's Wing." Reunited with Lon Chaney, Jr. and Boris Karloff, and supported by the marvelous Martita (*Great Expectations*) Hunt, Lorre and his friends re-created their old familiar monster roles. Despite its flaws, the production was a nostalgic feast that won a high share in network ratings.

American International Pictures recruited Lorre again for *The Raven,* scripted by Richard Matheson (*The Omega Man, The Legend of Hell House,* etc.), and directed by Roger Corman. Karloff and Price co-starred. Notwithstanding its title, this horror takeoff had, like most of AIP's Poe adaptations, little to do with Poe. It is set

Lorre on a publicity tour in New York for *The Raven* (AIP, 1963).

in some indefinite period between the eleventh and thirteenth centuries in England, and Lorre plays the inebriated Dr. Bedloe, who is transformed by Karloff into a raven. A friendly fellow sorcerer, Dr. Craven (Price), tries to undo the spell.

Expertly produced in magnificent color, *The Raven* abounds in magic, wizardry, and some excellent humor. With its release in January 1963, Lorre made a series of personal appearances with Karloff around the country to promote the film. Lorre commented that he loved this tour for making it possible to be before live audiences again.

Subsequently, AIP signed him up to an exclusive four-year contract that would include eight pictures. In August Lorre's lawyer protested in court against a former real-estate salesman who desired to go into show business and was about to change his name legally to "Peter Lorre." Angrily, Lorre protested publicly that this "fink" had no right to trade on his name after the many long and hard years it had taken him to build it up. The suit was settled to the "real" Lorre's satisfaction. At this time, too, Lorre had separated from his third wife and was living alone.

219

Another tour in a screen adaptation of Verne: *Five Weeks in a Balloon* (20th Century-Fox, 1962).

Vincent Price and Lorre having a little fun on the set of *The Raven*.

Karloff, Lorre, and Price stare menacingly for the photographer's benefit in this production shot on the set of *The Raven*.

Publicity shot for *The Comedy of Terrors* (AIP, 1964). Standing, Basil Rathbone; sitting (*left to right*), Boris Karloff, Lorre, and Vincent Price.

Lorre and Price in *Comedy of Terrors*.

Released in January 1964, AIP's *Comedy of Terrors* was Lorre's next film, co-starring Price, Karloff, and Rathbone. With such an impressive cast, AIP felt that it could repeat the earlier success of *The Raven.* Once again horror accouterments were contrived to create satire and to burlesque the genre. But while superficially entertaining, it proved a one-gag plot and disappointingly inferior to *Raven;* its slight story line revolved around undertaker Trumbull (Price) who "digs up" customers to bury them when rent time comes around. Lorre did his best with the role of the quavering, timid burial assistant, Felix Gillis. Elaborately mounted with some eerie scenes, it was the least effective of the AIP horror parodies since the studio's low-budgeter days.

Jerry Lewis then borrowed Lorre from AIP for his Paramount production of *The Patsy,* co-starring Keenan Wynn and John Carradine. Crowded into a supporting role, Lorre plays one of a group of leeching sycophants surrounding a show-business success, Jerry Lewis, whom they find dead one day. Fearful of losing their meal ticket, Lorre and friends discover a look-alike (also Lewis) to take his place.

On Tuesday, March 24, 1964, Peter Lorre's housekeeper entered his home to begin another day's chores—only to discover the great actor dead at the age of fifty-nine. Cause of death was revealed to have stemmed from the acute high blood pressure for which he had been undergoing treatment through the years. He was survived by his separated wife, his daughter Cathy, and two brothers.

Few ever realized that Lorre nurtured

The Raven. Lorre (*left*) and Price have an undertaking problem with Basil Rathbone (in coffin) playing a "customer" who refuses to stay dead no matter what they do to him.

a profound lifetime interest in psychoanalysis, spending much of his spare time helping out patients in mental asylums. Those who knew him well believed that had he not gone into show business, he could have made a name for himself in the field of psychiatry, for his knowledge of the subject was highly professional and many leading specialists with whom he had contact had high respect for his views.

Though he played so many distorted and misanthropic types, friends knew him as one of the fairest, friendliest, and most normal humans one could ever find. A highly cultivated and sensitive man, Lorre once said: "The development of friends is the most important thing in my life. You can buy the services of people, but you can't buy friends."

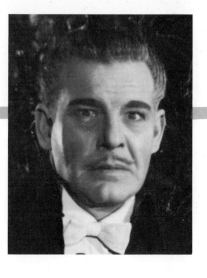

Lon Chaney, Jr.
1906-1973

In the history of Hollywood, certain personalities loomed so large that with the passage of time their film achievements assumed legendary proportions. Their accomplishments were unequalled; their shoes remained unfilled, and their reputations achieved Olympian stature. Occasionally, some of their offspring tried to create their own niche in films, only to find their efforts stifled by the inevitable comparison. A case in point is that of Lon Chaney, Jr. For as long as Chaney, Sr. lived, Lon, Jr. remained unknown. Even after his father's death, when he had begun a career of his own, he found himself living in the shadow of the great master

of horror. Another cross he had to bear was growing up with the realization that his idolized father was more dedicated to his profession than to his family. Thus whatever Lon, Jr. accomplished in his youth, he did on his own, without parental influence or assistance.

Finally, after many years of being ignored, of struggling through small supporting roles in undistinguished films, and of virtual anonymity, he was persuaded to change his baptismal name from Creighton Chaney (with which he began his career) to Lon Chaney, Jr.

Of all sons of famous fathers, Chaney probably came closest to not realizing his

225

full potential. The horror roles he did get could not measure up to the classical status of his father's Hunchback or Phantom. This was not entirely because of any lack of ability on Lon, Jr.'s part, although there are two schools of opinion holding equally strong views: one brooks no criticism of his rightful place in that pantheon reserved for the horror-film greats; the other, while admitting that Chaney, Jr. may have been competent as a colorful character actor, vociferously declares that his temperament, style, and personality made him completely unsuitable to the horror genre.

By the time he played the Frankenstein monster or the Mummy, the roles were no longer fresh. Only in his roles as Lennie in *Of Mice and Men* and as the Wolf Man was he able to bring a new character to the screen and create a monstrous yet sympathetic personality.

Creighton Tull Chaney was born prematurely on February 10, 1906, weighing all of two and a half pounds. Failing to respond normally at birth, he was swooped up by the doctor and dashed into the freezing water of Belle Isle Lake, situated on the outskirts of Oklahoma City. It was the only way the doctor knew of shocking life into the infant. Beside the doctor stood the worried young father, Lon Chaney, destined for fame and fortune; but this would still be years away—now he was struggling to find work and barely making ends meet.

In the months before Creighton's icy entrance into the world, his parents had been members of a small theatrical troupe traveling through the Southwest. His pregnant mother had worked hard up till the last minute, and it is not surprising that the rigors she underwent induced a risky premature birth. Now that fatherhood had come upon Chaney, Sr., he needed money, so he went to work for Doc and Bill's Furniture Store as a carpet layer; such work was not unusual—he had practiced

carpet laying earlier between other odd jobs, and when barnstorming work had been unavailable, he had also labored in the Colorado mines and been a decorator's assistant. Then Chaney heard of a job opening with a traveling troupe, and moved his family out of their small cottage to begin a long series of road tours.

Most of the time Baby Chaney lived backstage in a cotton-lined shoebox with holes punched in the lid. "This was probably one of the world's first incubators," recalled Chaney, Jr. with a laugh. Sometimes he would sleep in a small hammock woven by his dad and slung over a dressing table. Chaney remembered a special occasion during this barnstorming period when his parents were playing Chicago; their job unfortunately faded and they were down to their last quarter:

"As a last resort, Pop could always break into a dance in front of any of them oldtime bars and get enough nickels and pennies to buy some food," Chaney said. "But this particular Christmas Eve is still clear in my memory. Dad put most of his precious twenty-five cents into the gas meter. Then he started out with me. When we came to the first saloon he sat me on the bar close to the free lunch. Then he did his dance and picked up the small change. Meanwhile I filled my overcoat pockets with pretzels and sandwiches. Do you know what else he did when we got home? After I was asleep, he went out, broke a limb off a park tree, fixed it in a box in our room, and spent the whole night making tree decorations out of a roll of red crepe paper he had bought with a few pennies. He told me afterward he made paste out of cold baked potato and water."

When he couldn't find employment singing and hoofing in small shows, Chaney, Sr. worked as a stagehand. It was at this time that he separated from his wife, Cleva Creighton, though he tried to continue supporting his boy as best as he could. As the younger Chaney said, "I

Chaney, Jr. (*third from left*), age sixteen, watches as his famous father shakes the hand of a friend before embarking on a tour.

was put out to live." He lived in boardinghouses and schools while his father clowned and danced in theaters throughout the country. Then, because motion pictures in Los Angeles promised steady work without travel, Chaney, Sr. started on his film career.

By 1915 Chaney, Jr. found himself with a stepmother, Hazel Hastings, and a real home for the first time in his life. Despite his first taste of steady schooling, he was restless. "Regular schooling wasn't for me. I liked getting around," he recalled. "I never remember not working. I was going to school and then during the vacations I'd hitch-hike my way to the fruit ranches up near Bakersfield and pick apricots. You can't get rich picking apricots. I remember I got three cents a basket—a deep basket— and the rawest sunburn on my neck you ever saw." He remarked how invaluable this experience proved for his portrayal of Lennie, the migratory fruit-picker in *Of Mice and Men*.

Young Lon would often accompany his father to the studio. At the corner of Hollywood and Vine, both would sit on a wooden bench waiting for the trolley car to Universal City. (The bench is no longer there—a special edifice, dedicated to the memory of Chaney, Sr., replaced it two decades later.) Years later when his father was a top star, young Lon recalled how his dad would pass by that very same bench and pick up carloads of extras waiting for a lift.

When Lon, Jr. was ten, his father decided to remove him completely from theatrical surroundings, and sent the boy to live with his deaf-mute grandparents in Los Angeles. This experience instilled deeply within the youngster an understanding and feeling for the handicapped, which he always retained. As in his father's case, it may have accounted for his ability to bring a human quality to even the most freakish and wild screen portrayals.

Young Lon attended Hollywood High

(two of his schoolmates were Fay Wray and Joel McCrea, who starred together years later in *The Most Dangerous Game;* Wray also attained fame in *King Kong*). Lon's biggest ambition then was to play on the school football team. When he was turned down—he was six feet tall but weighed only 125 pounds—he looked for some other afterschool activity. Many of the other students were working as extras at the nearby movie lots on odd days, especially on Saturdays. In fact, the whole school was movie-conscious. One day young Lon seemed to realize that all his life he had wanted to act without really being aware of it.

He mentioned his ambition to his father and asked for his aid. The elder Chaney not only refused to help him but transferred him from Hollywood High to a business college. The young man was dejected, but not embittered. He harbored a deep, healthy respect for his father. Besides, as he once explained, his father always admired businessmen, possibly because he wasn't one himself. Chaney, Jr. said:

"His ideal of someone to look up to was the head teller of a bank. He wanted me to become someone like that.

"Dad never seemed like a star or actor to me. He had a curious suspicion of his newfound success. He always doubted it, always feared it would end. He kept up his membership in the stagehands' union to his dying day, just in case. He was so unassuming that when he died I suddenly realized I didn't have a single picture of him, didn't own a single clipping of him or his work. He wouldn't have any publicity stuff around the house. Somehow, he always feared it."

Perhaps Lon, Sr. was jealous or, since he became Number One in his field, he could not tolerate the thought of anyone, even his own flesh and blood, stealing any of his thunder. Even if he had reason to secretly loathe Hollywood's rat race and overall ambience, it was hardly logical that, having spearheaded a gold mine of his own, he would permit personal prejudice from letting his son have a stake in such an inheritance.

Meanwhile, young Chaney pursued afterschool and vacation jobs in butchershops and abattoirs. Occasionally he traveled on promotional tours of his father's big pictures.

Shortly after Lon finished his schooling, romance entered his life, and he married Dorothy, who gave him two sons, Lon III and Ronald. At the time of his marriage he was working for the General Water Heater Corporation; undoubtedly his father's attitude toward a screen career for his son had created in Lon a strong psychological block, for the idea of looking for any kind of film work—which was readily available—never occurred to him during this period.

Then, suddenly, in that black year of 1930, Lon Chaney, Sr. died.

"I can remember the huge funeral service," said Lon, Jr., "the crowds fighting and scrambling to get in, the organ playing the theme from *Laugh, Clown, Laugh* [one of his father's hits]. All the major studios shut down for five minutes in homage to his memory."

For nearly two more years young Lon continued plugging away at various unattractive jobs to support his family, apparently receiving very little, if anything, from the large fortune his father had earned. Eventually he became secretary of the water-heater corporation where he'd started as a boilermaker.

One evening he went with friends of his father to a party at which an assistant director was present. Lon said, "So I sang a song I'd written myself. The assistant director said, 'Look, why don't you take it around to our music department?' and made an appointment for me. When I went to the studio, I had to pass through the casting office. The casting director looked at me and said, 'You're Lon Chaney's son. You ought to be in pictures!'

That hit me right. I was fed up with regularity and thought he had a good idea.

"'How about it?' I asked. He told me he'd have a job for me in a couple of days."

Lon then quit his "regular" job and waited for the studio to call. They never did. Smiling, he said, "I haven't heard from that casting office yet!" It was a heartbreaking experience; but seven months later, another opportunity presented itself.

"My pal, the assistant director who took me to the studio in the first place, felt sort of responsible," Lon recalled. "He took me over to RKO and introduced me to the casting director there. He also said I ought to be in pictures. Only he did something about it and sold David O. Selznik [then head of the studio] on the idea. I got a contract and two hundred dollars a week."

So young Chaney had to persevere for two years after his father's death before he began, hesitantly, to follow in his footsteps. As his first role, he was given a bit part in the 1932 version of *Bird of Paradise*. Later he was offered the leading role in a serial, *The Last Frontier*. As the hero, a masked, black-clad figure patterned after Zorro, Chaney was expected to do his own stuntwork, riding, fighting, and falling.

"I'd never really ridden a horse—not to barge out and jump on one and ride like the devil. And the first thing they had me do was to get twenty feet up in a tree and leap on the villain as he galloped by beneath me."

Remarkably, Chaney managed to perform his assignment without incident. In addition to his dual identity as hero and mystery man, he also did a brief stint as an Indian. "We did a hundred scenes a day," said Chaney. But at least it was a start, rough though the riding was.

RKO made him work hard, and he hoped even harder. Perhaps some important movie mogul would "discover" him and realize he had greater potentialities, that he was not cut out to go on playing

Lon, Jr. and his horse, Wild Irish Rose, in a publicity shot for his first film, *Bird of Paradise* (RKO, 1932), in which he played a small role.

Lucky Devils (RKO, 1933). *Left to right:* Lon, Bill "Hopalong Cassidy" Boyd, William Gargan, and Bob Rose are ex-World War I pilots who turn their talents to profit as Hollywood stuntmen. Here they sit solemnly, in memory of their departed friends.

B- and C-westerns. But when the cowboy parts kept coming, he decided on a confrontation with the studio heads. To appease him, they gave him a role in *Virgie Winters,* a contemporary story. But all he got out of the part was a little personal satisfaction, for *Virgie* was only a pause between horse operas, and the cowboy pattern continued unbroken.

When he had signed with RKO the studio executives had wanted him to change his name to Lon Chaney, Jr., but he had refused. "As I see it now," he said later, "I was foolish. I'd have gotten ahead much faster if I had. But I didn't feel I was entitled to take my father's name. I didn't feel I was an actor yet."

Actually, Chaney, Sr. had named his son after his wife; Creighton was her maiden name. Lon—or Creighton as he was still known—preferred it, if for no other reason than out of love and respect for his mother.

More than a year and a half of rough riding on the RKO studio range convinced a saddle-sore Chaney to abandon the celluloid corral. He swore that he had to break out of the western mold; but, already, this early in his career, he had become a victim of the Hollywood Curse: typecasting. Worst of all, producers had only seen him in cowboy roles, if at all. He wasn't a star; why should they accord him any special privilege? Lon found the big studio executives were polite but reluctant.

Persistently, Chaney continued making the rounds, rebuffed at every turn. He was the first to admit that by leaving RKO, he had burned his bridges behind him. Before long, his cash reserves reached rock bottom, and he was now willing to take almost any part. Nearly at the point of applying for Home Relief, an offer finally did come—from a producer of westerns!

Chaney swallowed his pride and took the part. From this point on his career resembled a roller-coaster ride filled with ups and downs. He would make a picture or two, perhaps get a short-term contract with some producer of cheap quickies; then once more he would be "between pictures" —that is, unemployed.

During those days, the parts—in B- and C-westerns—were monotonous and cut from one cloth; they called more for brawn and athletic skill than for acting artistry.

"I was in a new picture practically every two weeks, always as a heavy. I'll swear I spoke the line 'So you won't talk, eh?' at least fifty times, and I'd rather not think about how often I had to say, 'Don't shoot him now—I have a better plan!'"

But even if he could bring the house down with the performance of his life, Hollywood wouldn't have known about it. Westerns were not fit for Sunset Boulevard. "Now I knew what Dad meant when he said, 'I've taken the bumps,'" reflected Chaney. "Well . . . I'd taken them. I did every possible tough bit in pictures. I had to do stuntwork to live. I've bulldogged steers, fallen off and gotten knocked off cliffs, ridden horses into rivers, driven prairie schooners up and down hills—everything."

Chaney didn't delude himself into believing that he was destined for "great drama" or that he was a potential Barrymore; but he refused to believe that all he could do were oatmeal westerns. Educationally and culturally held back by his eccentric father, he had never had any dramatic training. This he remedied, however, by enrolling in an evening dramatic school under an assumed name. For a time, an observer would have witnessed the odd sight of this experienced film actor wiping off the greasepaint, leaving the set every day, and hurrying to the classroom to study—acting!

This incongruous situation soon became obvious to the teacher. After several sessions, he took Chaney aside and confided, "You know as much about all this as I do," and with that, he authorized him to teach half the class.

Chaney later was recommended to a famous dramatic coach, but, after one conference, he was told, "I have nothing to teach you." Yet, despite this, he failed to get his long-awaited break. "I never got anywhere. I just marked time for years. Only one thing buoyed me up: the gambler's hope that *next time* I'd draw three aces."

Problems developed. His first marriage ended in divorce, and under California's vicious community property laws, he was compelled to turn over to his wife a tiny inheritance from his father. It was then that he learned what real hunger was. Once he starved for four days. "People who might have helped me didn't," he said. Then he beamed, "I found three real friends in this town: Wally [Wallace] Ford, Lewis Milestone, and—that little lady over there." He motioned to the pretty woman who had become his second wife, Patsy. They were married in Colton, California, in October 1937.

At this time Chaney took the step he had so long avoided and changed his name to Lon Chaney, Jr. "Why? Because they starved me into it. After that, I had a chance, at least."

Burgess Meredith and Lon in the internationally acclaimed *Of Mice and Men* (UA, 1939).

He surmised that the magic name of Lon Chaney would at least get him past the studio guards. This time he thought he struck oil. At the close of 1937, Fox signed him to a contract—as Lon Chaney, Jr.

Glowing with optimism, he felt that an immediate turning point had arrived in his career. It hadn't. Though lured by promises of a variety of good character roles, he was given tiny "bits." He became only part of the scenery, briefly on screen, if his little scenes didn't end up on the cutting-room floor. Aesthetically and morally, this was harder to accept than going hungry.

In 1938, on location in the Ozarks, he played a bearded outlaw in *Jesse James*. While shooting a scene on horseback he took a bad spill, and the horse behind galloped over him. Luckily, he escaped death or permanent crippling; in fact, his injuries were minor, and he was able to finish his scenes.

On January 15, 1939, his contract with Fox ran out and was not renewed. Two months later, with all his money gone, what had the future to offer?

Reports reached him that RKO was planning a remake of his father's classic film, *The Hunchback of Notre Dame*. No actor had yet been signed for the lead, and Chaney thought he saw his golden opportunity. To his great dismay, after an extensive screen test, the studio turned him down, and gave the part to Charles Laughton. Interviewed by the press, Chaney said he wasn't sorry; but this was said much later, after he had gotten a *certain part*. For it was this role which finally brought him the fame and happiness that he had long been denied; and, in an utterly different kind of characterization, he became established at last as a serious actor. The role: Lennie in *Of Mice and Men*.

What actually led up to his landing of this prize-winning role started when Lon and his wife Patsy, out of cash, had gone hungry for twenty-four hours. Unexpectedly, his agent appeared with the good news that he had gotten Lon a chance to

231

Lon, as Lennie, depends on Burgess Meredith for guidance and security in *Of Mice and Men*.

test for a part in a West Coast company's stage production of *Of Mice and Men*, based on John Steinbeck's famous novel, which had already been a success on Broadway. Five members of the original New York cast were to appear in the Los Angeles production. But Broderick Crawford, the original Lennie, had resigned from the cast to accept another role, so a replacement was being sought.

"I can never be grateful enough to Brod Crawford," said Chaney. He then went to the El Capitan Theater where the producer and veteran film star Wallace Ford was holding tests. Lon had never read the book or, of course, seen the play, so he had only the faintest idea of the role. "I was pretty bad the first time I read the lines. The only way I got the part was through the kindness of Wally Ford. He was willing to give me a chance. You can't explain it any other way," said Chaney, visibly moved.

Unaccustomed to the rigors of the theater, Chaney had to follow a new regimen: he arose at six every morning to learn his lines; then at two in the afternoon he went to the theater for regular rehearsals. This continued for three weeks, and by the end of that time he had his role down pat.

Opening night. He admitted he was scared stiff; this was, after all, his debut on the legitimate stage. Quite different from acting in films. An item in the local press didn't help to bolster his spirits either; it read: "His father was a great actor. Now we'll see what *he* can do." The inevitable comparison, which he had so long avoided by not using his father's name, was finally about to happen. But Lon's inner fears didn't permeate his calm exterior. He said, "Self-consciousness is one thing hard knocks teach you to squelch." Then he went on and gave a fully professional performance, and the play became a hit.

It seemed only just that the movie moguls *must now* acknowledge his acting prowess, he thought. There was also word traveling around of a film adaptation of the play. Chaney wondered if director Lewis Milestone would consider him for the role; he paced up and down his room filled with doubts, but hoping.

Milestone had only seen the original Broadway production, but *not* the Los Angeles version starring Chaney. "I had made up my mind who should play all the featured roles," Milestone said, "Lennie included. Everyone in town knew that. Then one day into my office came this great big

232

Of Mice and Men. Production shot with Lon,
Betty Field, and Burgess Meredith.

Of Mice and Men. Betty Field plays the unfaithful, hare-brained wife of the ranch's boss, who is
spurned by the ranch hands out of fear of her
husband. She turns to the retarded Lennie (Lon)
for affection, unaware of what the consequences
will be.

Of Mice and Men. Betty Field and Lon.

fellow with the open face, asking me, 'Can't I have a test?' But things aren't done that way in Hollywood. Agents usually come around asking for tests for their clients, never actors. I was so amazed, I said yes.

"The next day I was testing a girl for the part of Mae. I had to have someone to read Lennie's lines with her. So I asked Lon if he would. I told him he would get a separate test later. He agreed. In fact, he read Lennie's lines for *all* my tests of the other roles. When it came time to test him, I didn't have to. I couldn't see anybody else in the part."

In this manner Lon Chaney's son finally came into his own, and film history was made. Later, to an interviewer, he expressed his relief at not having gotten the part of Quasimodo in *Hunchback:* "I'm not sorry now. It's asking a lot to expect me to come up to my father's performance. I saw a revival of the film just a few weeks ago, and it made me realize more than ever how good he was and what a tough time anybody will have in the part Anything I might had done would have been a carbon copy."

Chaney, Jr., in fact, was never to play Quasimodo, except briefly; this was when he and his old friends Boris Karloff and Peter Lorre united in 1962 to appear in a horror spoof for "Route 66" on TV. In all of Chaney's subsequent horror roles, it is notable that he never tried to duplicate any of his father's performances.

He now had an opportunity to carve his own cinematic niche in the role of Len-

234

nie and prove himself to the world. Shooting started in the fall of 1939 for United Artists. His hair was dyed a brick-red, and he wore special shoes to add six inches to his height. In reality he was just six feet tall. "From that film on," he said, "people thought I was much taller." The special shoes made a number of action and running scenes sheer torture; but he bore up under his pains by remembering that his father had suffered more in some of his own grotesque roles.

At the conclusion of his big scene, something very unusual happened: the electricians and the rest of the crew broke into rapturous applause—a rare event for such hardened veterans who had worked with hundreds of actors. One still-photographer, who once photographed the elder Chaney

Lon is being outfitted by the studio prop man to portray Quasimodo in a small vignette for a 1962 segment of television's "Route 66."

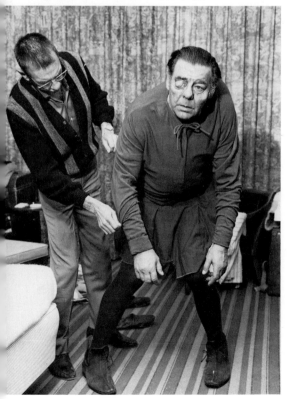

"back in the palmy days," commented on the resemblance:

"Like father, like son, whether he likes it or not!"

The public and critics echoed this acclaim, not only for Chaney, naturally, but for the entire film: Milestone's direction, Aaron Copland's brilliant score, the acting of Burgess Meredith and Betty Field. Now began the fan magazine and press interviews and gushy notices. Lon had finally emerged from total obscurity to fame—but not overnight.

Even before *Of Mice and Men* was released, producer Hal Roach had signed him for his next picture—his first *monster* film: *One Million B.C.* "Lennie was a wonderful help to my career," Lon said, "because he gave me a chance to show I wasn't just another of those boys who ride along on a father's name. A fellow's not smart to be a second-string halfback at the same college where his father made All-American. Even if he makes the varsity, too, much is expected of him. He ought to go to a different school. That's what I did."

On a trip East, he had flown over Oklahoma City, his birthplace:

"I looked down and saw it for the first time since that dousing I got the day I was born. I thought of all the things that had happened since. Sure, I crossed up my Dad's wishes. But somehow, I think he'd be happy now. Maybe I can get the name of Chaney back up in the theater lights across America again."

Overjoyed by Lon's work as Lennie, Hal Roach stated that a deal was pending to star him in *Cup of Gold*, a story of pirate adventure, based on the John Steinbeck novel. Steinbeck personally felt that the novel would be the perfect vehicle for Lon, but the project was held up indefinitely and never materialized.

For a long time Roach had been planning to produce *One Million B.C.* with film pioneer D. W. Griffith; the story was based upon the lives and adventures of prehistoric peoples. Chaney was cast as one

One Million B.C. (20th Century-Fox, 1940). Very rare shot of Lon as Akhoba, chief of the Rock people, being gored in a battle with a prehistoric bull.

Rescuing one of his tribe from a disaster in *One Million B.C.*

of the principal characters: Akhoba, tribal leader of the Rock People and father of Victor Mature. Originally, Lon's role was intended to be longer, but plot restrictions and editing minimized it. Different kinds of makeup were also experimented with; one very painstaking and elaborate job, making Lon appear quite subhuman, was scrapped when it was decided that it would create horror overtones which the producers thought undesirable—the final decision was that he and the rest of his tribe could look "wild" but, at least, more human.

Due to bitter arguments arising from conflicting opinions concerning cast and script, director Griffith withdrew from the production, demanding his name be deleted from the credits. Griffith felt that his original plans were being too distorted by Roach's more commercial approach. He (Griffith) had been profoundly impressed by Willis O'Brien's monumental animation for *The Lost World* and *King Kong* in 1925, and he was seriously considering using O'Brien's services in *B.C.* Griffith was therefore thunderstruck at Roach's pedestrian ideas, and finally blew up when Roach said "No animation—we'll blow up little tiny lizards to make them look like huge dinosaurs!" Which was exactly what they did look like in *B.C.*

Despite his resignation, the entire film bears Griffith's unmistakable hand and inspiration; in fact, much, if not all of the story, could have been drawn from his own films or unused backlog of material. Apart from this, it was important in association with Chaney's career, because for the first time he began utilizing *special* makeup in the tradition that had made his father famous.

Even in this bright moment, frustration arose again: he had originally created his own makeup for the part of Akhoba (the subhuman type mentioned above), only to be told that union regulations not only absolutely forbade actors from applying their own makeup but that the makeup itself could only be created under the supervision of a member of the Cosmeticians' Union. Times had certainly changed since his father's day. Unions had now taken over complete control of film-making activity, although the day when Hollywood would have to pay four men to do the work of one and, literally, be forced into overseas productions to survive, had not yet arrived. Costs were a little higher in the late thirties but within reason. And union makeup geniuses like Bill Madsen and Jack Pierce were vital to the industry.

Madsen's makeup expertise, in fact, enchanced *B.C.* and was used also for Chaney's outstanding "cripple" scenes—as Akhoba, he sustains a terrible accident after a prehistoric musk ox gores and tramples him, leaving him pathetically disfigured. Special makeup for these scenes alone required four and a half hours' preparation.

For location scenes Roach sent his scouts searching for wild, primitive locales, and they found them in Fire Valley, a red gash in the Nevada hills. The topography of this area consists of sandstone formations which time and weather have eroded into strange grotesque chasms, peaks, and pillars. To "face-lift" the valley back in time for shooting, studio workmen preceded the actors by a couple of weeks to install smoke pots in the ground that simulated volcanic spas and to add prehistoric-looking vegetation; many of the live animal sequences that didn't require special effects were taken there. After ten days the rest of the film was shot in the Roach Studios, where one of the most unusual sets ever seen by Hollywood was constructed. Part of the complex work involved the outstanding earthquake and volcanic scenes, for which Roach's special-effects department was especially commended.

Chaney's scenes were completed in December 1939, while special animal sequences stayed in production until the following spring. Chaney received third billing in the cast with Victor Mature, Carole Landis, and John Hubbard; direction was by Hal Roach and Hal Roach, Jr. Released in 1940, *One Million B.C.* was given mixed reviews. Though praised for its spectacle and exceptional special effects, it was criticized for glaring anachronisms that, for dramatic effect, had both man and dinosaur on earth at the *same time.* While paleontologists agreed that saurians and homo sapiens existed several million years apart, *B.C.*'s special effects are so splendid that fans have forgiven and forgotten such discrepancies; and even the small chameleons, gilas, and other contemporary lizards were transfigured (via photography and special effects) into such awesome, spellbinding monstrosities that for the next twenty-five years they kept on reappearing in stock footage in dozens of other films.

During *B.C.*'s release, Lon appeared on the "Inner Sanctum" radio show cast as a Lennie type, then traveled to New York to do another Lennie scene for CBS Radio. On his return to Hollywood he found that only Lennie-type roles were available. How many more times could he tolerate saying, "Tell me more all about the rabbits, George! I love rabbits!" Not wanting to risk getting typed in this category, he persevered in his efforts to get other roles; but learning that patience was futile, he capitulated and accepted a small supporting role in De Mille's *Northwest Mounted Police*—the part was as a Matis, a group of half-breeds who revolted against the Canadian government in 1885. It called for Lon to bumble along as a lovable giant-sized chap, obviously a takeoff on Lennie, but injected in the film for buffoon comedy relief.

Signed up by MGM for an elaborate Technicolor production of *Billy the Kid,* Lon appeared in another depressing minor role under the shadow of the star, Robert Taylor. Playing a heavy, his brief scenes for this whitewashed bio-pic of the famous psycho-outlaw (born in Brooklyn, not in the West as many believe) were shot on the studio lot, and the New Mexico scenes were, of course, shot elsewhere—in Arizona's Monument Valley.

Lon was minus a contract once more, and his future looked bleak, unless a surfeit of Lennie-type parts and droll heavy roles were by any stretch of the imagination "jobs with a future." To him they looked like poison.

Then—a ray of sunshine. Universal Studios was now starting to ride the crest of the second big horror cycle started the previous year (1939) by the monumental success of *The Son of Frankenstein.* Recalling Lon's successful portrayals as Lennie and Akhoba, and hoping that the Chaney name would again mean box-office magic, Universal offered Lon a contract, which he accepted, trusting it would set him on the shiny, Oz-like yellow-brick road to better deals.

Thus, at the studio where his father had achieved his greatest success, Lon made his horror-acting debut in an old property, *The Electric Man* (originally meant for Karloff and Lugosi), that Universal dusted off and retitled *Man-Made Monster.* It was another version of the mad-doctor theme, with more emphasis on electrobiology than on surgery or chemistry. Lon was put in the hands of the redoubtable Jack Pierce —who personally supervised all of Universal's makeup work and who, as previously mentioned, had been the creator of Karloff's immortal Frankenstein Monster makeup—and played a good-natured carnival-sideshow "electric man" with a capability for tolerating unusually high doses of voltage. His phenomenal immunity tempts Dr. Regas (superbly played with just the right dash of madness by Lionel Atwill) into feeding Chaney increasingly larger charges of electricity in order to fulfill his insane dream of "creating a race of living zombies." This results in chaos for all concerned, including Chaney and Atwill.

Despite Chaney's and Atwill's efforts, *Man-Made Monster* was somewhat disappointing. It did not exceed average B-budget programmer standards, for it lacked much of the verve and gusto that distinguished Universal's earlier hits. What was

Lon as a half-breed Canadian in Cecil B. D Mille's *Northwest Mounted Police* (Paramoun 1940).

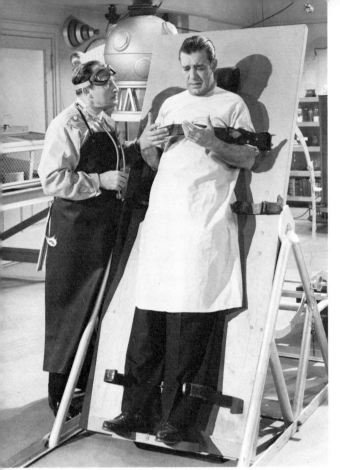

Lon is strapped to a lab table for Dr. Lionel Atwill's terrible experiment in *Man-Made Monster* (Universal, 1941).

important, however, was that it was the first film since *Of Mice and Men* to use Chaney's talent to best advantage.

During the time that the studio had been having *Man-Made Monster* rewritten and Chaney was waiting to start his scenes, he had been cast as a heavy in that almost forgotten 1941 super-serial, *Riders of Death Valley*, starring Buck Jones, Dick Foran, and Charles Bickford. Location scenes for the fifteen chapters were made in the Mojave Valley. Later, Lon went into three minor 1941 efforts. In the worst of them, *Badlands of Dakota*, he played a heavy, together with another well-known supporting player, Glenn Strange; he next proceeded to *Too Many Blondes* as a truck driver with cultural aspirations; and in *San Antonio Rose* he appeared as a musclebound gangster.

Ever so rarely a role appears guaranteeing immortality. If lightning could strike once with a role like Lennie in *Of Mice and Men*, could it happen again?

Man-Made Monster. Atwill's fiendish experiment is successful—Lon is now a monstrous, walking electric dynamo.

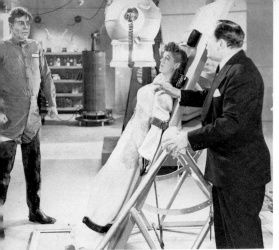

This mad-lab in *Man-Made Monster* scene is so reminiscent of that in *The Bride of Frankenstein* that it's almost an homage.

Jack Pierce applies finishing touches to Lon's makeup for *The Wolf Man* (Universal, 1941).

It did! Chaney was cast in the lead in *The Wolf Man,* one of Universal's most original creations since *Frankenstein.* As the studio's most important film that year, it served as a forerunner to the pyramiding growth of the second horror cycle. Though Universal had already made a film covering the subject of lycanthropy—*Werewolf of London* in 1935 (starring Warner Oland and Henry Hull, playing men who are both afflicted in the same way)—*Wolf Man* bore no resemblance to *Werewolf;* it was better scripted and directed, and adhered more factually to certain established theories. The cast *par excellence* featured Claude Rains, Bela Lugosi, Warren William, Ralph Bellamy, Maria Ouspenskaya, and Evelyn Ankers. An atmospheric musical score, splendid sets such as the unforgettable mist-clad moor sequences, and Chaney's fascinating makeup and ability to project terror, all combined to establish *The Wolf Man* as one of a handful of horror films deserving the label "classic."

The creation and planning of the *Wolf Man* makeup is alone a fascinating story. It is not generally known that Jack Pierce worked out a makeup style for Henry Hull in *Werewolf of London* that was never used because of the time that would have been involved in its application; consequently, a tamer, less effective one was used. For *Wolf Man,* Pierce, working from

The Wolf Man. Left to right: Patric Knowles, Evelyn Ankers, and Lon.

a life-mask of Chaney's face, fashioned a long wolf-like rubber nose and a thick wig. The hair was meticulously applied piece by piece, taking roughly five hours to do; though it took only forty-five minutes to remove, it was sometimes painful if the hair stuck on too well. Pierce also created the wolf-like hands and feet, and costumed Chaney in a black shirt and trousers so that the ordeal of body make-up would be avoided.

241

The Wolf Man. Lon as Larry Talbot, the were-wolf, suffers a temporary setback in a bear trap.

Evelyn Ankers and Maria Ouspenskaya attend to Lon's unconscious form after he has been bitten by a werewolf in *The Wolf Man.*

Lon in *The Wolf Man*.

Another publicity shot of Lon as the Wolf Man.

Between takes, Evelyn Ankers and Lon spoof things up in these exclusive publicity shots from *The Wolf Man.*

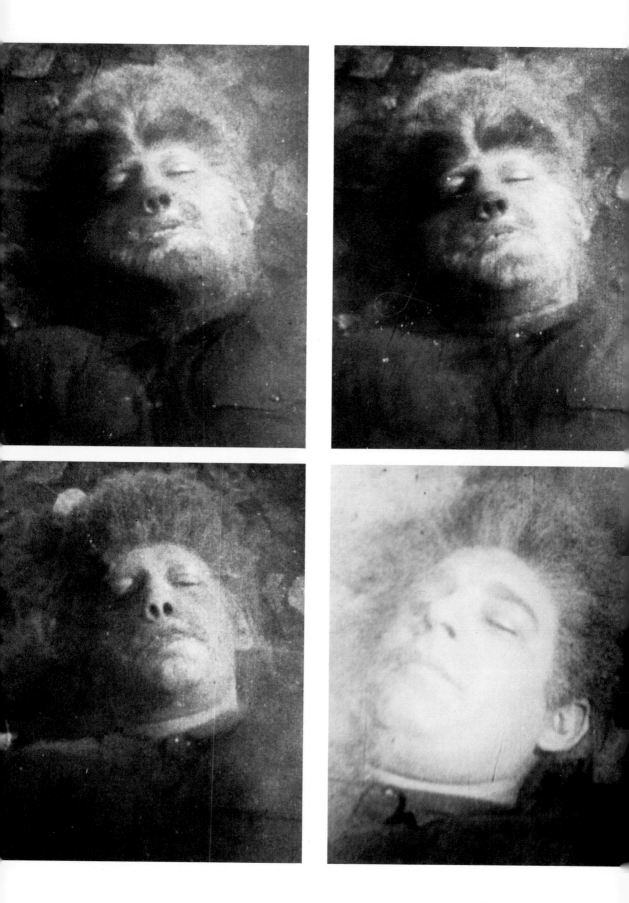

One of the other most interesting behind-the-scenes stories is that before Chaney was selected for the role, Lugosi was the one Universal had in mind for the part; instead, he was reduced to playing a relatively minor role: the son of Maria Ouspenskaya named, ironically, "Bela."

The film's church scenes were made on the original set of *Hunchback of Notre Dame* in which Chaney, Sr. had starred. A strange and unfortunate occurrence later developed: an original scene in *The Wolf Man*, showing Chaney wrestling with a six-hundred-pound bear, somehow mysteriously vanished when the film became available for TV and has never again been seen.

Wolf Man's quality notwithstanding, the horror film field had become equated with second-feature, mass-produced grindhouse fare; consequently, this A-budget production was never accorded the high recognition it deserved.

Upon *Wolf Man*'s completion Lon was rushed into a routine serial, fifteen chapters of *Overland Mail* shown in as many weeks for kiddie matinees but, fortunately for Lon, shot within two weeks. Lon also broke western-programmer tradition by playing a black-shirted hero. Though this was his last serial for Universal, his next job was another potboiler: Jack London's *North to the Klondike* (1942).

Because of *Wolf Man*'s financial suc-

Here and on opposite page: Lon as the unhappy werewolf changes back to normal in these unusual transition scenes from *The Wolf Man.*

247

Left to right: Don Terry, Lon, Helen Parrish, and Noah Beery, Jr. in the serial, *Overland Mail* (Universal, 1942).

Lon and Noah Beery, Jr. fighting it out with the Indians in *Overland Mail.*

248

Captured by the Indians, Lon runs into scorching problems in *Overland Mail*.

cess Universal planned a fourth sequel in the Frankenstein series, *The Ghost of Frankenstein*, starring Chaney as the Monster. For a long time Boris Karloff resisted offers to play the Monster for several reasons (covered in the Karloff chapter), one being that he was the laureated star in the long Broadway run of *Arsenic and Old Lace*. Chaney, therefore, subjected himself once again to the rigors of heavy makeup, personally applied by Jack Pierce. Reporting in every day at 4:00 A.M. to comply with an 8:00 A.M. shooting schedule, Lon learned that Pierce was dedicated to making this Monster another artistic triumph. Pierce made it similar to Karloff's Monster by recreating the same headpiece design; but an allergy caused by the rubber base put Lon out of action for a week.

Continuing where *Son of Frankenstein*

left off, and with Lugosi re-creating his famous Igor role, *Ghost of Frankenstein* was surprisingly good for a fourth-generation sequel, with its impressive scenes such as the one in which the Monster is raised from the sulphur pit, and the spectacular one in which his body is given a tremendous "tonic" and a charge of "even-greater strength" after getting struck by lightning. Though he attempted to make the Monster seem more unsympathetic than ever, Chaney's fresh approach created a highly interesting characterization. And at this time Universal decided to drop the "Jr." from Chaney's name permanently.

Though Universal was undoubtedly still producing its important horror films with care, *Ghost of Frankenstein* marked the last "quality" production in its horror series—subsequent ventures such as *House of*

Ralph Bellamy, Sir Cedric Hardwicke, Lon, and Lionel Atwill in *The Ghost of Frankenstein*.

Frankenstein, House of Dracula, and *A & C Meet Frankenstein* are regarded as good but, nonetheless, exploitation potpourris and not purist extensions.

Lon's next assignment was in a minor 1942 gangster film, *Eyes of the Underworld*. He was billed second to Richard Dix in a role ill-suited to his talents—as a moronic ex-convict—though one unkind critic commented, "Chaney's back in his right metier . . . Lennie-type roles become him."

Next—two Universal shorts, produced to aid the war effort: these *America Speaks* short subjects concerned victory gardening and the duties of citizens during air-raid blackouts.

Chaney's horror-film fame now made him Universal's ace box-office attraction, inspiring them to revive the Mummy series originated by Karloff ten years earlier. In *The Mummy's Tomb*, Chaney inherits the role played by Tom Tyler in the previous film in the series (*The Mummy's Hand*), and is now cast as Kharis, the three-thousand-year-old mummy, revived and manipulated by evil high priest Turhan Bey, who was billed as "the Man of Mystery." Pierce created for Lon a rubber mask which was horrific though not as chilling as the Karloff and Tyler makeup. Whereas previous *Mummy* films were left with ambiguous endings, this script attempted continuity and made an effort to relocate the

Lon, as the Frankenstein Monster, carrying off Evelyn Ankers against Ygor's (Bela Lugosi) advice in *The Ghost of Frankenstein* (Universal, 1942).

251

Mummy in New England; but trite dialogue was self-defeating, making the Mummy's prowlings in search of Princess Ananka seem humdrum. A few moody moments followed by a dubious death-by-fire could do little to keep this from being the weakest offering in the series; nor was it helped even by a few stock shots from the original *Frankenstein* film showing torch-bearing villagers searching for the Monster.

Universal now sallied forth to combine two of its most potent monsters in one film, *Frankenstein Meets the Wolf Man*. This dramatized the further adventures of Chaney as Larry Talbot who, in searching for death as a release from the torment of lycanthropy, discovers the comatose body of Frankenstein's Monster preserved in glacial ice. Hoping to find a welcome death by submitting himself to an experiment, he engages instead in a battle royal with the Monster who, with the Wolf Man, disappears amid the flooded ruins of Chateau Frankenstein.

A good script and tight, imaginative direction, however, didn't mitigate the subtle B-quality that Universal was less and less trying to camouflage in its films. Yet in *Frankenstein Meets the Wolf Man*, Lon gives one of his best performances; his natural feeling for pathos was very impressive and the film's highlight. Maria Ouspenskaya was recruited once again to repeat her part as Maleva the traveling gypsy. Ilona Massey (of *Balalaika* fame—opposite Nelson Eddy—and other prominent films) slipped in her career as the daughter of Dr. Frankenstein, but at least preserved her poise and dignity, and calmed down audiences by being very charming and one of the "good guys." Lugosi, frail-looking and almost sixty years of age, was totally unsuited for the Monster role (see Lugosi chapter). Production went along smoothly until an almost-fatal accident: a horse-cart carrying Chaney and Mme Ouspenskaya toppled; Lon was bruised but uninjured, but the aging actress suffered a leg fracture.

Frankenstein Meets the Wolf Man (Universal, 1943). Lon emerges from a glacial tomb in his second appearance as Larry Talbot, the werewolf.

Frontier Badmen, an above-average minor western, had Chaney as a supporting heavy, and starred Diana Barrymore in the usual cast of Universal's stock players. Between scenes, Lon visited the 1943 *Phantom of the Opera* production company—the sets employed for this brilliant remake were the same ones (with some slight alterations) used originally for his father's version.

By this time it was obvious that Lon was suffering from the usual contract player's occupational disease: his non-horror roles were being limited to heavies.

Lon tries restraining a boisterous Lugosi Monster in *Frankenstein Meets the Wolf Man.*

What else could he do? Even today, some so-called purists and uninformed, but well-paid, "critics" continue damning him out of the same prejudice that kept him down during those years when his star should have ascended even higher: "If he doesn't have monster makeup on and a cast of other good bravura actors to bail him out, Lon Chaney, Jr. is back to Lennie again," they kept saying. This odious canard was refuted, however, by Lon's role—possibly the most distinguished one of his career—as the lead in *The Son of Dracula.*

Actually the title was a misnomer, since

Lon in *Frankenstein Meets the Wolf Man.*

Frankenstein Meets the Wolf Man. One good monster turn deserves another—when Lon was freed from his icy grave, he decided to unfreeze the Lugosi Monster, conveniently frozen nearby.

he was actually the old Count himself and not the "son." The film was excellently directed by Robert Siodmak from a well-conceived script by Curt Siodmak, author of *Donovan's Brain.* Not since the original *Dracula* and *Dracula's Daughter* (1936), had Universal done anything on vampires. Expecting something on a much lower order, fans were quite elated at the film's quality. But, again, creativity and Siodmak's careful direction did little to offset the budget slashes that Universal was making on its horror product and that were quite evident in this film. To save money, they brought the good Count and his activities inside the low-cost shingled frame-house atmosphere of the United States (as in the cheap *Mummy* sequels); setting up a more atmospheric middle-European or

Lugosi as the Monster monitors a conference between werewolf expert Maria Ouspenskaya and Lon in *Frankenstein Meets the Wolf Man.*

Publicity shot of Lon as Count Alucard in *Son of Dracula* (Universal, 1943).

Transylvanian unit would have cost a few dollars more.

Emigrating from his native Transylvania, Chaney arrives in the United States of the forties, traveling incognito as Count Alucard, searching for "fresh blood." Trying to get control of an aristocratic southern family's estate as a means to power and riches, he wins the affection of their beautiful daughter, and then turns her into a vampire. But the hero frees her accursed soul by destroying her body the only way she can be purged of this evil. Foiled at the eleventh hour by Professor Van Helsing (very well played by the late J. Edward Bromberg)—who must have strange powers himself, since he does not look a day older than he did in the 1890s—Dracula meets his end when he is unable to get back in his coffin in time (it's been set afire by the hero), and the sun's first rays begin demolishing him.

Despite slight anachronisms and the low budget, Director Siodmak's scant resources were put to ingenious use. Each character, particularly Dracula, has such deep strong identity and good lines that one is more concerned with motivational development than with sets and the usual studio paraphernalia. Scenes of a fog-swept countryside, the graveyard night sequences, and Dracula's coffin emerging from the misty

In *Son of Dracula,* Lon calls himself Count Alucard, a name which actually is Dracula spelled backwards.

waters of a midnight lake are imaginatively creative and visually excellent.

Unlike his other characterizations, Lon's Dracula makeup consisted simply of an altered hairline, grayed temples, a suave moustache, and a thin coat of bluish-gray greasepaint on his face to impart a pale, undead look.

In comparing his various roles, Chaney said:

"Dracula is certainly more potentially terrifying than those roles which required gruesome makeup. I feel there is no doubt that the mind's own sinister subtleties can be far more frightening than a semihuman beast."

Around this same time an incident occurred that serves to illustrate the extent of Lon's public popularity, especially with the young. During a visit of the Quiz Kids (a group of acclaimed preteen intellectuals on radio for many years in the forties) to the Universal lot, a car drove past them containing a familiar passenger. On being informed "That was Lon Chaney in there!" the child prodigies chased the car until it stopped and the star signed autographs for them. One eight-year-old intellectual interrupted with, "Really, Mr. Chaney—you're quite good-looking. You don't scare me at all!"

Although pleased with Chaney's success Universal began (perhaps, unintentionally), to destroy Lon's career by thrusting him into a new series of highly execrable films, emanating from negotiations with Simon and Schuster publishing company (then noted for the mystery novels which gave birth to radio's famous "Inner Sanctum" mystery series). After a working script had been assembled, production began immediately on the first of the *Inner Sanctum* movie series. The initial offering, *Calling Dr. Death*, starred Chaney as Dr. Mark Steele, a neurologist who, following his wife's unsolved murder, is subjected to the relentless suspicions of a police detective (J. Carrol Naish) and

Lon uses hypnosis on Patricia Morison to discover the true identity of a murderer in *Calling Dr. Death* (Universal, 1943).

plagued by his own possible guilt. He solves his wife's murder by hypnotism. By the use of stream-of-consciousness narration by Chaney to link the various segments of the drama, these slim semi-radio-style programmers, though slanted specifically for whodunnit fans, were excruciatingly boring and Chaney was badly directed. In addition, Universal's advertising and exploitation seemed to be nonexistent.

Lon started working in 1944 in his second *Inner Sanctum* film, *Weird Woman*, adapted from Fritz Leiber's *Conjure Wife*. This disappointing production, about a college professor (Chaney) who suspects his wife (Anne Gwynne) of witchcraft, is the weakest segment of the entire series. Eighteen years later Leiber's frightening supernatural novella was remade into an exquisite horror film by a British company

257

Lon Chaney, Jr.'s various Mummy roles:

Discovered by Turhan Bey (*left*) in *The Mummy's Tomb* (Universal, 1942).

and titled *Burn, Witch, Burn* (*The Night of the Eagle* in Britain), and it benefited substantially from a script devised by SFantasy veterans Charles Beaumont and Richard Matheson.

Chaney's next contractual ordeal called for him to appear in the Technicolor *Cobra Woman*—another of the forties' Maria Montez costume adventures which provided simple-minded escapist entertainment for war-weary audiences. Considering its juvenile plot, perhaps it was fortunate that Chaney's role as a mute aide to hero Jon Hall was small.

Lon romped through Olsen and Johnson's comedy *Ghost Catcher*, and then tackled the Kharis role once more in *The Mummy's Ghost*—fourth in the lower budget Mummy horror programmers. Yousef Bey (John Carradine) arrives in America

(RIGHT) All wrapped up in his work, giving others good *gauze* to worry, in *The Mummy's Tomb*.

With Turhan Bey in *The Mummy's Tomb*.

Ramsey Ames is up in arms in this production shot from *The Mummy's Ghost* (Universal, 1944).

to guide the destiny of Kharis, who has returned from the fiery death that had concluded the previous film in the series. Kharis gains possession of the reincarnated Princess Ananka, who undergoes a chilling aging process as he carries her away in his arms, and they sink together in a bed of studio quicksand. An improvement over the third Mummy film, true—but the formula plot was now worn and begging for a badly required retread job.

In the third *Inner Sanctum* film, *Dead Man's Eyes*, Chaney plays an artist, temporarily blinded by his jealous model, who is suspected of murdering his fiancée's father. Feigning permanent blindness, he reveals the true killer. Even though this is the best of the series because of its intriguing theme and several neat scenes with Chaney, plodding direction and a

C-budget atmosphere wrote the final ending.

In the ambitious *House of Frankenstein*, the Wolf Man (Chaney) joined a sterling cast starring "mad doctor" Karloff, a psychopathic hunchback (J. Carrol Naish), Professor Bruno Lampini (George Zucco) and his Chamber of Horrors, Dracula (John Carradine), the Frankenstein Monster (Glenn Strange), and, of course, the inevitable mob of howling villagers in the last reel. The title is misleading—there are no members of the eminent Frankenstein family in this sixth semi-sequel; by this time their descendants were all happily married (e.g., Ilona Massey in *Frankenstein Meets the Wolf Man* falls in love with Patric Knowles) or are fleeing from the horrors of the Second World War.

Chaney wasn't disinterred from his icy

The Mummy's Ghost. Another rare production shot of Miss Ames and Lon.

Jean Parker and Lon in *Dead Man's Eyes* (Universal, 1944).

tomb until late in the story, but his Wolf Man again succeeded in projecting a quality that elicited pity mixed with horror. His tragedy is softened by his love for teen-aged Elena Verdugo, lately Marcus Welby's secretary-nurse on TV (whose Spanish ancestors, incidentally, owned most of the area where Universal City now stands). Their relationship arouses the jealousy of Daniel the Hunchback, a pathetic character reminiscent of Chaney, Sr.'s interpretation of Quasimodo two decades earlier. To accommodate the large number of actors requiring special makeup, makeup artist-director Jack Pierce increased his staff.

Inheriting not only his father's acting blood but fondness for outdoor life, Lon

Lon as the Wolf Man for the third time around in *House of Frankenstein* (Universal, 1944).

purchased a thirteen-hundred-acre ranch in California's Eldorado County which he worked with the help of his two teenage sons. Yet even though monster parts had brought him some success, he confessed at times that he was weary of them and yearned for roles where "I don't have to get killed off in the last reel." His relationship with the studio was also strained by his constant efforts to retain "Jr." in his screen credits. He was now, however, financially secure enough to adopt an eight-year-old boy; this was so characteristic of this big, gentle person who more than once avowed, "I only wish I had enough money to give countless deserving orphans a good home; the lousiest thing in this world is to grow up without love."

Following a role in Abbott and Costello's *Here Come the Co-eds*, Lon donned the Mummy wrappings for the third and final time in the fifth Tale of the Tana Leaves, *The Mummy's Curse*. His bachelorhood was now becoming predictable; to relieve the Mummy's monotonous quest for Princess Ananka, the writers helped in continuing a low budget atmosphere and switched the locale to the Louisiana bayous where Ananka makes an eerie return from her quicksand coffin—after engineers had drained the swamp—and Kharis, under the guidance of Peter Coe, his new priestly mentor, terrorizes swamp dwellers and archaeologists. After a series of Mummy murders, giving the villagers good *gauze* to worry, Kharis is "killed" again, and

Ananka reverts to her ancient state. While imaginatively this was the best film in the series, the Mummy wouldn't mumble again until his next encounter with Abbot and Costello a decade later.

Continuing in the disastrous *Inner Sanctum* series, Lon mesmerized his way through *The Frozen Ghost*, a very minor mystery in which he portrayed Gregor the Great, who fears he may have killed some-

Evelyn Ankers and Lon stand over murder victim in *The Frozen Ghost* (Universal, 1945).

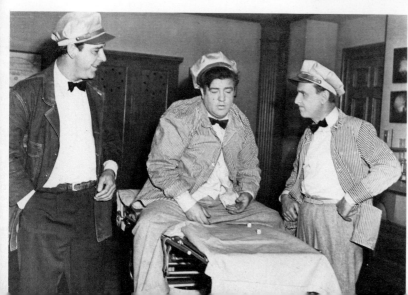

Lon with Lou Costello and Bud Abbott in *Here Come the Co-eds* (Universal, 1945).

263

one through hypnosis. He fared only slightly better in his next *Sanctum* that year (1945), *The Missing Head*. This remake of the Claude Rains and Lionel Atwill thriller, *The Man Who Lost His Head*, retained the original basic plot of a hardworking idealist (Chaney) whose existence is threatened by his ambitious and overly demanding employer (J. Carrol Naish). Naish pays for his misdeeds and callousness when his head is severed by the crazed Chaney. Lon's performance was good, but missing from *Missing* was the original's less-commercial approach and stylishness.

For *The House of Dracula*, Chaney repeated his popular Wolf Man for the fourth time, partially overshadowed by the Jekyll-Hyde activities of Onslow Stevens, who shone brilliantly enough to make one wonder why this fine artist had been so badly wasted and underrated throughout his career. The plot was notably superior to *House of Frankenstein*, eschewing its predecessor's erratic episodic nature and ghoulish ghoulashness:

Dr. Onslow Stevens has a reputation for humanitarianism and for helping the afflicted; consequently, he's visited by Count Dracula (who announces himself to the receptionist as "Baron Laotos") who is seeking a cure for his vampirism. When the villagers imprison Chaney, the Wolf Man, they call upon Stevens, who witnesses the lycanthropic change at a safe distance outside a prison cell, and who is made Chaney's custodian in the hope that he may cure him. Chaney, though, has misgivings, especially since matters start getting out of hand when Dracula begins to revert to his evil ways. In a transfusion scene, the kindly Stevens cleans out the Count's blood, believing such treatments and a special "for-

With mad doctor Onslow Stevens dead on the floor, Lon is at last cured of his lycanthropy (at least until *Abbott and Costello Meet Franken-stein* in 1948), but he still faces another problem with Monster Glenn Strange in *House of Dracula.*

mula" of his own will make monster into man. The experiment backfires when the Count places Stevens in a hypnotic sleep and infects him with his own vampire blood. Horrified at what has happened to him, Stevens bravely continues searching for a means to cure Chaney, still not aware of the full consequences of Dracula's tam-pering. Meanwhile, he also has on his hands the Frankenstein Monster whom he had earlier discovered unconscious in a remote grotto. Realizing now that Dracula's blood is in his veins, Stevens fights off its evil force with lessening resiliency, occasionally lapsing into a Hyde-like state, but he is happy to have brought Chaney's

A great non-Lon scene of Onslow Stevens as the tragic mad doctor and Glenn Strange as the Monster in *House of Dracula* (Universal, 1945).

torment to an end by curing him of lycan-thropy. In one of his last heroic gestures, he finds Dracula's coffin and destroys him by exposure to sunlight. Overwhelmed by gratitude, Chaney is concerned about his benefactor's deterioration and later goes forth to investigate strange sounds and screams in Stevens' laboratory. The good doctor, however, has now become totally evil and has brought the Monster back to greater power than ever. Rushing to attack the former Wolf Man, Stevens is shot down by Chaney and dies, finding peace at last. A fire, accidentally caused by the Monster, then destroys everything while Chaney and the heroine flee in safety.

In trying to economize, the producers used for the climax of *House of Dracula* the lab-Monster-fire footage from 1942's *Ghost of Frankenstein;* thus, in a sense, Chaney destroys himself! Despite its un-usually high quality in a period when the genre was being denigrated by lowered standards and fly-by-night C-companies, *House of Dracula* received bad reviews, no doubt resulting from prejudice based upon the critics' exposure to many of the poor products of the time. The second horror cycle was now about over; Uni-versal realized this, and decided to shelve the series permanently.

A routinely directed horse opera, *The Daltons Ride Again*, proved that Universal was also losing interest in Chaney. And *Pillow of Death* (1946), sixth and last of the *Inner Sanctum* mysteries, was a sad climax to his Universal contract.

Theatrical work continued to fascinate Lon and he was pleased to star as the lead in the national touring company of *Born Yesterday.* For his next film, he returned to Hollywood to appear as a comedy-villain in Bob Hope's private-eye takeoff, *My Favorite Brunette* (1947). His obvious parody of Lennie (which he satirized also in *The Counterfeiters*) prompted Chaney to complain:

"It still haunts me. I get a call to play a dumb guy, and the director tells me *not* to be Lennie. But he's never happy until I do play the part like Lennie; and then he doesn't know why he likes it."

Other film companies were on the move. Consequently, new potions were being con-cocted in the Universal conference-room cauldrons. The success of rival studios with screen comedians such as Hope, Red Skel-ton, and Danny Kaye had made rough com-

Lon, who had complained about being thrust back into Lennie-type roles, is seen here after giving Elisha Cook, Jr. a going-over in *My Favorite Brunette* (Paramount, 1947)—one of Bob Hope's best vehicles.

petition for the slapstick tradition of Abbott and Costello. Universal had, in less than eight years, invested tremendously and profited hugely from the famous comedy team. Indeed, during a long critical period in the early to mid-forties, A & C films saved Universal from total bankruptcy. It seemed unthinkable that Bud and Lou were in danger of being filed away in dusty vaults with old horror films.

Abbott and Costello Meet Frankenstein was designed to combine both waning trends. Playing to a new generation unfamiliar with the great early horror films, *A & C Meet* and its sequels proved so remunerative that both the comedy team and the horror-star veterans were able to re-establish themselves as box-office material. (Years later, American International used the same gimmick to break into big-time film competition when they coupled

Brenda Joyce *seems* menaced by Lon in this publicity photo for *Pillow of Death* (Universal, 1946).

horror with the j.d. trend in *I Was a Teen-Age Frankenstein*.)

In *A & C Meet Frankenstein*, Bela Lugosi, Glenn Strange, and Chaney re-created Dracula, the Frankenstein Monster, and the Wolf Man. Apparently forgetting how much trouble Onslow Stevens underwent to cure him in *House of Dracula*, Chaney again falls under the moon's influence, frustrating Dracula's evil plot to restore the Monster in America. The horror scenes were executed with sincerity, and the result was satisfying satire that paid homage to its source. In addition to the Wolf Man, Chaney also appears briefly in Frankenstein Monster makeup! Glenn Strange injured his leg during filming, and Chaney, enlisted as a substitute, thus appears as both Wolf Man and Monster in two different sequences. This highly unusual "inside" movie moment can be spotted by paying close attention to the scene near the

Abbott and Costello Meet Frankenstein (Universal, 1948). Despite appearing completely cured of lycanthropy in *House of Dracula*, Lon makes a comeback as Larry Talbot, bothered once again by his old problem when the moon is full. Bud and Lou stand by Lon, unaware of his *changeable* personality. Universal may have been inconsistent, but the results were terrific.

John Payne and Lon battle together in *Captain China* (Paramount, 1949).

end of the film where the Monster throws Lenore Aubert through the window.

The decline of horror to comedy curtain calls ended any opportunity for full use of Chaney's potential as a serious actor, and he fell into a rut of routine B-films. In the *16 Fathoms Deep* remake, he was the star. In *Only the Valiant* (1951), his sympathetic enactment of an Arab cavalry recruit who hates Gregory Peck made script limitations regrettable. *Bride of the Gorilla* found him in a better role for a change, starring opposite Barbara Payton, whose personal publicity in the press added

sensationalism to the film. Fantasist Curt Siodmak wrote and directed this Wolf Man–influenced story of mysterious killings in a tropical country. Surprisingly, the "man-into-gorilla" character was given to Raymond Burr instead of Chaney.

To promote *Gorilla*, a ten-day personal appearance tour was scheduled. Once underway, however, the trip stretched into four and a half months covering forty-five hundred miles—fantastic, considering how much the film was, and looked, of B-programmer level. Chaney commented: "What the people want, I discovered, was not for

A specially devised exploitation still of Lon and a large primate in *Bride of the Gorilla* (Realart, 1951).

our Hollywoodites to appear in a theater and say, 'It's nice weather and I'm glad to be here.' The audience expects a real acting job when a movie personality appears on the stage."

In 1952 he was contracted for an important supporting role in *High Noon*, playing the aged sheriff who is unable to help Gary Cooper; in this role he proved to the skeptics that he was still valuable as a straight actor.

In the early fifties Chaney portrayed on TV the Frankenstein Monster in "Tales of Tomorrow," a high-caliber, live SFantasy

Lon and Caesar Romero in *Once a Thief* (UA, 1950).

Battles of Chief Pontiac (Realart, 1952). Barry Kroeger, portrayer of numerous film heavies, sits at his desk in his role as an evil British officer thinking up new ideas for making life unpleasant for others, particularly Indians. Lex Barker (in buckskin shirt) stands heroically, with his friend Chief Pontiac (Lon) at his right.

series noted for its imaginative use of electronic special effects. His makeup was an original and creative conception by Vincent J-R. Kehoe. Special libations for outstanding occasions kept on preoccupying Lon more often with the passage of time (some even hinted that the "special occasions" happened several times daily). Consequently, after a four-hour makeup session with Kehoe, Chaney lost complete track of time and went through a live performance thinking it was a dress rehearsal. The way he explained it, he said that it took him several weeks to recover from this "encounter" and blamed it on the askew world of early TV.

He put in an appearance on "You Asked for It," explaining his father's famous make-up tricks, and then returned to Universal to enter *The Black Castle* in 1952—his first important horror production in four years, playing opposite his old friend Karloff.

The following years yielded inconspicuous roles in unmemorable films, and occasional starring and supporting TV roles. *The Indestructible Man* (1956) bears a

270

As a uniquely different Frankenstein Monster on TV in a segment of "Tales of Tomorrow" (1952).

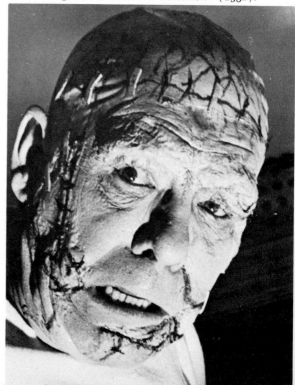

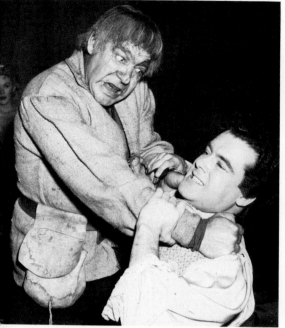

Lon in *The Boy From Oklahoma* (Warners, 1954).

Lon fights with Richard Greene (Robin Hood of TV fame) in *The Black Castle* (Universal, 1952).

The Black Castle. Lon obviously is still in a murderous mood.

Marian Carr and Lon in *The Indestructible Man* (Allied, 1956).

slight resemblance to the earlier *Man-Made Monster* but has little else to recommend it.

In *The Black Sleep*, portraying a madman, he was reunited with his old chum Lugosi for their final appearance together. The 1957 TV series, "Hawkeye and the Last of the Mohicans," was such a waste of film that the phrase "idiot box" was no longer a joke.

The 1957 apotheosis of Chaney, Sr. in Universal's *Man of a Thousand Faces* biopic was a tough act to follow; Lon, however, succeeded admirably with an impressive straight part in Stanley Kramer's *The Defiant Ones*.

In 1959 he headed south of the border —where he was something of an idol—for the grotesque *House of Terror*; later, he left for Sweden to star as Satan in a Siodmak TV series, "No. 13 Demon St" (turned into a feature and released in the United States as *The Devil's Messenger*).

The Black Sleep (UA, 1956). *Left to right:* Tor Johnson, Lon, George Sawaya, and John Carradine.

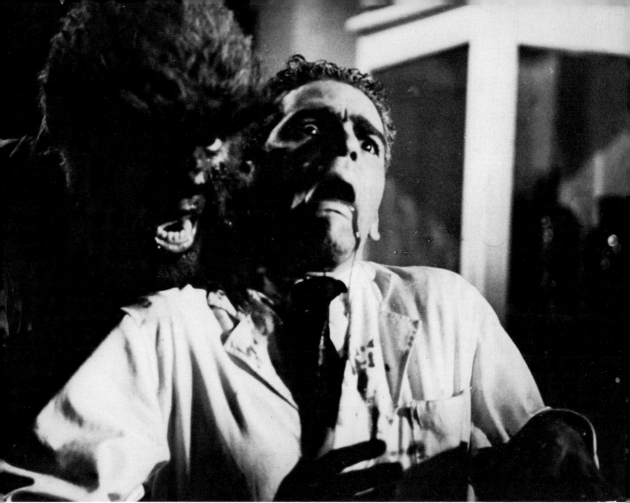

House of Terror (Des Fuentes, 1959). Lon in a
semi-reprise of the Wolf Man, spiked with tequilla.

During the summer of 1962, "Here's
Hollywood" invaded his castle in the San
Fernando Valley, and his nostalgic memories of his early film struggles and his
father's career made for an unforgettable
evening. Several months later, he, Karloff,
Lorre, and Martita Hunt appeared in a
"Route 66" Halloween special, "Lizard's
Leg and Owlet's Wing." Playing themselves, Chaney and Karloff re-created their
Mummy, Wolf Man, and Frankenstein
characterizations; Chaney also re-created
his father's famous Hunchback characterization, but this seemed out of place.

After Chaney appeared in American International's *The Haunted Palace* in an
interesting supporting role, the star of the
film, Vincent Price, remarked:

Lon in the Cuban-made *Rebellion in Cuba* (International, 1961; alternate title: *Betrayer*).

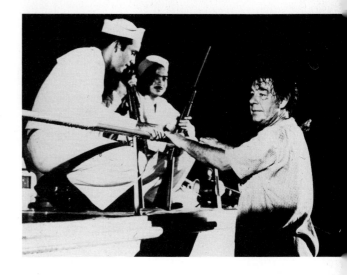

273

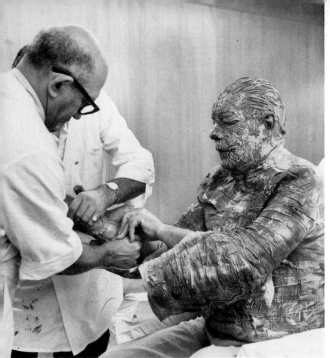

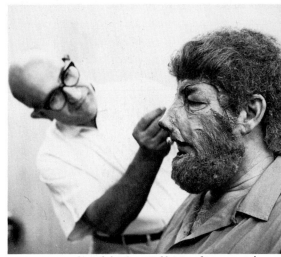

. . . and *voila!* The Wolf Man lives again!

Besides featuring Karloff, Lorre, and Martita Hunt, "Route 66's" special Halloween TV program focused heavily on Lon Chaney, Jr.'s several vignettes offering reprises of some of his early roles (including an homage to his father as Quasimodo). Makeup is being applied here for his Mummy takeoff.

Down the corridors of memory lane with dear old Boris Karloff for "Route 66."

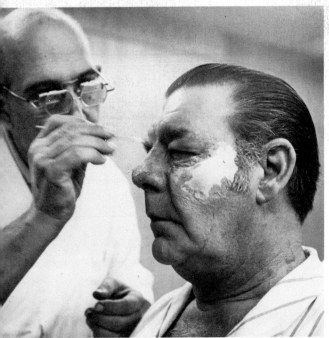

More makeup being applied for his Wolf Man stint on "Route 66."

Lon Chaney, Jr. in 1964.

Lon, Vincent Price, and Debra Paget in *The Haunted Palace* (AIP, 1964).

"Lon Chaney is one of the most talented actors in films today. He has none of the high-class attitude of today's stars; in fact, he is undoubtedly one of the most unassuming men I ever had the pleasure of working with."

In the mid-sixties, Chaney made national headlines by bitterly attacking "Fractured Flickers," a TV comedy series that specialized in cutting up old film and adding funny dialogue and weird sounds—one of the desecrated classics was his father's *The Hunchback of Notre Dame*. Lon saw red and probably various other shades. "Later, I found I didn't have a leg to stand on. I couldn't sue them. I was told the film had fallen into public domain. But I think that's a cheap, crummy way

A moment of anxiety between Price (*left*) and Lon in *The Haunted Palace*.

276

of making a living when anyone does a thing like that."

Comparing himself to his father: "He couldn't have read a speech of more than a paragraph; it wasn't necessary in those days. On the other hand, the things he could do with his eyes and even with his facial muscles have never been duplicated."

Asked why horror films have unending appeal: "I don't know, but I get a lot of fan mail from prominent people, doctors and lawyers, for example. After all, is there anything more horrible than prizefights which have plenty of appeal, judging from the audience?"

The next ten years saw Lon Chaney's sad decline into a morass of minor roles in films that rarely deviated from mediocrity and too often exemplified the inherent defects of an industry that on one day could say, "You're a star! You were a fabulous Lennie and a great Wolf Man. And you made a lot of money . . . *for us!*" and not long after say, "Sorry—nothing important here except a few days' work, provided you don't mind standing near a horse's rear end. Take it or leave it, kid. Those are the breaks!"

Disillusionment, chronic drinking, and age had their effect on him. Plagued also by serious illnesses on several occasions, he underwent major surgery several years ago for a throat malignancy that kept him on the critical list for some time. An apprehensive entertainment world waited each day for the latest news of his condition. It finally arrived: the gentle giant had pulled through. Looking battered and baffled by the ordeal, he recuperated and resumed his film work. Time hadn't been too gentle and his appearance had altered considerably. But his stamina, loyalty to his profession, and sheer enthusiasm for enjoying life each day at a time won for him a degree of admiration and affection that was envied by most of his colleagues.

For many years Lon Chaney lived about a mile and a half from the main gate of Universal City and, because his

On the good side of the law and friend of Western sheriff Dana Andrews, Lon is being treated for wounds sustained during an altercation with the local baddies in *Town Tamer* (Paramount, 1965).

films were everywhere on TV, he received more fan mail than ever before. There was no doubt in the minds of his fans that important films still awaited him. "There certainly wouldn't be any doubts in the minds of good directors if they studied his brilliant portrayals in *Of Mice and Men, One Million B.C.* and *Son of Dracula,*" his fans would rightfully say.

Lon's last home was in San Clemente. His doctors believed the climate there would be better; for, though he seemed to have rallied from the throat surgery undergone a few years previous, he was a sicker man than any of his fans imagined or that he himself would care to admit. He was wracked by a whole series of ailments (gout, beriberi, hepatitis, etc.), and after undergoing surgery for cataracts during the month of April in 1973, Lon ventured to try acupuncture to relieve his debilities.

Lon's pains and disappointments, sorrows and frustrations finally came to an end one morning during July 1973. The sad-looking giant had passed away.

Ironically, the date of his death was Friday the 13th.

277

Vincent Price

1911-

The King of Leer and Prince of Smirk, Vincent Price, first achieved fame as Prince Albert on the Broadway stage in *Victoria Regina* in 1935; by the early seventies he had ascended to become the King of Horror.

By the time the early forties rolled in, Price was already universally established as a versatile actor able to play straight as well as sinister roles. Shortly after attaining critical recognition opposite Helen Hayes in *Victoria Regina,* he went on to win further praise as the cruel Mr. Manningham in *Angel Street,* opposite Judith Evelyn. (This play was later adapted for the screen under the title, *Gaslight,* starring Charles Boyer and Ingrid Bergman.)

Price is a direct descendant of Peregrine White, the first colonial child born in Massachusetts, and of Jean-Pierre Desnoyers, the first state treasurer of Michigan, and he is the fourth male in direct succession to bear the family name of Price.

Born on May 27, 1911, in St. Louis, Missouri, to Vincent Leonard and Margaret Cobb (Willcox) Price, Vincent is one of four children—the others are his brother James and his two sisters Harriet and Laura Louise. He comes from an affluent background—his father was president of the National Candy Company, which supplied sweets to five-and-dime stores and thousands of retailers throughout the nation. Price attended Community School in St. Louis and the St. Louis Country Day School. In 1929 he matriculated at Yale, majoring in fine arts; much of his college leisure time was spent in swimming with the college team and rowing on the varsity crew.

His parents first discovered that Vincent had been bitten by the theatrical bug at the age of five, after an aunt arranged for him to appear in a kindergarten version of *The Angel of the Annunciation*. Through grade school, high school, and college, he maintained an interest in theatrical activities though he was unaware into what this "hobby" would eventually develop. But hobby or no, he had avowed his love for the theater since childhood.

Upon graduating from Yale with a B.A., he started making the theatrical rounds, seeking auditions; but good looks and an impressive six-foot-four height proved of little advantage in the beginning when producers listened to him reciting his school-play experience.

"Meanwhile," he said, "I drove a bus for the students at Riverdale Country School and after that I was an assistant teacher of English, German, and dramatics and art. I had to eat. I could have written home for funds, but somehow that wasn't playing the game."

Candidly, he admitted, "I was down, all right, but not out—and it occurred to me that if I went to London and saw the stage producers there, I'd be able to wangle some sort of an acting job. I knew London like a book, knew where to go and whom to see, so it wasn't like going into a strange land. I'd spent several summers abroad during my college vacations. I had been a research student at the universities of Nuremberg, Vienna, Frankfurt, and London. In 1932, during one of these vacation periods, I had spent my days piloting tourists through museums and art galleries, tutoring in history and English, while at night I sang in a Vienna night

club. Oh, I knew my way around—but that's about all. But my knowledge and acquaintance of Europe never fazed the London producers at all. They said, even more politely than the American producers: 'You can't get a professional stage job without professional experience, and you can't get professional experience anywhere outside a professional theater'—all of which left me not only more than slightly bewildered but completely nonplussed. For a week or so, that is. Then, desperately, I lied my head off to an English producer, and with such good effect, that in no time at all I was given a part in the London production of *Chicago*. That was in 1935, and I made my professional bow at the Gate Theater as a squeaky-shoed cop, doubling as a judge in the last act! Now I slapped myself on the back; I was actually getting somewhere in this acting business."

Two months later, at the same theater, he played the most coveted leading role of the London season—Prince Albert, in *Victoria Regina*. Gilbert Miller, then in London, had bought the play for an American production to star Helen Hayes. At last Broadway, which had snubbed the young Price and given him a royal runaround, became aware of him as an actor, for all Miller had to do was to watch Price during the first act of the play's London engagement to realize he would be perfect opposite Helen Hayes. The critical reaction was spontaneous enthusiasm—paeans of praise for Price's acting were long and loud: "The young actor is perfect in the role of Prince Albert. . . . A great new star has appeared—he should shine long in the heaven of show business." And he did, too, for two straight box-office hit years without a break in the role of Prince Albert.

But the rest of the country was denied the opportunity of witnessing the excellence of his stage talents in this play. Helen Hayes cautioned him against a nationwide tour. "I want very much to have you come with us," she said when the play was ready to go on tour. "But if you did, I, personally, should be very sorry. You will be typed forever in Prince Albert parts. My advice to you is to stay here in the East and play summer stock for all that you're worth. All sorts of parts and every part you can get. Vary them as much as possible. It will be the greatest experience for you."

Vincent followed her advice. That summer he played in stock companies in Westport, Connecticut, Mt. Kisco, New York, and Skowhegan, Maine. In September 1937 he was put under contract to play opposite Elissa Landi in the Broadway production of *The Lady Has a Heart*, which ran for three months; then he went directly into Orson Welles' Mercury Theater production of *The Shoemaker's Holiday*, playing the role of Master Hammon. Following this, Price appeared as Hector Hushabye in Welles' production of *Heartbreak House*.

Even amid heavy theatrical commitments, romance loomed for Vincent. A young actress, Edith Barrett, who appeared with him in several plays, became his wife on April 23, 1938. They were married in New York's St. Thomas' Episcopal Church, and increased their togetherness a few years later by playing together in 20th Century-Fox's *The Song of Bernadette* and *The Keys of the Kingdom*. Out of this union came their son, Vincent Barret Price, who is today a noted poet and student of anthropology, and the father of two children.

At last Hollywood beckoned. Film producers, ever on the hunt for promising new talent, had been following Price's rave reviews. Universal Studios eagerly signed him up, but with a special contractual arrangement that would allow him to appear on the stage six months of the year. For his first film, Vincent appeared opposite Constance Bennett in *Service De Luxe*.

He was not very delighted with the outcome, and later commented, ". . . I was cast as Constance's leading man in this small turkey. The only reward I had from the venture was an expensive wardrobe which took me the rest of the year to pay for and which immediately went out of style."

Service De Luxe was followed by a number of other Universal films, but thanks to another flexible working arrangement which Vincent had inserted as a contract clause, he would not be monopolized by only one company; thus his second film was for Warner's in *The Private Lives of Elizabeth and Essex*, one of this studio's most opulent A-budget spectacles. It was adapted from Maxwell Anderson's stage play—in which Price had also appeared—and directed by Warner's ace director, Michael Curtiz. Bette Davis starred as Elizabeth, and Errol Flynn as Essex. Despite Helen Hayes' admonition, Price remained a member of England's royal court by being cast in the role of Sir Walter Raleigh.

Between films Price bounded back to Broadway, and in December 1939 took on the role of the Reverend William Duke in *Outward Bound*. This was followed by a heavy lineup of off-off-Broadway productions, such as *Parnell* and *What Every Woman Knows*, among others.

Anxious to have Price back on their cast-roster and having been impressed by his appearance as Raleigh in the Warner's film, Universal thrust him back into English court life as Richard III's brother, Clarence, in *Tower of London*. It starred Karloff as Mord the Executioner, and Basil Rathbone as Richard, who eliminated Vincent as a possible contender for the throne by drowning him in a wine vat, after a drinking bout set up by Vincent to prove that he could drink Rathbone under the table.

During the rest of 1940 Universal cast Price in such varied films as *Green Hell* (he dies in the South American jungle by a poisoned arrow), and *The House of the Seven Gables*, in which he is framed by his evil brother, George Sanders, and is

Tower of London (Universal, 1939). Price is unaware, during a drinking bout with Basil Rathbone, that he's about to be drowned in a wine vat by Basil, who will be assisted in the deed by Boris Karloff (*left*).

House of the Seven Gables (Universal, 1940). *Second, third, and fourth from the left:* Egon Brecher, Dick Foran, Nan Grey; *first and second from the right:* Margaret Lindsay and Vincent Price.

forced to waste many years in prison, eventually to be released, exonerated, and to witness Sanders' bitter end. It was also one of Price's rare moments in a heroic-type role.

Quite unaware of it at the time, he began establishing himself in the genre that was eventually to become his trademark by assuming the lead in *The Invisible Man Returns*. Made on a smaller budget and lacking *The Invisible Man*'s expensive hoopla and publicity seven years earlier, this sequel was released by Universal under average double-bill standards; but despite this, it was directed from a well-plotted and tight script by Curt Siodmak, author of "Donovan's Brain," a horror-sci-fi favorite adapted several times for the screen, radio (starring Orson Welles on CBS' "Suspense" in the mid-forties) and TV. The advantage of the 1933 original over the sequel was that it not only had an expensive nationwide publicity campaign but was also directed by James

Whale, who had already helmed *Frankenstein* and *The Old Dark House,* and it made an overnight star of a then-unknown Claude Rains. The real star of this sequel—primarily because of his name value—was Sir Cedric Hardwicke, playing Price's treacherous brother. Invisibility created a further disadvantage by keeping Price swathed in bandages and "unseen" for nearly the entire film; but as in Rains' case, Price's distinguished voice partly overcame this handicap. Becoming an almost complete hero, Price avenges himself upon an evil brother and other conspirators, and returns to normal at the end of the film in one of the screen's better transformation sequences: from invisibility his body slowly shows a skeletal frame that gradually acquires blood vessels, muscles, skin, and finally, becomes a complete Vincent Price . . . on screen at last—for not more than two minutes!

The Invisible Man Returns (Universal, 1940). Famous character actor and supporting star Alan Napier is being scared by Price's invisibility. Actually, Vincent was far more invisible than this publicity shot makes it seem.

Price was quite happy that 1940 marked the end of his Universal contract and that now he could take advantage of a far better offer from 20th Century-Fox. The deal would place him in at least twelve distinguished productions over the next seven years, with several emerging as some of the most opulent spectaculars of the forties.

While working for Universal and during his first year with Fox, Price had not engaged in any stage activity. But in 1941 he was notified by the producers of *Angel Street* that the play, with Judith Evelyn, was being revived for another Broadway run and that he was wanted for the role of Mr. Manningham once more. The second run, which opened December 5, 1941, proved even more successful than the first; it lasted a year and was a personal triumph for Price, who received ecstatic reviews. For example, Richard Watts in the New York *Herald-Tribune* wrote: "In his days in the theater, Vincent Price has never been nearly so fine as the cold, sneering, implacable husband."

Prior to this Broadway success, his films at Fox had been many and varied. He had played the part of Joseph Smith, founder of the Mormons, in *Brigham Young*, opposite Dean Jagger, Tyrone Power, and other prominent Fox contract players. This was followed by his role as Charles II in *Hudson Bay*, starring Paul Muni and Gene Tierney, and directed by Irving Pichel.

After *Angel Street* closed, Price went back to Fox as the very merciless prosecutor who tries to commit Jennifer Jones to an asylum in *The Song of Bernadette. PM*'s film reviewer neatly summarized Price's performance as ". . . the perfect symbolization of ruthless intellect." The film, though, was more of an ordeal than a treat. "It took nine months to make, and the boredom of waiting [between takes] for a call from the studio began to pall," Price revealed. "I like the discipline of the theater. In movies and on TV there is no

continuity in learning a role. You have just a little to do at a time as told to you by the director. I have never been satisfied by this. So, in making a film, I take the whole script home and learn the role as if I were appearing in a stage play. I dislike playing only a little of the part each day."

It was around the time he was making *Bernadette* that Vincent's second career opened up—in the art field. Indeed, if acting hadn't proved so lucrative, he would more seriously have contemplated making art his full-time profession, for he had received an M.A. in fine arts from the University of London in 1935 before winning acclaim in his first important role in New York in *Victoria Regina*. Now, together with George Macready (who had also appeared in *Regina*), Price started The Little Gallery in early 1943 and maintained it for two years, both partners keeping it supplied with parts of their own collections and the works of aspiring unknown artists. This experimental gallery was to become an important inspirational basis that would eventually establish Price in the art world as a respected lecturer and authority.

Speaking of his years with Fox, Price said that his two favorite films were *Dragonwyck* and the Otto Preminger hit, *Laura*. Bosley Crowther, commenting in *The New York Times* about Price in *Dragonwyck*, wrote: "He makes a formidable Bluebeard and his moments of suave diabolism are about the best in the film." The part called for Price to play a feudal-like patroon in the early nineteenth century who holds sway over his upper Hudson River estates and who does not try to adapt to the changing times of a growing America; instead, he considers himself above the law and unanswerable to the outside world. Though it was gilded with distinct Gothic touches, *Dragonwyck*, in Price's opinion, is not a horror film. "I played the part of an egomaniac who thought the world should be run his way."

Laura—still thought of by many as Preminger's best film—includes one of the

Clifton Webb, Price, and Dana Andrews in Otto Preminger's best film, *Laura* (20th Century-Fox, 1944).

screen's most witty confrontation of two sophisticated cynics (when Price locks intellectual horns with Clifton Webb) since *All About Eve*'s brilliant verbal duels between George Sanders and others in *Eve*'s memorable cast.

In 1947, with the expiration of his Fox contract, Price signed up with RKO and began playing the kinds of roles with which audiences now usually identify him. Until that time his parts had been varied; most, however, had been in historical-period dramas, though he had done occasional turns in marginal terror-suspense films. His best brushes with the macabre had been in two films, *The Invisible Man Returns* and *Dragonwyck* which, as previously mentioned, Price rejects as too mild to qualify as a "horror" film. Now his transitional stage started with his first role at RKO as a malevolent Svengali-like character in *The Long Night*. Greatly underrated by the critics and public alike, *The Long Night* featured a notable cast headed by Henry Fonda as the man who perceives Price's evil and unsuccessfully tries to foil his mesmeric-like control over his (Fonda's) girl, Barbara Bel Geddes. Price gloats over the fact that his diabolical intellect is superior to Fonda's earthy simplicity, but he brings about his own death by a long barrage of derogatory sarcasm that taunts Fonda into killing him. Creatively arranged and stylish,

the film was directed by Anatole Litvak, who was laureated for such successes in the thirties as *Mayerling, The Amazing Dr. Clitterhouse, Confessions of a Nazi Spy,* and in 1948, a year after the Price film, *The Snake Pit* and *Sorry, Wrong Number.*

After finishing *The Long Night*, Price returned to Universal to take a part in *The Web* as an eccentric Howard Hughes-type tycoon steeped in intrigue and conspiracy. His next encounter with horror occurred the following year, and was more like a gag: all he did was an Invisible Man voice-over for less than a minute in the punch-line ending of *Abbott and Costello Meet Frankenstein.* Price was unbilled, to boot, but there was no doubt about whose voice it was.

In 1948, together with art-aficionado friends such as Edward G. Robinson, Fanny Brice, and others, Price promoted another venture in Hollywood, the Modern Institute of Art; unfortunately, it failed after two years from lack of financial aid.

Vexed because the movie industry had refused to support such a worthwhile institution, Price has often decried its cultural apathy: "I went into the theater thinking an actor was a cultured man. This is often true in England and in other parts of Europe. But here in Hollywood, actors have been made freaks. An actor is not supposed to participate in the community. Why shouldn't an actor use his fame to advance the cultural life?

"The entire movie industry," he continued, "did not give one cent to the museum. One of the top executives dismissed the entire project as a publicity stunt—as though Fanny Brice, who had already retired, needed the publicity. Or as though Eddie Robinson, whose name was already very well known to the art world, needed this kind of attention."

Quite capable of expressing righteous indignation at the drop of a hat, with a zeal uncommon among most actors, Price outlined to what degree he felt movie-acting should be part of an actor's life, and emphasized how important it is for him to be involved in other activities and to appear in at least one or two plays a year regardless of how many film assignments he gets. In 1959 alone, covering fifty-five cities in only sixty days, he gave seventy lectures before various organizations. In these talks, he charged that Hollywood's theory of film-making as a twenty-four-hour-a-day lifestyle was utterly unrealistic and possibly damaging: "The career should always support your life," he said, "but you can also miss a lot if you make your career in movies your entire life."

With the closing of the museum which Robinson, Brice, he, and so many others had lovingly nurtured, Price became a member of the Los Angeles County Museum's board of directors, a post he still holds to this day.

In 1948, following his divorce from Edith, Price met Mary Grant, a costume designer at Paramount; they were married on August 25, 1949. Besides her knowledge of art and fashion designing, Mary was a respected gourmet chef, and husband and wife collaborated on several best-selling cookbooks, including *A Treasury of Great Recipes* and *A National Treasury of Cookery.*

During this period Price was appointed to the Fine Arts Committee of the White House, and to the Latin Arts and Crafts Board of the U.S. Department of the Interior of which he has been chairman to date; included in the department is the Indian Arts and Crafts Board, which keeps Price active among Indian student and art groups in the Southwest. In these sessions the enthusiastic Price also stresses the cultural importance of poetry: "For years and years I dedicated myself to trying to make the American people visual-minded. Then when I went on the board I saw that we'd done it—that there was a tremendous concentration on the visual arts. But nothing was being done about poetry. And when I read the poetry the Indian boys and girls were writing, I saw that here was really

one of the things inherent in the Indian spirit." He read some examples of Sioux poetry, pointing out that they contained "the short statement in verse of the Indian's emotions."

The Indian poetry that Price mentions are by students or alumni of the Institute of American Indian Arts at Santa Fe, New Mexico, which represents eighty-five different tribes from all over the country. Each year Price presents a creative-writing award. "We're trying to encourage poetic drama, narrative poems, the use of poetry in documentary films," says Price. "Through the interest of Stewart and Mrs. Udall, when he was Interior Secretary, we got enough money to build a superb theater, and students have written some fine things for it."

After his powerful performance as Cardinal Richelieu in a spectacular MGM color remake of Dumas' *The Three Musketeers*, scripted by Robert Ardrey (1948), Price played the brains behind a Caribbean smuggling ring in *The Bribe*. In the same year (1949) he showed up in *Bagdad,* wearing a fez and eye-patch ("the studio thought it'd make me more menacing"), as a nefarious Turkish pasha who frightens desert princess Maureen O'Hara—the epitome of Arabian female pulchritude complete with flaming red hair, blue eyes, and Irish brogue!

Following these action potboilers Price, in 1950, was assigned two roles in succession—in *Champagne for Caesar* and *The Baron of Arizona*—that are hailed as among his best. In addition, the films themselves were remarkable and very untypical.

Champagne for Caesar lets Price have a field day as the semi-comedic soap-company tycoon who sponsors a weekly TV quiz show hosted by none other than Art Linkletter. Ronald Colman plays a brilliant but obscure intellectual with an encyclopedic memory whose contempt for commercial radio and TV festers into a plot to disgrace and undo the medium by appearing on Price's show. Instead of collecting his prize money, Colman returns and doubles it each week. Eventually he becomes a national-headline celebrity, serving to bring an unparalleled windfall of publicity to Price's products. As Colman's winnings mushroom, Price fears he's created a monster and decides to take the program off the air. Furious public reaction, however, forces Price to revive the show; and after a total of several months Colman nears the point of winning all of Price's business empire. In a particularly juicy scene, while he is escorting Colman around his factory, Price is momentarily tempted to shove him into a boiling soap vat but half-heartedly relents. An outrageous, biting satire of Madison Avenue and a little ahead of its time, *Champagne for Caesar* remains surprisingly undated after more than two decades.

The Baron of Arizona, which is one of Price's personal favorites, was directed by the controversial Samuel Fuller, admired devoutly by many cineastes as a brilliant but unjustly overlooked film auteur.

Said Price: "It was an extraordinary film in that it is the true story of a man who tried to forge documents that would make him own practically an entire state— but then he tries to sell it back to the government for five million dollars, and they begin to get suspicious."

Aside from having good casts and being entertaining time-wasters, his next four films were almost unmemorable except for his presence and for two delightfully similar roles. One was in *Curtain Call at Cactus Creek* (1950), where as a poor man's Edwin Booth heading an early Western touring theater group, he endures— and survives—playing opposite Donald O'Connor (in what was a hack-written western spoof). In *His Kind of Woman,* he showed up as a hammy matinee idol who turns amateur detective, rescuing Jane Russell and Robert Mitchum from Raymond Burr's evil clutches.

In late 1952 Price participated in a long-running stage recital of George Bernard Shaw's *Don Juan in Hell,* with Sir Cedric Hardwicke and Charles Boyer. He assumed the Devil's role, originally read by Charles Laughton but vacated by him because of other commitments. Meanwhile, Price completed narrative work in *Pictura,* a documentary covering the works of six outstanding painters.

During the genre's 1940–1945 "cycle" and until 1951, few SFantasy-horror flicks of any importance were produced, and those made were nearly all of B-budget to Z-quality status. Warner's, however, was impressed by the favorable reaction generated by RKO's *The Thing* and Fox's *The Day the Earth Stood Still,* and thought they would go one step further by remaking their 1933 success, *The Mystery of the Wax Museum.*

For a number of obscure reasons, *Wax Museum* had, except for sporadic showings, been virtually withdrawn from general circulation after its initial release. As the years passed all that remained of it was a dim memory, and it was classified as one of the famous lost films of the century. (However, around 1972 an original negative was unexpectedly discovered hidden away in one of Jack Warner's "forgotten" files.) The studio, recalling how highly regarded the film had been in 1933, decided to remake it. Late that year they announced that the new version would be titled *House of Wax* and have Vincent Price in the top role. And so it was that Price, after skirting the fringes of many tame macabre films in marginal "weird" roles, was at last able to fulfill his burning desire to star in a definitive horror shocker.

Taking advantage of the then-current 3-D movie fad, yet wisely sensing its limitations and transitory appeal, Warner's—unlike other studios which were shooting mostly in black and white and using cheap tints to create a 3-D illusion—shot *House of Wax* in 3-D *and* full color. This permitted theaters to rent the picture as a regular color film, if they chose—an option especially attractive to exhibitors when 3-D

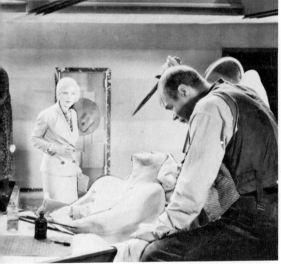

Two scenes from Warners' 1933 *Mystery of the Wax Museum*.

House of Wax (Warners, 1953). As the creative artist Henry Jarrod, designer of an opulent wax museum, Price tries to prevent his evil partner from starting a fire to collect insurance.

quickly fell out of favor, not only because people became tired of squinting through the little cardboard glasses, but because CinemaScope had arrived.

Few have been the times when Price reveled in a part so hugely and literally made a film his own—a production that seemed tailor-made for him. As Henry Jarrod, Price plays the co-owner and creator of exhibits in a wax museum in New York City around the turn of the century. However, his greedy partner has other notions and sets fire to the place to collect a handsome sum of insurance. Trying to stop him in a battle royal, his labors of love melting and burning all around, Price

is knocked unconscious and left for dead as open gas jets detonate, leaving the building a flaming ruin. Months later Price, his face now horribly scarred as a result of the fire, returns to avenge himself by garroting his partner and then hanging him by the neck in an elevator shaft to make his death seem a suicide. Murderer though he may be, Price proves himself an astute businessman by removing his ex-partner's ill-gotten insurance money after the struggle. Shortly, Price kills his partner's girlfriend, Carolyn Jones, in her apartment; later, in the unnerving atmosphere of the morgue, a shrouded body on one of the slabs stirs eerily, rises, and . . . Price sets forth to steal the girl's body. At his laboratory he converts her into a waxen image of Joan of Arc. With the financial aid of Paul Cavanaugh, Price goes back into the wax-museum business, pretending to be disabled and confined to a wheelchair—his horrible features hidden by a unique lifelike mask identical to his original face. Phyllis Kirk, who lived with the murdered girl, had seen the killer hovering in semidarkness. Price pursues her in what

287

In vain does Price attempt to put out the destructive fire in *House of Wax.*

House of Wax. After murdering her in her room, Price goes to the morgue to steal Carolyn Jones' body to convert her into a wax image of Joan of Arc.

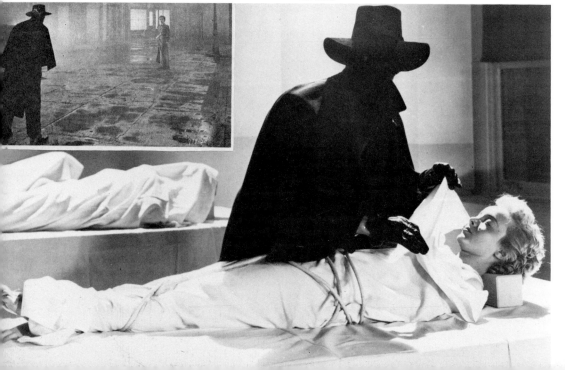

must be one of the best-made, breathtaking chase scenes in film history, up and down alleys and along gaslit streets, his dark and impressive cloaked figure striding along like the Angel of Death. Kirk survives the night, mystified about her assailant's identity; later, her curiosity piqued by the disquieting way that Joan of Arc's wax image resembles her deceased friend, she returns to the museum after closing hours, and to her horror, discovers her friend's head under layers of wax. "You shouldn't have done that, my dear," says Price, getting up from his wheelchair. As she strikes him on his face, his lifelike mask crumbles, revealing the horror of his charred features.

She faints and is carried off by Price to his wax workshop below. A model of total derangement, Price prepares to convert her into a wax-covered figure, fussing busily with his boiling vat and components, all the while reassuring her that the pain she is about to experience will reach the height of supreme exquisiteness: "The end will come quickly my love. There is a pain beyond pain, an agony so intense, it shocks the mind into instant beauty. We will find immortality together, and they will remember me through you." Her rescue, however, is at hand; the police arrive, and in an ensuing scuffle, Price is brought to his end by falling into the boiling wax.

House of Wax. Phyllis Kirk, the murdered girl's roommate, is pursued by Price.

Here and on opposite page: Feigning disability, and hiding his madness, Price is back in the wax-museum business, thanks to the financial aid of Paul Cavanaugh (standing behind wheelchair in "Bluebeard" scene).

House of Wax. Plucky Phyllis Kirk is unaware of danger while passing by a row of wax heads; one of them (*second from right*) is Charles Bronson's.

The Mad Magician (Columbia, 1954). Vincent goes berserk once more in a film that was almost a remake of *House of Wax*.

The Mad Magician. The climax—Vincent falls victim to his own invention and burns to a crisp in an incinerating machine.

Going on to earn more than five million dollars, rated by *Variety* among the all-time top box-office winners and elevating Price to even greater prominence, *House of Wax* has rightfully joined ranks with other classics in the genre as a creatively directed masterpiece of enthralling terror.

The advantages that would be ultimately created by Price's ascendancy to the ranks of the horror film masters such as Chaney, Karloff, and Lugosi, would, in the meantime, be outweighed by stigmatization. He was now definitely typed as a horror heavy; until the horror-film cycle would begin blossoming again in the late fifties, his roles were to be varied but unexceptional supporting parts, including several far beneath him, such as his role as Sinbad's "friend," Omar Khayyam, in *Son of Sinbad,* co-starring several of the screen's most ungifted players—Dale Robertson, Sally Forrest, and Lilli St. Cyr.

The exception was Columbia Pictures' *The Mad Magician,* in 3-D, with Price as an insane magician out to avenge himself against real and imagined persecutors. There are some slightly absorbing scenes and a complement of excellent supporting players (John Emery, Patrick O'Neal, and Jay Novello); but its main claim to fame is for being a shameful and flagrant though pallid imitation of *House of Wax,* dully directed by the fading John Braham who, ten years before, had achieved renown for his powerful direction of *The Lodger* and *Hangover Square,* both starring Laird Cregar.

A year earlier Price had continued to retain his status as a serious stage actor by signing up for Jose Ferrer's production

293

of *Richard III* as the Duke of Buckingham; this was followed by summer-stock work in 1954 in *The Winslow Boy;* next, at year's end, he appeared in the short-lived *Black-Eyed Susan* on Broadway. Between films he played in the La Jolla Playhouse in a summer 1954 production of *Billy Budd,* then contracted to repeat his role in *Richard III* in December 1955 at New York's City Center under Richard Whorf's direction. In 1956 Price began appearing all over television, first menacing Gladys Cooper and Cathleen Nesbitt in "Sisters," then putting his knowledge of art to profitable use by winning on "The $64,000 Question" (appearing on the same show next year to compete with his old friend Edward G. Robinson). In 1957 CBS-TV aired "The Revolution of the Eye," filmed in the Museum of Modern Art, narrated and co-scripted by Price. Despite sufficient public acclaim of the art documentary to warrant retelevising it at a later date, CBS and other networks coldly rejected Price's proposal to use it as the basis for a regular art series.

Then, quite suddenly, the film business started taking a profound interest in horror. It first began with Hammer Films' production of *The Curse of Frankenstein,* starring two relatively unknown players, Christopher Lee and Peter Cushing. Made on a rather small budget of approximately $250,000, it added a newer, more modern dimension to the macabre and had the definite advantage of full, blazing color; and it made a fortune, establishing this hitherto minor film-making company into an important production firm. But while Hammer stirred interest, it was Universal Pictures that climaxed horror's importance when, in 1957, it decided to place all of its SFantasy films of the thirties and forties in one basket and to release them to television in a promotional package called "Shock Theater." What resulted became show-business history. "Shock Theater" was an immediate sensation, garnering some of the highest ratings known to TV; and in-

cluded in the package, of course, were several of Price's earliest trips in terror, such as *The Invisible Man Returns.*

Although there was really no absence of SFantasy production until the 1957 boom, the accent had been more on an occasional giant animal, bug, or other out-sized creatures, or mostly minor hack-written science fiction with only a few better efforts, such as *The Thing, War of the Worlds, The Day the Earth Stood Still, It Came from Outer Space, This Island Earth,* and *The Forbidden Planet.*

Now, though, with the phenomenon of the Hammer and horror hurricane created by Universal's TV revivals, the pendulum swung to the macabre, which was responsible for advancing the next and greatest phase of Vincent Price's career.

As in Peter Lorre's case, the mere name of Vincent Price on a movie marquee was now enough to imply all sorts of macabre moments—even red-herring roles as in *The Fly,* a big box-office hit in 1958. Based on the *Playboy* prize-winning story by George Langelaan, Price is the worried brother of a well-meaning scientist (Al Hedison) who experiments with a machine capable of transmitting solid matter. After the device has proved successful with inanimate objects, Hedison tries transmitting himself. But the results are terrible—he emerges from the receiving end with the arm and head of a fly, not aware beforehand that the little creature had been buzzing around in the transmitter's isolation booth. A small fly now has his arm and head. Changes in Hedison's reasoning begin taking place as his character becomes more "fly-like," and he secludes himself in his laboratory while Price and the rest of the family chase about the house trying to catch the part-human fly. Notches above the usual creature feature, the film stresses human heartaches and sorrow, and turns what could have been the routine shock value of average horror fare into stark, dramatic tragedy. The climactic scene has to be among the most memorable in film annals: brooding over Al Hedison's death (who, in a final moment of mental clarity decides to commit suicide rather than become a total monster, and allows a huge power press to squash him as if he were a giant bug), Detective-Inspector Herbert Marshall and Price are walking in the garden when they hear a tiny voice shrieking weirdly, "Help . . . help me!" over and over. Looking closer in the bushes, they see a large spider's web. Entrapped in it is The Fly, with one tiny human arm, the tiny Hedison head crying, "Help . . . help me!" Just at that moment the spider charges forth to claim its victim. Hurling a large rock upon this horror, Price and Marshall bring the poor creature's misery to an end.

In his autobiography, *I Like What I Know*, written in 1958, Price recounted his experiences in *The Fly*. He said: "Herbert Marshall and I had to examine a spider's web which held the small fly which was supposed to be my brother. It took a whole day to film the scene, for we kept laughing ourselves sick. In the end, we had to film it standing back to back—we just couldn't look each other in the face."

Price, incidentally, authored another book in 1961. This, an inspiring and moving work, was written after the death of his favorite dog, and was called *The Book of Joe*. In it, he expressed his deep sentiment and love for his pet of fourteen years.

The following year *The House on Haunted Hill* starred Price under the skillful direction of veteran chill-master William Castle, who scooped up every known haunted-house-of-mystery cliché ever used and added several newer ideas, the primary one being an acid bath that strips its

The Fly (20th Century-Fox, 1958). Price relates how this climactic scene put him and Herbert Marshall in stitches, resulting in several retakes. The child is Charles Herbert.

One of the devices Price used to lead his guests to their doom in *The House on Haunted Hill* (Allied, 1959).

victims down to the skeleton, and a typical Castle gimmick: "Emergo," a skeletal-type apparition strung on a wire in the theater; this appeared to come at the audience from the screen, clear across to the back of the orchestra. Price appears quite unsympathetic in his role as he helps his victims along to their corrosive ablutions.

The same year an old chestnut from the early twenties, *The Bat*—based on Mary Roberts Rinehart's stage play, and remade several times for the screen—starred Price in the role of a doctor hiding out in a remote country house. He is suspected of robbery and of being a strange hooded murderer known as "the Bat"; but the killer turns out to be someone else in this by now-outdated theme which had the further disadvantage of boring direction.

Roles in the genre were now coming in droves, though an occasional benign

House on Haunted Hill. Guests in this "house" were invited and *died* to regret it.

part was offered to capitalize on his name value, such as his ringmaster's role in *The Big Circus,* an above-average A-budget circus mystery. David Nelson—who else?— turns out to be the psychopathic trapeze-artist killer, and in a "happily-ever-after" finale Price, Peter Lorre (another herring), and the cast exude delight as they watch Gilbert Roland walking on a cable across Niagara Falls without falling and breaking his neck.

The Return of the Fly that year was rather unwelcomed, falling under the dreaded spell of "sequel curse," unlike sequel exceptions such as several of the *Frankensteins* and, more recently, those of the *Planet of the Apes.* Price appears in the same role, but now Al Hedison's orphaned son has grown up to carry on his dad's experiments but is not mature enough to avoid a traditional mistake and a poor

script. All ends well as Price saves the nephew from death and a B-budget potboiler.

The next year, 1960, William Castle cast Price in an excellent shocker, *The Tingler,* with another Castle theatrical gimmick that really added nothing to the film: a "Tingler" was attached beneath certain seats in the theater, and the house manager pushed a button to coincide with certain appropriate moments on the screen, giving a mild jolt to each chair's occupant. It was quickly abandoned in subsequent releases since the gadget either failed to work at all, or worked too well, much to the consternation of some theatergoers. A combination of nostalgia and modern science-horror, *Tingler* stars Price as a doctor who discovers a "thing" dormant in all humans that is nourished by fear and can kill unless one screams and thus destroys it by yelling.

The Bat (Allied, 1959). A publicity shot of Vincent in a red-herring role.

Vincent is annoyed by the monster Fly in this staged publicity shot for *The Return of the Fly* (20th Century-Fox, 1959).

Taking the ultimate "trip" in an experiment to
learn the true horrors of fright in *The Tingler*
(Columbia, 1960).

The Tingler. Price now knows the terrible effects
of true fright.

Philip Coolidge, manager of a revival movie theater—focal point of several charming sequences involving old films—is married to deaf-and-dumb Judith Evelyn and decides to do away with her by frightening her to death, for, since she is unable to give voice to a scream, she will die from the Tingler. Finally, Price himself almost dies when the creeping Tingler is released from its cage; but he survives by emitting a long scream. Several times throughout the film, audiences are urged by Price to "scream for your life's sake!" while the Tingler buzzers under the theater seats were also supposed to convey this message —or, unwelcomed *massage,* as was often the case.

Until 1960 the name of American International Pictures, co-owned by two extremely clever hardworking men, Samuel Z. Arkoff and one-time science-fiction fan, the late James H. Nicholson (who passed away on December 10, 1972), was almost entirely equated with rock-bottom grindhouse and drive-in cheapies. While a number of AIP's fifties' productions have fallen into a predictable limbo (the majority being dragstrip and motorcycle-gang adventures), all had the tremendous asset of unparalleled economy—most filmed in several days to a week, never more than twelve or fourteen days—and tantalizing distribution deals for exhibitors, including guarantees of all kinds. By shrewd reinvestment of profits and *leasing* instead of wasting money by *buying* studio space, Arkoff and Nicholson were now ready, after eight years, for better productions. Signing up Price to a special three-film contract for the lead-spots, AIP suddenly shifted to quality film-making under the slick control of Roger Corman, a hard-nosed director, renowned even at this date for being a very hard driver and one who knew how to cut corners mercilessly.

The productions were known throughout the world as AIPoe, and the first in which Price was to star was *The House of Usher* (1960), adapted by Richard Mathe-

son (author and scripter of *The Incredible Shrinking Man, The Legend of Hell House, The Omega Man,* etc.) into brooding Gothic horror. Price, as Usher, gave everything he had, which was more than can be said of most of the others in the cast, among whom were the leftovers from previous AIP gangland and 'cycle programmers who would reappear in a few more AIP films. Made in color on a budget of less than $175,000 (but expensive for a company that once averaged $6,000 to $10,000 for a black-and-white teenage actioner), director Corman's tight-fisted control and characteristic martinet discipline made *Usher* look like a million dollars— a production formula from which AIP never deviated and which would put them into the position of being able to vie with major companies in another ten years, while less budget-minded studios headed into crises or bankruptcy in the interim.

Another Corman, *The Pit and the Pendulum,* was begun a few months later, following *Usher's* success, and was also scripted by Matheson. Shock values went even further this time as every possible torture device was brought into play. Price is lord of a sixteenth-century Spanish castle, hounded by his late father's evil reputation as an official Church Inquisitor and torturer. Though Price at the start is well-meaning and trying to live down the family stigma, his beautiful wife, Barbara Steele, conspires with her secret lover to drive him insane in order to gain his possessions. Blood will tell, though, and Price snaps out of his catatonic state, now madder than a monster, thinking he is his own father; he improves on his parent's perversion and deals sweet, albeit sanguinary, vengeance upon his enemies, ending by sequestering Miss Steele in an Iron Maiden. Even more expensive-looking than *Usher, The Pit and the Pendulum* served to raise Price in the entertainment world's esteem and AIP as an important film-making company.

Matheson's adaptation of Jules Verne's

300

The House of Usher.

Price shows houseguest Mark Damon portraits of his weird ancestors in *The House of Usher*.

For the kind of man Price plays in *The Pit and the Pendulum,* nothing can serve to drive him to greater madness than an unfaithful wife like Barbara Steele.

(LEFT) *The Pit and the Pendulum* (AIP, 1961). Madness slowly starts taking possession of Price.

(RIGHT) *The Pit and the Pendulum.* Now utterly deranged, Price becomes a throwback and imagines himself to be his Inquisitor father.

Master of the World was also released about the same time. Charmingly creative and in period style, it starred Price as Robur the Conqueror, an ingenious man of science who is fanatically opposed to war and who travels about in a Verne-type flying machine, forcing world powers to attain peace in his way. But valuable though the Verne name had been for other studios, *Master of the World* made far less money than either of the Poe films because it stressed science fiction and had no horror. To become profitable it would have required exploitation that only companies of Paramount's or Fox's capacity could afford.

On the termination of his first AIP contract, Price was called to Italy in 1961 for three films: *Queen of the Nile* (with Price cast as an insidious Egyptian high priest trying to force his daughter to marry the Pharaoh's demented son), *The Black Buccaneer* (from a former white-slaver in the Caribbean, Price takes over San Salvador, steals the governor's daughter for himself, and is finally foiled by Ricardo Montalban, a buccaneer-turned-hero), and *The Last Man on Earth*. This latter, a worthy horror entry, was ostensibly finished in late 1961, but didn't arrive in the United States until late 1964. Loosely adapted from Richard Matheson's gem of a horror novel, *I Am*

As Robur the Conqueror who seeks to destroy the armed forces of the world in *Master of the World.*

Legend, by two other writers *sans* Matheson, the story still managed to retain some of its original quality. Even on what was obviously a low budget, director Sidney Salkow created strong impressions of death and putrescent horror permeating a world in which all normal life has ceased and been replaced by wandering hordes of vampire-like ghouls who have been transformed to this state by a mysterious modern plague that has decimated the entire world. Through flashbacks, Price is seen as an industrial biochemist who witnesses the destructive effects of the plague that finally claims his own family. By some

strange circumstance he survives and now, all alone, he barricades himself against the "undead," venturing out only during the daytime (when they are asleep) to destroy them in their resting places; thus he becomes a "vampire-killer." There are others in the land, though, who resent Price's presence: they themselves are all former ghouls who have found an antidote to the plague's effects and wish to restore the rest of the world's victims to normalcy. Regarding Price as the embodiment of a system that all but destroyed the earth, they kill him in an excellently filmed climax. (The film, starring Charlton Heston, was re-

307

Master of the World (AIP, 1961) didn't do well at the box office, though it was a fine sci-fi production, starring Price as a nineteenth-century anti-war militant.

Price is besieged by roving vampire-like ghouls in *The Last Man on Earth* (AIP, 1964). It became almost a prototype for other successful SF-horror films—such as 1968's *Night of the Living Dead,* itself a minor classic—and was remade as *The Omega Man* (1971) in an even more powerful version.

made as *The Omega Man* in 1971, scripted, this time by Matheson, with a number of variations.)

Naked Terror, allegedly detailing barbaric Zulu tribal practices for quickie documentary shock appeal, was narrated by Price and ended his chores for 1961. In 1962 he walked through and stole every scene as the lead in *Confessions of an Opium Eater;* based on De Quincey's famous essay, it dealt less with opium and more with Chinese tong wars. Price braves the eerie sanctum of an evil tong to help a Chinese journalist friend escape from the

insidious minions of the hatchet man in turn-of-the-century San Francisco. In *Convicts 4,* Price has another uncharacteristic and sympathetic part as Carl Carmer, an actual author and columnist, who strives to get a reprieve for a reformed convict presently in the death house. The film was adapted from the true experiences related in the bestselling autobiography of convicted killer John Resko.

Richard III was never depicted as more depraved than when Price played him in United Artists' 1962 remake of *Tower of London.* In this film, more Grand Guignol than anything Shakespeare had ever dreamt of, Price was outfitted with a Veronica Lake wig and a hump that would have been a credit to Quasimodo, and he raved and gloated through his King-of-

England role with enough twistedness to outdo Dr. Frankenstein in the creation of his Monster. History rarely ever was so much fun.

AIP signed Price to a new three-year contract; under its terms, however, he would be allowed to work for other studios as well. In *Tales of Terror* (1962) he starred in three different segments, all Poe adaptations by Richard Matheson: in *A Cask of Amontillado,* which also borrowed several ideas from *The Black Cat,* Price is the winetaster Fortunato, who lusts after Peter Lorre's wife and winds up being entombed behind a wall by Lorre. In *Morella* he is the slightly dotty alcoholic recluse who mourns over the mummified corpse of his wife. Morella's spirit arises in revenge to claim Price and his daughter. In *The Facts in the Case of M. Valdemar,* Basil Rathbone co-stars as a mesmerist who, while conspiring to take over Price's daughter and possessions, places Price in a trance to keep him from dying. Rathbone's plans backfire, and Price melts away in his bed in a butterscotch-fudge ooze. The atmosphere, settings, and mood of *Tales of Terror* managed to hold up well under Corman's direction, even though it was not one of his most spirited ventures; besides, anthology films have rarely worked well in sustaining the continuity achieved by feature-length films.

The Raven (1963) proved a remarkable change of pace for everyone involved; scripter Matheson and director Corman combined their gallows-humor talents to concoct one of the finest black comedies ever put before a camera. In *The Raven,* Price and Boris Karloff appeared together for the first time since Universal's *Tower of London* as competing sorcerers trying to out-zap each other for supremacy. Peter Lorre is the Raven, of course, who plaintively asks to be changed back to human form. The film proved that while professional comedians may be polished and adequate in their work, professional screen villains of such mettle as Price, Karloff, and Lorre can outshine even veteran comics. Following its completion, Price stated very enthusiastically that he would like to do more comedy.

After Price finished narrative work for the Oscar-winning documentary, *Chagall,*

Price, with an opium pipe, in a lethargic mood in *Confessions of an Opium Eater* (Allied, 1962).

United Artists signed him for *Twice-Told Tales*, another screen anthology adapted from two of Nathaniel Hawthorne's short stories, "Dr. Heidegger's Experiment" and "Rappaccini's Daughter," and including a truncated version of *House of the Seven Gables*. In the first tale, Price discovers an elixir that brings his former fiancée back to young womanhood and restores his and Sebastian Cabot's youth; but the experiment fails and they all become old again. In the next tale, Price is a diabolical scientist who contaminates his daughter with a form of poison that brings death to anyone whom she touches. The final tale has the "House" bringing down its traditional curse upon a greedy Price while he is searching for a hidden treasure. Styled well and set in nineteenth-century New England, the film has a goodly quota of shocks that almost compensate for its anthology filmic deficiency.

Because of so many macabre productions in 1963, Price was asked if he didn't think it paradoxical that a man of his extreme culture should appear in myriad horror roles. "This is not so," he answered. "Culture and terror films have a lot in common. People often ask me how I can talk about art and then come back to Hollywood and do thriller pictures. I answer, 'baloney.' Some of my terror films were taken from classic stories by such authors as Edgar Allen Poe, Verne, De Maupassant, and Hawthorne." Price went on to emphasize that the genre has its deepest roots in classical written art:

"These pictures go on forever because they can't become dated. They are like fairytales, and fantasy has been one of our greatest literary exports for years."

When it was pointed out that some critics felt that many of the films were quite frightening, he replied, "If you're

Veteran heavy Michael Pate (*right*) looks on as Price tortures a victim in the 1962 version of *Tower of London* (UA). Richard III never appeared more insane.

Price and Joyce Jameson attack Peter Lorre in a
scene from "The Black Cat" segment of *Tales of
Terror* (AIP, 1962).

In "The Case of M. Valdemar" segment of *Tales
of Terror,* Debra Paget stares in disbelief at the
horrifying butterscotch fudge disfiguring Vincent
Price.

Price plays a good warlock in *The Raven* (AIP, 1963).

The Raven. Vincent is almost paralyzed by fright when his father's mummified corpse acts belligerently.

Price in *Twice-Told Tales* (UA, 1963).

going to do movies, you might as well do some that people see."

The time was when Hollywood cut back on horror-film production, concentrating more on realism. Price contended that such films were real "horror pictures" since they dealt in personal problems and true-to-life conflict. "Television took over the role of the entertainer when movies went serious," he explained. "There's a difference between horror and terror pictures. A horror picture depicts real problems as they exist today. They frighten you because you think the situation could involve you. Terror movies are make-believe. A hand comes out of nowhere. It's contrived to make you scared, just as comedy is contrived to make you laugh."

During the remainder of 1963 Price was cast in *Diary of a Madman*, based on several De Maupassant stories, including "The Horla": Price is a respected judge who degenerates into a murderer after being cursed by a man he has sentenced to death. AIP produced another black-comedy romp, *Comedy of Terrors*, starring Price; also in the film were Karloff, Lorre, and Rathbone, who tried to drum up new business for their failing mortuary by *making* their own customers. AIP then thrust Price into the first of its many successful teenage seashore pinhead series, *Beach Party*. Price does a small "guest" role as Big Daddy, manager of the teenagers' hangout.

Before 1971, when Price appeared in *The Abominable Dr. Phibes*, he was to star in three successive AIP films credited among his best: *The Haunted Palace* (1964), *The Masque of the Red Death*

Price is in a groggy condition as a bungling undertaker in *Comedy of Terrors* (AIP, 1963).

Price and Debra Paget in *The Haunted Palace*
(AIP, 1964).

315

An atmospheric poster design for *The Haunted Palace*.

The Haunted Palace. One of the most eerie scenes, with Price and Debra Paget.

Price, as the cruel devil-worshiper Prospero, and
Jane Asher in *The Masque of the Red Death*
(AIP, 1964).

The Masque of the Red Death. Price falls prey to
the Red Death in the climax.

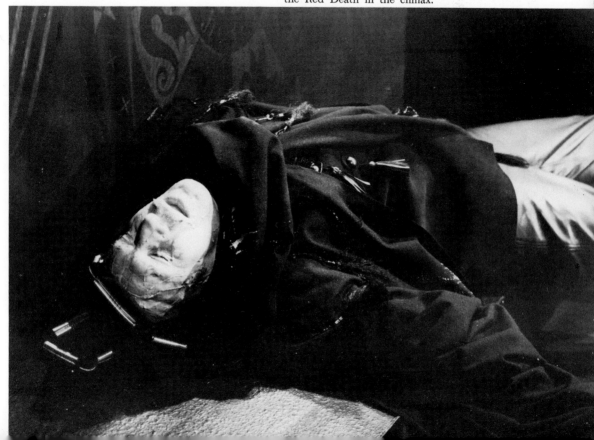

(1964), and *The Tomb of Ligeia* (1965). The late Charles Beaumont succeeded in capturing H. P. Lovecraft's own special brand of New England Gothic terror in his adaptation of "The Case of Charles Dexter Ward" for *Palace,* under Corman's direction. Set in a strange nineteenth-century New England village inhabited by deformed half-humans, some without eyes or facial features, Price is a lineal descendant of an eighteenth-century warlock who was burned at the stake. Price's part turns into a dual role as the warlock takes possession of the mind of his great-great grandson as a means of restoring his own evil. Though mostly the work of Lovecraft, AIP decided, in one of its typically exploitative moves, that *Palace* would be more commercial if publicized under Poe's name rather than that of a lesser-known author.

Audience and critical acclaim of *Red Death* and *Ligeia* was justified by the excellence of both Corman-directed productions; these films also marked AIP's and Price's first experience with British-based productions. One of Beaumont's last scripts, *Red Death* is based almost wholly on Poe's original, though it includes ideas from several of his other stories. Price, of course, is Prospero, cruel, sardonic, Devil-worshiping ruler of an immense twelfth-century palace, who believes he is above everything and can flout God, man, and nature with impugnity, and who goes forth to gather about him his debauched friends and acolytes to protect them from the danger of the Red Death plague which is ravaging the countryside. But Prospero's castle walls turn into a death trap rather than a haven, and a bacchanal ball becomes the Dance of Death as the spectral form of the Red Death claims all for his domain. Undoubtedly Corman's best film, it was greatly enhanced by Nicolas Roeg's brilliant photography and a performance by Price which he himself esteems.

Drug addiction and a strange power from his wife's grave haunt Price in *Ligeia,*

notable for being Corman's last fine film (though he has made more since 1965) and the end of his association with Price.

While more films in and out of the genre were still ahead, Price's schedule was getting increasingly crowded with his other "careers": numerous TV appearances; stage work; college tours; lectures on art, cooking, films. As a result of what he calls "my blatting my mouth off on television," he has made, at times, more money from his "nondramatic" *sidelines* than from what most film producers ever offered. Representing Sears Roebuck's mail-order art department, Price personally purchased more than three thousand original works which sold at prices ranging from thirty to nine thousand dollars.

In view of all this—and especially since TV appearances alone would be enough for any other man—the question often asked is: Does Vincent Price ever sleep? His response: "I made up my mind in 1946 to go on every TV show that asked me. I go nuts when I'm not working. I guess I'm an old ham, really."

On several occasions between horror films, Price defended the genre against criticism:

"Our horror pictures are tremendously successful. Oh, it's great to make *Mutiny on the Bounty;* but when I went to see it there were only fifteen people in the theater, while next door *The Raven* was playing to a full house."

During the Boston pre-Broadway run of Arnold Bennett's *Buried Alive* (better known as the 1943 film, *Holy Matrimony,* starring Monty Woolley and Gracie Fields), Price took pains to detail his concern for stage work: "You people in the East think there is no theater anywhere but in Boston, New York, and Philadelphia. If the truth must be known in words of one syllable, the best theater audiences in America are in San Francisco, Denver, and a few other places west of the Mississippi.

"I am most unhappy in New York, since

In *The Tomb of Ligeia* (AIP, 1965).

Drug addiction makes the eyes of the character
Price plays sensitive to light, forcing him to wear
tinted glasses in *The Tomb of Ligeia*.

A slice of colorful publicity at the Hollywood premiere of *The Tomb of Ligeia*. *Left:* Carol Borland (reliving her most famous and, perhaps, only film role as the vampire girl of 1935's *Mark of the Vampire*) and Price. *Far right:* The "bride of Frankenstein" herself, Elsa Lanchester.

Another quaint publicity shot at the opening of *The Tomb of Ligeia*.

320

the audiences are almost wholly made up of tourists, whose standards depend wholly on how hard it is to buy tickets. There is no real love of the theater as there was in the old days, when people went because the play itself was worthwhile and because they enjoyed the acting of their favorite players. Now they demand 'hits.'"

When asked by one uninformed young lady why he was *back* in the legitimate theater, he answered, "My dear woman, I have never *left* the theater. I have been playing every year, but not on the East Coast. Sometimes I have done summer theater; sometimes plays in Seattle, San Francisco, and Denver. What plays, you ask? Well, they include *The Lady's Not for Burning, Peter Pan,* and *The Cocktail Party,* to name a few."

Concerning horror film-making, Price cautions: "It's becoming harder and harder to scare people. We still rely on the basic elements of fear: snakes, rats, claustrophobia. But we're adding all the time. I must say I've had a lot of fun with it all. I completed a recording called *Witchcraft.* I describe curses for those you hate, and how to summon up top witches—you know the sort of thing."

Asked if he believed in evil: "If there's a power of good, it follows that there must be a power of evil. And I've seen evil. Years ago, Hollywood used to be one of the most evil places on earth. No, I'm not joking."

Since 1965 Price's films have been fewer but his *price* has been much higher. After madly ruling an undersea kingdom in *City in the Sea* (1965), being a mad scientist manufacturing robots to take over the world in two horror spoofs (*Dr. Goldfoot and the Bikini Machine* in 1965, and *Dr. Goldfoot and the Girl Bombs,* 1966), he appeared in a few non-horror films. Then he became a bloodthirsty hunter of heretics and witches in *The Conqueror Worm* (1968), set in the time of Cromwell's England with a few prologue lines from Poe's poem to justify its exploita-

City in the Sea (AIP, 1965; American title: *War Gods of the Deep*). Vincent was thought mad because he wanted to rule an undersea kingdom in this British-based production.

The Gill Man arrives to terrorize everyone in *City in the Sea.*

International intrigue, smuggling, and white slavery in Tangiers is Price's game and the setting for *House of a Thousand Dolls* (AIP, 1967).

Cromwell's England allows Price (*right*) to persecute and burn people suspected of heresy and witchcraft in *The Conqueror Worm* (AIP, 1968).

322

Price and Christopher Lee in *The Oblong Box* (AIP, 1969).

The Oblong Box.

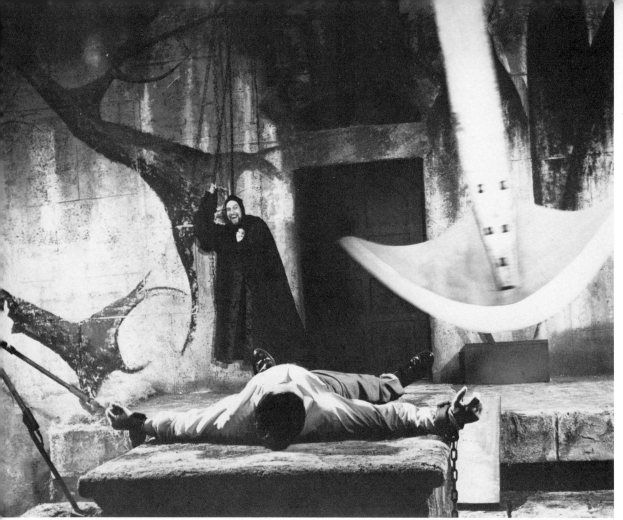

Price in a parodied scene from *The Pit and the Pendulum* in *Dr. Goldfoot and the Bikini Machine* (AIP, 1965).

In the TV situation comedy "F Troop" (1966), Price played an eccentric European actor (who talks like Bela Lugosi!) in the frontier country of the West who is mistaken for a Transylvanian vampire. It was a very entertaining spoof.

"F Troop." Forrest Tucker, Price, and Larry Storch.

"F Troop." Forrest Tucker, Price, and Larry Storch.

"F Troop." Forrest Tucker, Larry Storch, and Price.

Vincent has the power to turn puppets into humanoid replicas in the "Deadly Dolls" segment of TV's "Voyage to the Bottom of the Sea" (1967). Richard Basehart (*left*) and David Hedison (formerly Al Hedison and Price's co-star in *The Fly*) on the left.

Cry of the Banshee.

The Sidhi, a demon creature who destroys Price and members of his household in *Cry of the Banshee* (AIP, 1970).

In *Scream and Scream Again* (AIP, 1970).

tion as a "Poe" film. Blood spattered about everywhere in *The Oblong Box* (1969) under uneven direction and a thrown-together script as Price tries once again living down in Victorian times a family curse picked up from African natives while slave-trading in his younger days. *Cry of the Banshee* (1970), which contained the germ of an excellent plot wasted under hasty direction and a thudding low-budget look, starred Price as a deranged nobleman beset by a werewolf-like demon creature decimating his friends and household.

After a number of unnoteworthy productions, Vincent Price came back in 1970's *Scream and Scream Again*—science fiction with a strong accent on horror. Price runs a laboratory creating authentic-looking "androids" who resemble humans and are placed in high positions "to take over." Peter Cushing and Christopher Lee co-starred, with a top-flight supporting cast. The surprise is that not only is Price an android himself, but so is Christopher Lee (who demolishes Price in acid), after appearing to be a sort of anti-hero.

Over a period spanning nearly twenty years, Price had appeared in every kind of shocker that writers and directors could dream up. There didn't seem to be any more new worlds left to conquer . . . until *The Abominable Dr. Phibes* in 1971. While *House of Wax* may have been Price's finest horror trip in the past, *Phibes* is certainly his circus of horrors, involving enough elements for at least several other good films. Price said of his part: "I play a mad doctor, Anton Phibes, who visits the nine curses of Egypt on the nine doctors who he thinks killed his wife. Each murder is inspired by the biblical account of the plagues God is supposed to have wrought upon Pharaoh during the period of the Exodus. And this includes death by bats, rats, bees, frogs, and locusts. It was a wonderful part for me, with a super script. Robert Fuest, who made the new version of *Wuthering Heights,* is the best

young director I've ever worked with. It's also the first time I've acted with Joseph Cotton in thirty-two years." Price and Cotton appeared together in the mid-30s in Orson Welles' "Mercury Theater" productions. "We're great pals and see a lot of each other at home in Hollywood."

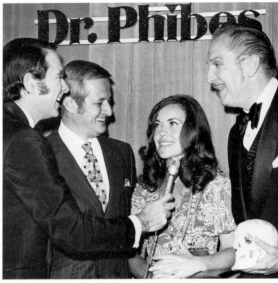

1971: The late president of American-International, James H. Nicholson, honors Vincent Price for his appearance in *The Abominable Dr. Phibes* at a charity world premiere. *Left to right:* Hollywood and TV newsman Army Archerd, Nicholson and his wife Susan Hart Nicholson, and Price.

Phibes was successful enough to produce a 1972 sequel, *Dr. Phibes Rises Again.* The two films, though similar, have enough remarkable and creative touches to endow each with its own unique identity and the advantage of being made in England. Price continued: "Brian Eatwell's sets are wonderful; he turned *Phibes* into a visual masterpiece. This puts it into a class above the average horror film where they use a lot of fog and dreary Gothic sets. Bob Fuest, who was a set designer before he turned director, realized at once that to make this film different and to give it integrity as a Grand-Guignol horror picture, it had to have a difference. The 1930s was a great period and it hasn't been used in this type of film before. It's much more

A gory moment in *Scream and Scream Again*.

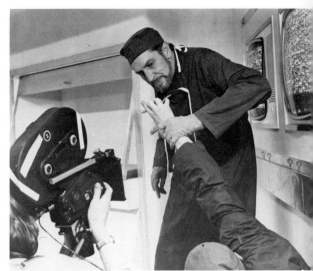

Setting up a take on the set of *Scream and Scream Again*.

Price in his laboratory engaged in creating humanoids in *Scream and Scream Again*.

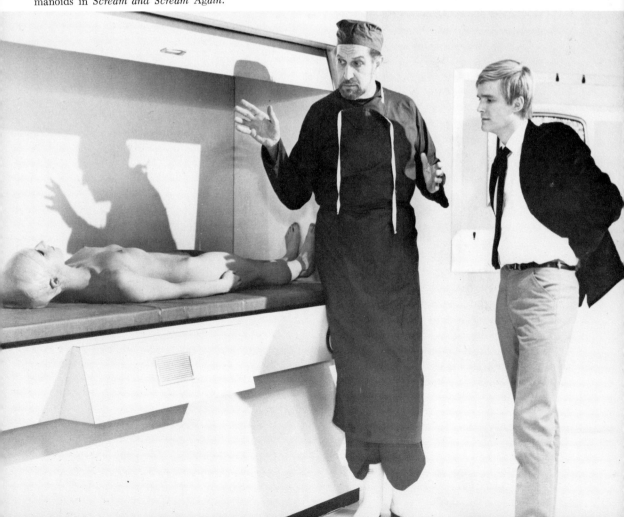

The Abominable Dr. Phibes. Horribly disfigured in an accident, Price takes horrible vengeance upon nine doctors whom he blames for his wife's death and his own skull-like face. At other times he wears a mask (which, by some odd coincidence, resembles Vincent Price).

The Abominable Dr. Phibes.

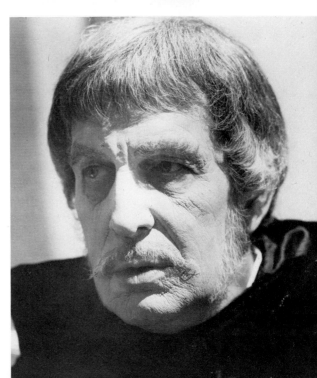

Love means
never having to
say you're ugly.

JAMES H. NICHOLSON and SAMUEL Z. ARKOFF present

VINCENT PRICE
JOSEPH COTTEN

the abominable
dr. phibes

also starring
HUGH GRIFFITH and TERRY-THOMAS   presenting VIRGINIA NORTH as Vulnavia

WRITTEN BY JAMES WHITON and WILLIAM GOLDSTEIN · PRODUCED BY LOUIS M. HEYWARD and RONALD S. DUNAS
EXECUTIVE PRODUCER SAMUEL Z. ARKOFF and JAMES H. NICHOLSON · ORIGINAL MUSIC COMPOSED BY BASIL KIRCHIN · DIRECTED BY ROBERT FUEST

GP ALL AGES ADMITTED   COLOR BY MOVIELAB   An AMERICAN INTERNATIONAL Picture
ONE SHEET

loff, whether the scripts were great or mediocre, or sometimes even downright bad, we all worked terribly hard to make them good. It isn't true what people say about comedy or horror films not being serious art. Those people think only in terms of problem dramas, but every single work of art that is ever done has to have some form of seriousness behind it. And that goes for comedy most particularly. There is this funny thing: All the classic horror pictures really had a seriousness of intent."

Asked what roles he favors most:

"I don't think that we actors know what is really suitable for us. I've played pretty darned near the whole gamut as an actor. I did *Peter Pan* on the stage a few years ago, and I have done musicals. I've also done quite a lot of Gilbert and Sullivan, and things like that. Sometimes an actor thinks that he should play only tragedy when he may be denying himself the marvelous expression of comedy, which is really much more difficult than drama. I have never turned down any kind of drama—I've done an awful lot of dramatic films—but what I really love to do is comedy. Even out-and-out slapstick for that matter."

Reminded that he is a transatlantic favorite, he answered:

"It's a marvelous feeling. I'm still astonished at the public recognition I get whenever I'm in London. My voice on the telephone is even recognized by anonymous operators."

Even though his career has brought him great success, does he feel completely fulfilled in his work and as a person?

"Yes, I think I am reasonably happy, and I attribute this mainly to lack of boredom. You can avoid boredom if you're a happy human being. Unfortunately, modern life, with its standardizations, is apt to impose boredom on people. And this is a great pity. In a way, I kind of solved one of my unfulfilled ambitions. I like to write, and to tell people all about the things I've seen. You really can't do that in conversation, because that is one art

horrifying to set the story in a period with which many people easily identify than in a creepy mansion in some ancient time and country unknown to them."

In describing his bizarre characterization, Price said: "It was difficult. You see, he has no throat. He can only speak if an extension cord from an electric-light socket attached to a receptacle in his neck keeps him functioning. He's all right so long as someone doesn't blow a fuse!" he added with a fiendish laugh. "You can take it from me that horror films are hard work. In the movies that I made with Boris Kar-

that has died in recent years—the art of conversation. It is a period of small talk. Television was responsible for this killing of conversation, although it is the greatest communication medium in the world. But don't think I'm knocking TV, because I grew up with the medium and I love it!"

What about present-day film trends?

"Permissiveness and nudity have become so commonplace in movies today, there's nothing left for them to show that hasn't been seen a million times already. General audiences are becoming sick of it. For myself, I think sex must have humor. If it doesn't, then forget it. I loved *Bob and Carol and Ted and Alice*—a wonderful movie which could only have been made in America. It was so true to life in showing the kind of thing that is happening in the States today—and funny, too."

Making all the Poe and horror films must have been tremendously gratifying to him personally, especially considering their international success.

"It has been. But, you see, I love to act. Making these horror films is a marvelous experience for me, especially when they're so different and creative like *Dr. Phibes*. I've never done anything like it before. It is made with a kind of imagination which is not expensive but has great artistic taste."

One of Price's most recent box-office successes is the British-made *Theatre of Blood*, completed in late November 1972, co-starring Diana Rigg, Robert Coote, Robert Morley, the late Jack Hawkins, Dennis Price, Diana Dors, and other outstanding players.

Vincent plays Edward Lionheart, a demented classical actor who believes that the Critic's Circle has unconscionably denied him his just award as the year's best actor. So, aided by his daughter-in-crime (Diana Rigg), he sets out to kill off each of the nine theater critics through gory deaths matching those described in the Shakespearean plays which formed his last acting repertoire.

The film may go down in film history as one of the most star-studded horror productions ever made. As Price said:

"When I first heard the big names they had assembled for this picture, I just couldn't believe it. This is my tenth British horror movie in eight years. During the course of the film I play scenes from a number of Shakespearean plays. A feast for any actor!"

For many years, with his daughter Mary Victoria (called Vicky) and his second wife, Mary, Price occupied a huge old sturdy mansion, not very unlike some of his eerie film chateaus, situated atop a rise in the Holmby Hills section of Los Angeles, near Beverly Hills. Price purchased it about twenty years ago for fifty thousand dollars, which, he explains, "was a real steal since nobody wanted edifices like this at the time." Containing twenty spacious rooms and surrounded by two acres, the house also has a totem pole standing across the patio near a three-story-high African plant that seems to reach out and grab you. The pole towers thirty feet and is believed to have contained the bodies of two natives. It was brought to Beverly Hills by the late John Barrymore, and the Prices bought it from his estate. Thousands of unusual items that would delight the heart of any collector could be found all over the place. The Price collection can include anything from exotic seashells to an antique-farmhouse front door; in addition his well-known art collection contains many rare works of the Old Masters and those of brilliant contemporaries.

In late January 1973, Price visited the New York area on a tour promoted by Sears Roebuck for the opening of a new interior-decorating course. He sat on the side of the bed in his suite at the Plaza Hotel, unbuttoned the collar of his blue shirt, and withdrew a dark-blue tie with one long, uninterrupted pull. Price was away from the public for a few hours, taking time out from a busy schedule of lectures and TV and radio interviews that had lasted for days and was only a part of a nationwide campaign. He admitted that traveling from town to town can be tiring. "But more than that," he sighed, "it is lonely. Oh, there are always people around. And they're always nice to you. An actor is seen by so many people so many times on the screen that he almost becomes family. But you know very well you can be surrounded by people and still remain lonely."

Accompanying Vincent was company promotion man Leo McCormack, who was trying to get the star to order some lunch.

"The shrimp salad appeals to me." But he vehemently turned down *coffee* and made a face that would have been suitable for one of his horror films. "God, I can't stand that stuff. It has my insides churning. Let me have some tea. Make it iced tea."

"What about a drink?" McCormack said.

"Never touch it on the road. I make it a habit," said Vincent, "not to drink when I'm on tour. After these few days, I've got a couple of stops before returning home for a short rest. Then we start a lecturing series that will cover thirty-three cities in thirty days. And everyone offers you a drink. If I accepted them all, I'd be soused. I wouldn't be able to make it back to the hotel."

He got up and hung the tie over the top of the black-and-white checked sports jacket he had placed on a chair.

"The old Plaza is really unique," he said, scanning the ornate moldings which run around the corners where the high ceilings meet the walls. "It's got class and dignity that the years haven't replaced. What did you order, Leo?"

Before he received an answer, there was a knock at the door and a smiling waiter, eyes glued on Price, pushed in a cart.

"My God," Price shouted, "he's ordered a cheeseburger at the Plaza. And a bottle of beer to go with it!"

Reiterating the way he has long felt about comedy acting, Price said, "With tragedy, everything's going with you. The audience suffers with you, feels, relates, to the emotional stress being portrayed. High comedy is the pinnacle test of an actor."

Asked who his favorite actor was, he replied: "Today? George C. Scott, without question. He is a real actor, not just in the theatrical sense. He is also capable of performing comedy flawlessly. For the actor I'd select covering the years, that would be Cary Grant. He was capable of fulfilling any role."

He admitted sadly that he doesn't see many of those he worked with over the years. "I'm on the road so much. But I do have contacts. Jane Russell called on New Year's. She's fine, but I don't see her. It's nice to keep up with people, though."

Apart from appearing on guest shows, he is little involved with TV these days; he said, "TV, unfortunately, has flunked its responsibility as a visual medium."

Commenting on *The Vincent Price Treasury of American Art*—a handsome book costing twenty-five dollars—he said, "I really enjoyed compiling those prints. It includes a collection of a hundred and forty-nine outstanding paintings by Americans from the very first colonial achievements in recording themselves for posterity, to the 1970's movements, including the resurrection of modern American Indian painting.

"I did the writing while on lecture tours and completed about four chapters a week. You have to understand that I do not type. I also can't write on white paper. Only yellow. I need the guidelines my pencil can follow.

"I make it a rule, and a very strict one, never to take drinks and to stay away from most breads, especially those which have the value removed, and starches. I stay out of the hotel restaurants, and prefer lobster or salads or cottage cheese. I can honestly say that when I finish a lecture tour I am in good condition. And this is because I don't eat a lot of junk."

He has a rule about restaurants that he's abided by for years: Whenever he goes to a French restaurant (his favorite kind) he always tries the *pâté maison* first. "I don't know why it is, but if that's good the rest of the food will be good. If it's not, then beware!"

Extensive tours and lecture engagements made him long to be with his wife and daughter and his writer-poet son who resides in Albuquerque. "He did the pulling together, the compiling of the art book; and it was a fine job," Price said.

"Yes, the family watched some of my old films, and my daughter would get very disturbed if I got killed—no matter how many times the film ran," he said, smiling.

"I believe a father's goal should be to be a friend to his children. Love is there. Friendship you have to work at. I was the last of four children, and my parents were mature, settled in their ways, when I came along. There was a built-in generation gap, to use a phrase from today. But we had that friendship I'm speaking about.

"Love is not always understanding. Sometimes it's misunderstanding. Friendship is understanding."

Does he have that relationship with his daughter?

"Ho, ho," he burst out laughing. "Who can tell?" Then, with a sly no-no wave of his finger, he said softly, "Little girls confide nothing!"

Vincent and his family were great overnight-trip fans, so whenever they had the opportunity, they used to zip around Southern California in a Cortez home-on-wheels camper which he drives, stopping along the way at every antique shop and scenic attraction. Even in the midst of shooting *Dr. Phibes*, Vincent didn't let six thousand miles between California and England separate him from his family at Christmas—they flew over to join him. He showed them some of the colorful sound stages; but his daughter Vicky never got a chance to see her father kill any of his victims as Dr. Anton Phibes: "There are some things a father just doesn't do in front of his daughter," he explained. "But really, I'm one of the most well-intentioned murderers you'd ever want to meet."

While Vincent stayed in London last year to star in *Madhouse*, he also also became a weekend commuter to Manchester to captain one of the teams on TV's "Movie Quiz," a weekly show transmitted from that city. "I love listening to the rich variety of English accents," he said. "I like to guess which part of the country people are from. These were my first visits to Manchester, and I loved them. I was fascinated by the 'Mancunian' dialect, and I had a great time deliberately stopping people in the street and asking questions, simply to hear them speak. The same thing happened on my first visit to Birmingham several years ago, but I have to admit that I find 'Mancunian' easier to understand than 'Brummagen.' My friends are now urging me to go to Newcastle and hear some 'Geordie.' I'm told it's something that every student of dialect should hear."

Price spoke of what a thrill it had been appearing on the "Movie Quiz" show: "I travelled up to Manchester on a Sunday afternoon, did the show and returned to London on the midnight sleeper train. At five-thirty A.M. a car would be standing by at Euston to take me to the set. One Monday morning I fell right off to sleep when I got back to the studio. I had been awake all night on the sleeper."

Engaged in another project, the busy Price took the underground from his Belgravia apartment to Tottenham Court Road to meet Canadian animator Dick Williams, who was making his first full-length cartoon, *The Amazing Nasruddin*, adapted from Idries Shah's Persian fantasy tale. Price is heard as the voice of the villainous Grand Vizier Anwar who, with his pet vulture, plots to take over the Persian kingdom. "Did you ever see Dick's film of *A Christmas Carol,* which won the Hollywood Oscar last year?" asked Vincent. "It was brilliant. I was absolutely delighted when he asked me to supply the voice of this cartoon character. I've never done anything like this in my career. It was fascinating watching these animators bringing all these thousands of drawings to life on the screen. Dick has a lot of Disney's artists from California working for him now in his London studios. *Nasruddin* has already taken him four years and it should be ready for release around the end of 1974."

Vincent seemed more industrious than ever at sixty-two and didn't hesitate to refute any rumors of retirement. "They'd have to bury me before I retire," he joked, "and even then my tombstone will read 'I'll be back!'"

With work in *Madhouse* barely completed, Vincent already had two more British feature-film contracts handed to him, tentatively scheduled for late 1974 production. Between engagements, he hopped back to the States and narrated a brilliant TV documentary, *The Devil's Triangle,* which did so well that it went into theatrical distribution. It's an eerie but factual film (consisting of authentic film footage and eyewitness interviews) about an area between Bermuda and Miami where ships, planes, and U.S. Navy craft have inexplicably vanished without a trace.

"I recently met a woman in New York who had cancelled her vacation in Bermuda after seeing it," said Vincent, not without a trace of pride. "She told me that the film scared hell out of her!"

Verifying what he's often said—"I'm a sucker for activity"—Vincent has also finished work on one more book *What the Hell Do You Do with Parsley?* He pointed out elatedly, "It's a facetious idea, but I think it will be fun. You see, in America our food is always covered in great mounds of parsley. You can barely find it. I am exploring a theory that the richest men in America are not the Paul Gettys or the Howard Hughes-type tycoons. They are the Parsley Kings. I was in Montana not long ago on a lecture tour and I decided to finish my dinner with an ice cream. And, yes—you've guessed it—it was served with a sprig of parsley!"

Madhouse, Vincent's most recent release, falls into the spirit of *House of Wax* and *Theatre of Blood.* Price co-stars with Peter Cushing, both playing veteran horror stars. Cushing's envy turns into malicious jealousy, twisting his mind. Attempting to displace Vincent from the plum lead in an important TV horror series, Cushing supplies a quota of corpses, not only to frame Vincent but to drive him to suicide. For a while, Vincent imagines himself insane; then he uncovers Cushing's plot, and in a final confrontation, they fight to the death. Cushing doesn't survive and is burned unrecognizably and mistaken for Vincent. Realizing that he can never exonerate himself, Vincent nevertheless makes a comeback—permanently disguised as Cushing.

Though Vincent Price has often expressed concern about being typecast, what he feared as stigmatization years ago has made him one of the world's most sought-after and best-paid actors. As he would wryly quip:

"After all, you can't look a gift hearse in the mouth!"

336

Epilogue

The seventies have seen the escalation of serious themes. Cornel Wilde's *No Blade of Grass* (1970), based on John Christopher's novel, was the first serious depiction of a future ecological disaster. *Beneath the Planet of the Apes* (1970) took its characters into the "forbidden zone" for the final destruction of Earth; *Escape from the Planet of the Apes* (1971), which scripter Paul Dehn calls "an ape love story," brought the apes to the present day where they become victims of political persecution; *Conquest of the Planet of the Apes* (1972) features the ape pre-history revolution (and its many parallels with the black revolution); and *The Battle for the Planet of the Apes* (1973) describes the events surrounding the rise of the ape civilization.

House That Dripped Blood (1971) and *Asylum* (1972) continued the series of Amicus Productions' feature/anthologies of Robert Bloch short stories which began with *Torture Garden* (1967). Audiences wondered whether to laugh or scream at Robert Fuest's *Abominable Dr. Phibes* (1971), a satirical horror character perfectly suited for Vincent Price's talents; better is the sequel, *Dr. Phibes Rises Again* (1972), with the satirical intent even more apparent. *The Mephisto Waltz* (1971) and *The Other* (1972) gave the decade two fine occult films. Robert Altman's *Brewster McCloud* (1970) is a literate allegorical fantasy of a boy who yearns to fly. Allegory was also the guiding force of a Borgesian and ambiguous study of life as labyrinth;

and *Performance* (1970), of decisive cues, entrances, and exits. In *El Topo* (1971) writer-director-star Alexandro Jodorowsky found a surrealistic lifestyle necessary to create this metaphysical metaphor ostensibly set in the framework of the western film.

THX-1138 (1971), the first major production by film-school graduates, used flickering TV images, computer print-outs, and real locations for a depressing vision of man's eventual dehumanization. It was equaled, if not surpassed, in 1972 by *ZPG* (standing for Zero Population Growth), a futuristic essay in which world pollution has destroyed all urban vegetation and poisoned the air, and childbearing is punishable by death. *The Omega Man* (1972) offered a brilliant science-fiction variation on Matheson's *I Am Legend:* the hero (Charlton Heston) believes himself to be the sole survivor of germ warfare and holes up in his apartment fighting off a diseased cult of antitechnologists.

Douglas Trumbull, special-effects innovator for *The Andromeda Strain* (1971), *2001,* and *Candy* (1968), made his directorial debut with the poetic tragedy, *Silent Running* (1972), borrowing his title from submarine terminology and his spaceship-interior setting from an abandoned aircraft carrier. Its ecological theme has an astronaut (Bruce Dern) countermanding his superior and murdering his co-workers in an obsessive effort to save the last of earth's vegetation. Ending with humanized robots tending the deep-space garden, the film is an antithetical outgrowth of the ideas in *2001.* Trumbull conceived of his robot drones—bilateral amputees inside lightweight molded plastic—after seeing Browning's *Freaks.* After *Silent Running,* Trumbull joined producer Jacobs to co-direct (with J. Lee Thompson) *Journey of the Oceanauts* (1973), an underwater tale of men-fish in the year 1991.

In the ranks of highly talented and inventive new directors, Trumbull is joined by John Boorman. After bringing critics to their feet with a nightmarish blend of psychological terror and realism in the film version of James Dickey's *Deliverance* (1972), Boorman leaped ahead light years for the science-fictional *Zardoz* (1973), an original story of immortality set in the far future.

In 1973 and 1974 the entertainment industry was shaken, though, when SFantasy and macabre films literally "took over":

Just as MGM announced dissolution of most company activity after a long string of failures, *Westworld* (a Disneyland-like pleasure park where robots go wild), MGM's final big budgeter of the year, became an overnight financial bonanza. Woody Allen's fantastic futuristic foray, *Sleeper,* also did extremely well. And so was the case with *Fantastic Planet,* a superb animated fantasy acclaimed by many as a potential classic. TV had an unusually large share of the genre, including a four-hour version of *Frankenstein,* with other versions of the Mary Shelley classic from Andy Warhol's company, and Mel Brooks' eagerly awaited spoof. *The Golden Voyage of Sinbad*'s success was also significant, since it was essentially planned as a children's film. There were many other entries, such as *Sisters, Don't Look Now, The Conversation* and . . . *The Exorcist,* now described as among the most profitable films ever made and, certainly, if not the most frightening, at least one of the scariest films ever added to the genre.

With this long-awaited synthesis of literate concepts and special-effects magic, plus the ever-increasing box-office receipts for fantastic films, the future holds promise of many wonders to come. The parlor trickery of Méliès has evolved into the artistry of visionaries.

338

Filmography

A checklist of the films of Lon Chaney, Sr.; Bela Lugosi; Boris Karloff; Peter Lorre; Lon Chaney, Jr.; and Vincent Price, compiled from all available data.

Films are listed according to year of completion or release, followed by the name of the studio/distributor. If the film was made abroad, the name of the country of origin precedes that of the studio/distributor.

Names of directors are given in parentheses.

1913 *Poor Jake's Demise.* Imp (Allen Curtis)

The Sea Urchin. Powers (Edwin August)

The Trap. Powers (Edwin August)

Almost an Actress. Joker (Allen Curtis)

Back to Life. Victor (Allan Dwan)

Red Margaret, Moonshiner. Gold Seal (Allan Dwan)

Bloodhounds of the North. Gold Seal (Allan Dwan)

1914 *The Lie.* Gold Seal (Allan Dwan)

The Honor of the Mounted. Gold Seal (Allan Dwan)

Remember Mary Magdalen. Victor (Allan Dwan)

Discord and Harmony. Gold Seal (Allan Dwan)

The Menace to Carlotta. Gold Seal (Allan Dwan)

The Embezzler. Gold Seal (Allan Dwan)

The Lamb, the Woman, the Wolf. Bison (Allan Dwan)

The End of the Feud. Rex (Allan Dwan)

The Tragedy of Whispering Creek. Bison (Allan Dwan)

The Old Cobbler. Bison (Murdock MacQuarrie)

A Ranch Romance. Nestor.

Her Grave Mistake. Nestor.

By the Sun's Rays. Nestor.

The Oubliette (Chapter 1, *The Adventures of Francois Villon,* of four 3-reel chapters; the second chapter, *The Higher Law,* also included Chaney in the cast). Bison (Charles Giblyn)

A Miner's Romance. Nestor.

Her Bounty. Rex (Allan Dwan)

Richelieu. Bison (Allan Dwan)

The Pipes of Pan. Rex (Joseph DeGrasse)

Virtue Is Its Own Reward. Rex (Joseph DeGrasse)

Her Life's Story. Rex (Joseph DeGrasse)

Lights and Shadows. Rex (Joseph DeGrasse)

The Lion, the Lamb, the Man. Rex (Joseph DeGrasse)

Her Escape. Rex (Joseph DeGrasse)

1915 *The Sin of Olga Brandt.* Rex (Joseph DeGrasse)

Star of the Sea. Rex (Joseph DeGrasse)

Threads of Fate. Rex (Joseph DeGrasse)

The Measure of a Man. Rex (Joseph DeGrasse)

When the Gods Played a Badger Game. Rex (Joseph DeGrasse)

Such Is Life. Rex (Joseph DeGrasse)

Where the Forest Ends. Rex (Joseph DeGrasse)

All for Peggy. Rex (Joseph DeGrasse)

The Desert Breed. Rex (Joseph DeGrasse)

Outside the Gates. Rex (Joseph DeGrasse)

The Grind. Rex (Joseph DeGrasse)

Maid of the Mist. Rex (Joseph DeGrasse)

The Girl of the Night. Rex (Joseph DeGrasse)

The Oyster Dredger. Victor (Chaney scripted and directed)

Steady Company. Rex (Joseph DeGrasse)

The Violin Maker. Victor (Chaney) DeGrasse)

The Stool Pigeon. Victor (Chaney)

An Idyll of the Hills. Rex (Joseph DeGrasse)

For Cash. Victor (Chaney)

The Stronger Mind. United (Joseph DeGrasse)

The Trust. Victor (Chaney)

Bound on the Wheel. Rex (Joseph DeGrasse)

Mountain Justice. Rex (Joseph DeGrasse)

Quits. Rex (Joseph DeGrasse)

The Chimney's Secret. Victor (Chaney)

The Pine's Revenge. Rex (Joseph DeGrasse)

The Fascination of the Fleur de Lis. Rex (Joseph DeGrasse)

Alas and Alack. Rex (Joseph DeGrasse)

A Mother's Atonement. Rex (Joseph DeGrasse)

Lon of the Lone Mountain. Rex (Joseph DeGrasse)

The Millionaire Paupers. Rex (Joseph DeGrasse)

Father and the Boys (5 reels) Broadway (Joseph DeGrasse)

Under a Shadow. Rex (Joseph DeGrasse)

Stronger than Death. Rex (Joseph DeGrasse)

1916 *The Grip of Jealousy* (5 reels). Bluebird (Joseph DeGrasse)

Dolly's Scoop. Rex (Joseph DeGrasse)

Tangled Hearts (5 reels). Bluebird (Ida May Park)

The Gilded Spider (5 reels). Bluebird (Joseph DeGrasse)

Bobbie of the Ballet (5 reels). Bluebird (Joseph DeGrasse)

Grasp of Greed (5 reels). Bluebird (Joseph DeGrasse)

The Mark of Cain (5 reels). Red Feather (Joseph DeGrasse)

If My Country Should Call (5 reels). Red Feather (Joseph DeGrasse)

Place Beyond the Winds (5 reels). Red Feather (Joseph DeGrasse)

Felix on the Job. Victor (George Felix)

The Price of Silence (5 reels). Bluebird (Joseph DeGrasse)

The Piper's Price (5 reels). Bluebird (Joseph DeGrasse)

1917 *Hell Morgan's Girl* (5 reels). Bluebird (Joseph DeGrasse)

The Mask of Love. Big U (Joseph DeGrasse)

The Girl in the Checkered Coat (5 reels). Bluebird (Joseph DeGrasse)

The Flashlight Girl (5 reels). Bluebird (Ida May Park)

All the following films that Chaney appeared in were of feature length (average *minimum* length having to be five reels), except for 1917's *The Empty Gun* (directed by Joseph DeGrasse), which had three reels and was the last short film in Chaney's career:

A Doll's House. Bluebird (Joseph DeGrasse)

Fires of Rebellion. Bluebird (Ida May Park)

Vengeance of the West. Bluebird (Joseph DeGrasse)

The Rescue. Bluebird (Ida May Park)

Triumph. Bluebird (Joseph DeGrasse)

Pay Me. Jewel (Joseph DeGrasse)

The Empty Gun. Gold Seal (Joseph DeGrasse)

Anything Once. Bluebird (Joseph DeGrasse)

Bondage. Bluebird (Ida May Park)

The Scarlet Car. Bluebird (Joseph DeGrasse)

1918 *The Grand Passion.* Jewel (Ida May Park)

Broadway Love. Bluebird (Ida May Park)

The Kaiser, the Beast of Berlin. Renown (Rupert Julian)

Fast Company. Bluebird (Lynn F. Reynolds)

A Broadway Scandal. Bluebird (Joseph DeGrasse)

That Devil Bateese. Bluebird (William Wobert)

The Talk of the Town. Bluebird (Allen Holubar)

Riddle Gawne. Paramount-Artcraft (Lambert Hillyer)

Danger—Go Slow. Universal Special (Robert Z. Leonard)

1919 *The Wicked Darling.* Universal (Tod Browning)

The False Faces. Paramount-Artcraft (Irvin Willet)

A Man's Country. Winsome-Robertson-Cole (Henry Kolker)

Paid in Advance. Universal-Jewel (Allen Holubar)

The Miracle Man. Paramount-Artcraft (George Loane Tucker)

When Bearcat Went Dry. C. R. Macauley Photoplays (Oliver Sellers)

Victory. Paramount-Artcraft (Maurice Tourneur)

1920 *Daredevil Jack* (15-chapter serial). Pathé (W. S. Van Dyke)

Treasure Island. Paramount-Artcraft (Maurice Tourneur)

The Gift Supreme. C. R. Macauley Photoplays (Oliver Sellers)

Nomads of the North. Associated First National (David M. Hartford)

The Penalty. Goldwyn (Wallace Worsley)

1921 *Outside the Law.* Universal-Jewel (Tod Browning)

For Those We Love. Goldwyn (Arthur Rosson)

Bits of Life (an anthology film of four stories). Associated First National (Marshall Neilan, James Flood, and William Scully)

The Night Rose. Goldwyn (Wallace Worsley)

Ace of Hearts. Goldwyn (Wallace Worsley)

1922 *The Trap.* Universal-Jewel (Robert Thornby)

Flesh and Blood. Irving Cummings Productions (Irving Cummings)

Voices of the City. Goldwyn (Wallace Worsley)

The Light in the Dark. Associated First National (Clarence F. Brown)

Shadows. Preferred Pictures (Tom Forman)

Oliver Twist. Associated First National (Frank Lloyd)

Quincy Adams Sawyer. Metro (Clarence Badger)

A Blind Bargain. Goldwyn (Wallace Worsley)

1923 *All the Brothers Were Valiant.* Metro (Irvin Willet)

While Paris Sleeps. Hodkinson (Maurice Tourneur)

The Shock. Universal-Jewel (Lambert Hillyer)

The Hunchback of Notre Dame. Universal Super Jewel (Wallace Worsley)

1924 *The Next Corner.* Paramount (Sam Wood)

He Who Gets Slapped. Metro-Goldwyn (Victor Seastrom)

1925 *The Monster.* Metro-Goldwyn (Roland West)

The Phantom of the Opera. Universal-Jewel (Rupert Julian)

The Unholy Three. MGM (Tod Browning)

The Tower of Lies. MGM (Victor Seastrom)

1926 *The Blackbird.* MGM (Tod Browning)

The Road to Mandalay. MGM (Tod Browning)

Tell It to the Marines. MGM (George Hill)

1927 *Mr. Wu.* MGM (William Nigh)

The Unknown. MGM (Tod Browning)

Mockery. MGM (Benjamin Christensen)

London After Midnight. MGM (Tod Browning)

1928 *The Big City.* MGM (Tod Browning)

Laugh, Clown, Laugh. MGM (Herbert Brenon)

While the City Sleeps. MGM (Jack Conway)

West of Zanzibar. MGM (Tod Browning)

1929 *Where East Is East.* MGM (Tod Browning)

Thunder. MGM (William Nigh)

1930 *The Unholy Three.* MGM (Jack Conway)

The Films of Bela Lugosi

* Lugosi appeared in film under the name Arisztid Olt.
** Lugosi's first American film.

1917 *Lulu.* Phoenix Films (Milhaly Kertesz, later Michael Curtiz)
**A Leopard.* Hungary. (Alfred Deesy)
**Az Elet Kiralya.* Hungary. (Alfred Deesy)
**Tavaszi Vihar.* Hungary. (Alfred Deesy)
**Alarcosbal.* Hungary. (Alfred Deesy)
Az Ezredes. Hungary. (Mihaly Kertesz)

1918 **Casanova.* Hungary. (Karoly Vass)
**Kuzdelem a Letert.* Hungary. (Alfred Deesy)
99. Hungary. (Mihaly Kertesz)

1919 *Nachenschnur des Tot* (Necklace of Death). Germany. Eichberg Film Co.
Der Tanz Auf Dem Vulken (Daughters of the Night) Germany.
Sklaven Fremder Willens. Germany.
Hamlet. Germany.

Lugosi probably made the following two films before he fled from Hungary, but they weren't released until 1920 and 1923, respectively:
Szineszno. Hungary. (Antal Forgacs)
Diadalmas Elet. Hungary. (Bela Gaal)

1920 *Die Frau in Delphin.* Germany.
Der Januskopf (*Dr. Jekyll and Mr. Hyde*). Germany. Lipow Co. (F. W. Murnau)
Le Dernier des Mohicans (*Last of the Mohicans*). Germany. Luna Films.
Johan Hopkins der Dritte. Germany.

1923 ***The Silent Command.* Fox (J. Gordon Edwards)

1924 *The Rejected Woman.* Distinctive Film Co. (Albert Parker)

1925 *The Midnight Girl.* Chadwick Films.
The Daughters Who Pay. Bonner Film Co. (George Terwilleger)
Prisoners. First National.

1928 *How to Handle Women.*
Wild Strawberries.

1929 *The Thirteenth Chair.* MGM (Tod Browning)
Veiled Woman. Fox.
Prisoners (sound version). First National.

1930 *Viennese Nights.* Warners.
Wild Company. Fox (Leo McCarey)
Renegades. Fox (Victor Fleming)
Such Men Are Dangerous. Fox (Kenneth Hawkins)

1931 *Women of All Nations.* Fox Films (Raoul Walsh)
Dracula. Universal (Tod Browning)
Broadminded. First National (Mervyn LeRoy)
Black Camel. Fox (Hamilton MacFadden)

1932 *The Murders in the Rue Morgue.* Universal (Robert Florey)
Chandu the Magician. Fox (Marcel Vanel, William Cameron Menzies)
The Death Kiss. World Wide (Edward L. Marin)
Island of Lost Souls. Paramount (Erle C. Kenton)
White Zombie. UA (Victor Halperin)

1933 *International House.* Paramount (Edward Sutherland)
Night of Terror. Columbia (Benjamin Stoloff)
The Whispering Shadow (12-chapter serial). Mascot (Albert Herman, Colbert Clark)

1934 *The Black Cat.* Universal (Edgar G. Ulmer)
Gift of Gab. Universal (Karl Freund)
The Return of Chandu (12-chapter serial). Principal Serial (Roy Taylor)

1935 *Murder by Television.* Imperial (Clifford Staniforth)
Mark of the Vampire. MGM (Tod Browning)
The Raven. Universal (Louis Friedlanders, later Lew Landers)
Mysterious Mr. Wong. Monogram (William Nigh)
The Best Man Wins. Columbia (Erle C. Kenton)

1936 *Shadow of Chinatown* (12-chapter

serial). Victory Pictures (Robert F. Hill)

The Invisible Ray. Universal (Lambert Hillyer)

Postal Inspector. Universal (Otto Brower)

The Phantom Ship (British title: *The Mystery of the Mary Celeste*). Hammer (Denison Clift)

1937 *S.O.S. Coast Guard* (12-chapter serial). Republic (William Witney, Alan James)

1939 *The Phantom Creeps* (12-chapter serial). Universal (Ford Beebe, Saul A. Goodkind)

The Gorilla. 20th Century–Fox (Allan Dwan)

Son of Frankenstein. Universal (Rowland V. Lee)

Ninotchka. MGM (Ernst Lubitsch)

1940 *The Human Monster* (British title: *Dark Eyes of London*). Monogram (Walter Summers)

The Saint's Double Trouble. RKO (Jack Hively)

You'll Find Out. RKO (David Butler)

Black Friday. Universal (Arthur Lubin)

The Devil Bat. PRC (Jean Yarborough)

1941 *The Invisible Ghost.* Monogram (Joseph H. Lewin)

The Black Cat. Universal (Albert S. Rogell)

Spooks Run Wild. Monogram (Phil Rosen)

The Wolf Man. Universal (George Waggner)

1942 *The Night Monster.* Universal (Ford Beebe)

The Corpse Vanishes. Monogram (Wallace Fox)

The Ghost of Frankenstein. Universal (Erle C. Kenton)

Black Dragons. Monogram (William Nigh)

Bowery at Midnight. Monogram (Wallace Fox)

Phantom Killer. Monogram (William Beaudine)

1943 *The Ape Man.* Monogram (William Beaudine)

Eyes of the Underworld. Universal (Roy William Neill)

Ghosts on the Loose. Monogram (William Beaudine)

The Return of the Vampire. Columbia (Lew Landers)

Frankenstein Meets the Wolf Man. Universal (Roy William Neill)

1944 *Voodoo Man.* Monogram (William Beaudine)

Return of the Ape Man. Monogram (Phil Rosen)

One Body Too Many. Paramount (Frank McDonald)

1945 *The Body Snatcher.* RKO (Robert Wise)

Zombies on Broadway. RKO (Robert E. Kent)

1946 *Genius at Work.* RKO (Leslie Goodwins)

1947 *Scared to Death.* Screen Guild Inc. (Christy Cabanne)

1948 *Abbott and Costello Meet Frankenstein.* Universal (Charles Barton)

1951 *My Son the Vampire* (alternate titles: *Mother Riley Meets the Vampire* and *Vampires Over London*). Renown Pictures (John Gilling)

1952 *Bela Lugosi Meets a Brooklyn Gorilla.* Jack Broder Productions (William Beaudine)

Glen or Glenda? George Weiss Productions (Edward D. Wood, Jr.)

1954 *Bride of the Monster* (alternate title: *Bride of the Atom*). Edward D. Wood, Jr., Productions (Edward D. Wood, Jr.)

1956 *The Black Sleep.* UA (Reginald LeBorg)

Plan Nine from Outer Space. D.C.A. (Edward D. Wood, Jr.)

Lock Up Your Doctors. (A semidocumentary compilation containing extracts from six of Lugosi's older films. In the prologue Lugosi described the film as his "obituary.") New Realm (Sam Katzman)

344

The Films of Boris Karloff

1919   *His Majesty, the American.* United Artists/Douglas Fairbanks Productions (Joseph Henabery)

1920   *The Prince and Betty.* Pathé (Robert Thornby)

The Deadlier Sex. Pathé (Robert Thornby)

The Courage of Marge O'Doone. Vitagraph (David Smith)

The Last of the Mohicans. Associated Producers (Maurice Tourneur)

1921   *The Hope Diamond Mystery* (15-chapter serial). Kosmik (Stuart Paton)

Without Benefit of Clergy. Braunton Productions (James Young)

The Cave Girl. Inspiration (Joseph J. Franz)

Cheated Hearts. Universal (Hobart Henley)

1922   *The Man from Downing Street.* Vitagraph (Edward José)

The Infidel. Preferred (James Young)

The Woman Conquers. Preferred (Tom Forman)

Omar the Tentmaker. Associated First National (James Young)

The Altar Stairs. Universal (Lambert Hillyer)

1923   *The Gentleman from America.* Universal (Edward Sedgwick)

The Prisoner. Universal (Jack Conway)

1924   *The Hellion.* Sunset (Bruce Mitchell)

Dynamite Dan. Sunset (Bruce Mitchell)

Parisian Nights. R. C. Pictures (Alfred Santell)

1925   *The Prairie Wife.* Metro-Goldwyn (Hugo Ballin)

Forbidden Cargo. R. C. Pictures/FBO (Tom Buckingham)

Lady Robinhood. R. C. Pictures/FBO (Ralph Ince)

Never the Twain Shall Meet. Cosmopolitan/Metro (Maurice Tourneur)

1926   *The Greater Glory.* First National (Curt Rehfeld)

Flames. Associated Exhibitors (Lewis H. Moomaw)

The Golden Web. Greater Gotham (Walter Lang)

Her Honor the Governor. R. C. Pictures/FBO (Chet Withey)

The Bells. Chadwick (James Young)

The Eagle of the Sea. Paramount (Frank Lloyd)

The Nickel Hopper. Pathé/Hal Roach (Hal Yates)

Flaming Fury. R. C. Pictures/FBO (James Hogan)

Valencia. MGM (Dmitri Buchowetzki)

1927   *Tarzan and the Golden Lion.* R. C. Pictures/FBO (J. P. McGowan)

Let It Rain. Paramount (Edward F. Kline)

The Princess from Hoboken. Tiffany (Allan Dale)

The Meddlin' Stranger. Action (Richard Thorpe)

The Phantom Buster. Action (William Bertram)

Soft Cushions. Paramount (Edward F. Kline)

Two Arabian Knights. Caddo/UA; Howard Hughes, producer (Lewis Milestone)

1928   *Old Ironsides.* Paramount (James Cruze)

The Love Mart. First National (George Fitzmaurice)

Burning the Wind. Universal (Henry MacRae, Herbert Blache)

Vultures of the Sea (10-chapter serial). Mascot (Richard Thorpe)

The Little Wild Girl. Hercules/Trinity (Frank Mattison)

1929   *The Fatal Warning* (10-chapter serial). Mascot (Richard Thorpe)

The Devil's Chaplain. Rayart–Richmont (Duke Worne)

Two Sisters. Rayart (Scott Pembroke)

The Phantom of the North. Biltmore (Harry Webb)

Behind That Curtain. Fox (Irving Cummings)

King of the Kongo (10-chapter serial). Mascot (Richard Thorpe)

The Unholy Night. MGM (Lionel Barrymore)

1930 *The Bad One.* United Artists (George Fitzmaurice)

The Sea Bat. MGM (Wesley Ruggles)

The Utah Kid. Tiffany (Richard Thorpe)

King of the Wild (12-chapter serial). Mascot (Richard Thorpe, B. Reeves Eason)

Mother's Cry. First National (Hobart Henley)

1931 *The Criminal Code.* Columbia (Howard Hawks)

Cracked Nuts. RKO (Edward F. Cline)

Young Donovan's Kid. RKO (Fred Niblo)

The Public Defender. RKO (J. Walter Rubin)

Smart Money. Warners (Alfred E. Green)

I Like Your Nerve. First National (William McGann)

Five Star Final. First National (Mervyn LeRoy)

The Mad Genius. Warners (Michael Curtiz)

Graft. Universal (Christy Cabanne)

The Yellow Ticket. Fox (Raoul Walsh)

The Guilty Generation. Columbia (Rowland V. Lee)

Business and Pleasure. Fox (David Butler)

Tonight or Never. Feature/Goldwyn (Mervyn LeRoy)

Frankenstein. Universal (James Whale)

1932 *Behind the Mask.* Columbia (John Francis Dillon)

Alias the Doctor. First National (Lloyd Bacon)

Scarface. Caddo/UA; Howard Hughes, producer (Howard Hawks)

The Cohens and the Kellys in Hollywood. Universal (John Francis Dillon)

The Miracle Man. Paramount (Norman Z. Leonard)

Night World. Universal (Hobart Henley)

The Old Dark House. Universal (James Whale)

The Mask of Fu Manchu. MGM (Charles Brabin)

The Mummy. Universal (Karl Freund)

1933 *The Ghoul.* England. Gaumont (T. Hayes Hunter)

1934 *The Lost Patrol.* RKO (John Ford)

The House of Rothschild. 20th Century–Fox (Alfred Werker)

The Black Cat. Universal (Edgar Ulmer)

The Gift of Gab. Universal (Karl Freund)

1935 *The Bride of Frankenstein.* Universal (James Whale)

The Raven. Universal (Lew Landers)

The Black Room. Columbia (Roy William Neill)

1936 *The Invisible Ray.* Universal (Lambert Hillyer)

The Walking Dead. First National/Warners (Michael Curtiz)

The Man Who Lived Again. England. Gaumont (Robert Stevenson)

Juggernaut. J. H. Productions/Grand National (Henry Edwards)

Charlie Chan at the Opera. 20th Century–Fox (H. Bruce Humberstone)

1937 *Night Key.* Universal (Lloyd Corrigan)

West of Shanghai. First National/Warners (John Farrow)

The Invisible Menace. Warners (John Farrow)

1938 *Mr. Wong, Detective.* Monogram (William Nigh)

1939 *Son of Frankenstein.* Universal (Rowland V. Lee)

The Mystery of Mr. Wong. Monogram (William Nigh)

Mr. Wong in Chinatown. Monogram (William Nigh)

The Man They Could Not Hang. Columbia (Nick Grinde)

The Tower of London. Universal (Rowland V. Lee)

1940 *British Intelligence.* Warners (Terry Morse)

Devil's Island. Warners (William Clemens)

The Fatal Hour. Monogram (William Nigh)

Black Friday. Universal (Arthur Lubin)

The Man with Nine Lives. Columbia (Nick Grinde)

Doomed to Die. Monogram (William Nigh)

Before I Hang. Columbia (Nick Grinde)

The Ape. Monogram (William Nigh)

You'll Find Out. RKO (David Butler)

1941 *The Devil Commands.* Columbia (Edward Dmytryk)

1942 *The Boogie Man Will Get You.* Columbia (Lew Landers)

1944 *The Climax.* Universal (George Waggner)

House of Frankenstein. Universal (Erle C. Kenton)

1945 *The Body Snatcher.* RKO (Robert Wise)

Isle of the Dead. RKO (Mark Robson)

1946 *Bedlam.* RKO (Mark Robson)

1947 *The Secret Life of Walter Mitty.* Goldwyn/RKO (Norman Z. McLeod)

Lured. United Artists (Douglas Sirk)

Dick Tracy Meets Gruesome. RKO (John Rawlins)

Unconquered. Paramount (Cecil B. DeMille)

1948 *Tap Roots.* Universal (George Marshall)

1949 *Abbott and Costello Meet the Killer: Boris Karloff.* Universal (Charles T. Barton)

1951 *The Strange Door.* Universal (Joseph Pevney)

1952 *The Black Castle.* Universal (Nathan Juran)

The Emperor's Nightingale (Karloff was narrator of this animated feature, adapted from Han Christian Andersen's fairytale). Czechoslovakia. Rembrandt (Jiri Trnka, Milos Makovec)

Colonel March Investigates. Panda/Criterion (Cyril Endfield)

1953 *Sabaka* (alternate title: *The Hindu*). UA (Frank Ferris)

Il Mostro Dell' Isola (*The Monster of the Island*). Italy. Romano (Roberto Montero, Alberto Vecchietti)

Abbott and Costello Meet Dr. Jekyll and Mr. Hyde. Universal (Charles Lamont)

1957 *Voodoo Island.* UA (Reginald Le Borg)

The Juggler of Our Lady (6-minute cartoon with Karloff as narrator). Terrytoons (Al Kousel)

1958 *Frankenstein 1970.* Allied (Howard W. Koch)

The Haunted Strangler. MGM (Robert Day)

Corridors of Blood. MGM (Robert Day)

1963 *The Raven.* A-I (Roger Corman)

The Terror. A-I (Roger Corman)

Black Sabbath. A-I (Mario Bava)

1964 *The Comedy of Terrors.* A-I (Jacques Tourneur)

Bikini Beach. A-I (William Asher)

1965 *Die, Monster, Die!* A-I (Daniel Haller)

1966 *The Ghost in the Invisible Bikini.* A-I (Don Weis)

The Daydreamer (animated feature of four Andersen fairy tales. Karloff was the voice of the Rat in "Thumbelina"). Embassy (Jules Bass)

The Venetian Affair. MGM (Jerry Thorpe)

1967 *Mondo Bizarro* (*Mondo Balordo* in Europe) (Karloff was narrator of this *Mondo Cane*-style documentary). Crown (Robert B. Montero)

The Sorcerers. Allied (Michael Reeves)

Mad Monster Party (animated feature, à la Pal's Puppetoons, with Karloff doing the voice of a Karloff puppet). Embassy (Jules Bass)

Cauldron of Blood (alternate title: *Blind Man's Bluff*). Hispamer (Santos Alcocer)

1968 *Targets.* Paramount (Peter Bogdanovich)

The Crimson Cult. A-I (Vernon Sewell)

Isle of the Snake People. Azteca/Columbia (Enrique Vergara, Jack Hill)

The Incredible Invasion. Azteca/ Columbia (Enrique Vergara, Jack Hill)

The Fear Chamber. Azteca/Columbia (Enrique Vergara, Jack Hill)

House of Evil. Azteca/Columbia (Enrique Vergara, Jack Hill)

The Films of Peter Lorre

1931 *M.* Germany. Nero Films (Fritz Lang)

The 13 Trunks of Mrs. O. F. Germany. Tobis.

Monte Carlo Madness. Germany. (Hans Schwartz)

1932 *White Demon.* Germany. UFA (Kurt Gestron)

F.P.I. Doesn't Answer. Germany. UFA (Karl Hart)

1933 *A Shot at Dawn* (British title: *Invisible Opponent*). Germany. (Sam Spiegel)

1934 *De Haut à Bas.* France.

The Man Who Knew Too Much. England. Gaumont (Alfred Hitchcock)

1935 *Mad Love.* MGM (Karl Freund)

Crime and Punishment. Columbia (Josef von Sternberg)

1936 *Secret Agent.* England. Gaumont (Alfred Hitchcock)

Crack-Up. 20th Century–Fox (Malcolm St. Clair)

1937 *Nancy Steele Is Missing.* 20th Century–Fox (Gregory Ratoff)

Think Fast, Mr. Moto. 20th Century–Fox (Norman Foster)

Thank You, Mr. Moto. 20th Century–Fox (Norman Foster)

1938 *Mr. Moto's Gamble.* 20th Century–Fox (James Tinling)

Mr. Moto Takes a Chance. 20th Century–Fox (Norman Foster)

I'll Give a Million. 20th Century–Fox (Walter Lang)

Mysterious Mr. Moto. 20th Century–Fox (Norman Foster)

1939 *Mr. Moto's Last Warning.* 20th Century–Fox (Norman Foster)

Mr. Moto Takes a Vacation. 20th Century–Fox (Norman Foster)

Mr. Moto on Danger Island. 20th Century-Fox (Norman Foster)

1940 *I Was an Adventuress.* 20th Century–Fox (Gregory Ratoff)

Strange Cargo. MGM (Frank Borzage)

Island of Doomed Men. Columbia (Charles Barton)

Stranger on the Third Floor. RKO (Boris Ingster)

1941 *You'll Find Out.* RKO (David Butler)

The Face Behind the Mask. (Columbia (Robert Florey)

They Met in Bombay. MGM (Clarence Brown)

Mr. District Attorney. Republic (William Morgan)

The Maltese Falcon. Warners (John Huston)

All Through the Night. Warners (Vincent Sherman)

1942 *The Invisible Agent.* Universal (Edwin L. Marks)

The Boogie Man Will Get You. Columbia (Lew Landers)

Casablanca. Warners (Michael Curtiz)

The Constant Nymph. Warners (Edmund Goulding)

1943 *Background to Danger.* Warners (Raoul Walsh)

Cross of Lorraine. MGM (Tay Garnett)

1944 *Arsenic and Old Lace.* Warners (Frank Capra)

Passage to Marseilles. Warners (Michael Curtiz)

Hollywood Canteen. Warners (Delmer Daves)

The Mask of Dimitrios. Warners (Jean Negulesco)

The Conspirators. Warners (Jean Negulesco)

1945 *Confidential Agent.* Warners (Herman Shumlin)

Hotel Berlin. Warners (Peter Godfrey)

Three Strangers. Warners (Jean Negulesco)

1946 *The Verdict.* Warners (Don Siegel)

348

The Beast with Five Fingers. Warners (Robert Florey)

The Chase. UA (Arthur Ripley)

Black Angel. Universal (Roy William Neill)

1947 *My Favorite Brunette*. Paramount (Elliot T. Nugent)

1948 *Casbah*. Universal (John Berry)

1949 *Rope of Sand*. Paramount (William Dieterle)

1950 *Quicksand*. UA (Irving Pichel)

1951 *Der Verlorene* (*The Lost One*). Germany. Pressburger (Lorre directed, starred, and co-produced)

1953 *Beat the Devil*. Santana-Romulus (John Huston)

Double Confession. England. Associated British-Pathé (Ken Annakin)

1954 *20,000 Leagues Under the Sea*. Buena Vista (Richard Fleischer)

1956 *Congo Crossing*. Universal (Joseph Pevney)

Around the World in 80 Days. UA (Michael Anderson)

1957 *The Buster Keaton Story*. Paramount (Sidney Sheldon)

The Story of Mankind. Warners (Irwin Allen)

The Sad Sack. Paramount (George Marshall)

Silk Stockings. MGM (Rouben Mamoulian)

Hellship Mutiny. Republic (Lee Sholen, Elmo Williams)

1959 *The Big Circus*. Allied (Joseph Newman)

Scent of Mystery. Mike Todd, Jr. Productions (Jack Cardiff)

1961 *Voyage to the Bottom of the Sea*. 20th Century–Fox (Irwin Allen)

1962 *Tales of Terror*. A-I (Roger Corman)

Five Weeks in a Balloon. 20th Century–Fox (Irwin Allen)

1963 *The Raven*. A-I (Roger Corman)

1964 *The Comedy of Terrors*. A-I (Jacques Tourneur)

The Patsy. Paramount (Jerry Lewis)

The Films of Lon Chaney, Jr.

1932 *Girl Crazy*. RKO (William A. Seiter)

Bird of Paradise. RKO (King Vidor)

Last Frontier (12-chapter serial; feature version: *The Black Ghost*). RKO (Spencer Gordon Bennet, Thomas L. Story)

1933 *Lucky Devils*. RKO (Ralph Ince)

Scarlet River. RKO (Otto Brower)

Son of the Border. RKO (Lloyd Nosler)

The Three Musketeers (12-chapter serial). Mascot (Armand Schaeffer, Colbert Clark)

1934 *Sixteen Fathoms Deep*. Monogram (Armand Schaeffer)

Life of Virgie Winters. RKO (Alfred Santell)

Girl of My Dreams. Monogram (Raymond McCarey)

1935 *The Shadow of Silk Lennox*. Commodore (Ray Kirkwood)

Scream in the Night. Commodore (Fred Newmeyer)

The Marriage Bargain. Hollywood Exchange (Albert Ray)

Captain Hurricane. RKO (John S. Robertson)

Hold 'Em, Yale. Paramount (Sidney Lanfield)

Accent on Youth. Paramount (Wesley Ruggles)

1936 *Undersea Kingdom* (12-chapter serial). Republic ("Breezy" Eason, Joseph Kane)

The Singing Cowboy. Republic (Mack Wright)

The Rosebowl. Paramount (Charles Barton)

Ace Drummond (12-chapter serial), Universal (Ford Beebe, Cliff Smith)

The Old Corral. Republic (Joseph Kane)

1937 *Cheyenne Rides Again*. Victory/Sam Katzman (Bill Hill)

Midnight Taxi. Fox (Eugene Forde)

Angel's Holiday. Fox (James Tinling)

Wild and Wooly. Fox (Lewis Creber)

Wife, Doctor and Nurse. Fox (Walter Lang)

Secret Agent X-9 (12-chapter serial). Universal (Ford Beebe)

Slave Ship. Fox (Tay Garnett)

Life Begins in College. Fox (William A. Seiter)

Charlie Chan on Broadway. Fox (Eugene Forde)

1938 *Road Demon.* Fox (Otto Brower)

Passport Husband. Fox (James Tinling)

Mr. Moto's Gamble. Fox (James Tinling)

1939 *Jesse James.* Fox (Henry King)

Frontier Marshal. Fox (Allan Dwan)

Charlie Chan in the City of Darkness. Fox (H. Leeds)

Union Pacific. Paramount (Cecil B. De Mille)

Of Mice and Men. UA (Lewis Milestone)

1940 *One Million B.C.* 20th Century–Fox (Hal Roach, Sr. and Jr.)

Northwest Mounted Police. Paramount (Cecil B. De Mille)

1941 *Riders of Death Valley* (12-chapter serial). Universal (Ford Beebe, Ray Taylor)

Man-Made Monster. Universal (George Waggner)

Too Many Blondes. Universal (Thornton Freeland)

Billy the Kid. MGM (David Miller)

San Antonio Rose. Universal (Charles Lamont)

Badlands of Dakota. Universal (Alfred E. Green)

The Wolf Man. Universal (George Waggner)

1942 *North to the Klondike.* Universal (Erle C. Kenton)

The Ghost of Frankenstein. Universal (Erle C. Kenton)

Overland Mail (15-chapter serial). Universal (Ford Beebe, John Rawlins)

The Mummy's Tomb. Universal (Harold Young)

Eyes of the Underworld. Universal (Roy William O'Neill)

Keeping Fit (an "America Speaks" short subject). Universal (Arthur Lubin)

1943 *What We Are Fighting For* (an "America Speaks" short subject). Universal (Erle C. Kenton)

Frankenstein Meets the Wolf Man. Universal (Roy William O'Neill)

Frontier Badmen. Universal (William McGann)

Crazy House. Universal (Edward Cline)

Son of Dracula. Universal (Robert Siodmak)

Calling Dr. Death. Universal (Reginald LeBorg)

1944 *Follow the Boys.* Universal (Edward Sutherland)

Weird Woman. Universal (Reginald LeBorg)

Cobra Woman. Universal (Robert Siodmak)

Ghost Catchers. Universal (Edward Cline)

The Mummy's Ghost. Universal (Reginald LeBorg)

Dead Man's Eyes. Universal (Reginald LeBorg)

House of Frankenstein. Universal (Erle C. Kenton)

1945 *Here Come the Co-Eds.* Universal (Jean Yarborough)

The Mummy's Curse. Universal (Leslie Goodwins)

The Frozen Ghost. Universal (Harold Young)

Strange Confession. Universal (John Hoffman)

The Daltons Ride Again. Universal (Ray Taylor)

House of Dracula. Universal (Erle C. Kenton)

1946 *Pillow of Death.* Universal (Walter Fox)

1947 *My Favorite Brunette.* Paramount (Elliot Nugent)

Laguna (short subject). Columbia.

1948 *Abbott and Costello Meet Frankenstein.* Universal (Charles Barton)

16 Fathoms Deep. Monogram (Irving Allen)

The Counterfeiters. Fox (Peter Stewart)

1949 *There's a Girl in My Heart.* Allied (Arthur Dreifuss)

Captain China. Paramount (Lewis Foster)

1950 *Once a Thief.* UA (W. Lee Wilder)

1951 *Inside Straight.* MGM (Gerald (Mayer)

Only the Valiant. Warners (Gordon Douglas)

Behave Yourself. RKO (George Beck)

The Bushwackers. Realart (Rod Amateau)

Bride of the Gorilla. Realart (Robert Siodmak)

1952 *Battles of Chief Pontiac.* Realart (Felix Feist)

Thief of Damascus. Columbia (Will Jason)

High Noon. UA (Fred Zinnemann)

Springfield Rifle. Warners (André De Toth)

Flame of Araby. Universal (Charles Lamont)

The Black Castle. Universal (Nathan Juran)

1953 *Raiders of the Seven Seas.* UA (Sidney Salkow)

Lion in the Streets. Warners (Raoul Walsh)

Bandit Island (3-D novelty), Lippert (Robert L. Lippert, Jr.)

1954 *The Boy from Oklahoma.* Warners (Michael Curtiz)

Jivaro. Paramount (Edward Ludwig)

Casanova's Big Night. Paramount (Norman Z. McLeod)

The Big Chase. Lippert (Arthur Hilton)

Passion. RKO (Allan Dwan)

The Black Pirates. Lippert (Allen Miner)

Big House U.S.A. UA (Howard Koch)

1955 *Not as a Stranger.* UA (Stanley Kramer)

I Died a Thousand Times. Warners (Stuart Heisler)

The Indian Fighter. UA (André De Toth)

The Silver Star. Lippert (Richard Bartlett)

1956 *Manfish.* UA (W. Lee Wilder)

The Indestructible Man. Allied (Jack Pollexfen)

The Black Sleep. UA (Reginald LeBorg)

Daniel Boone, Trailblazer. Republic (Albert Gannaway, Ismael Rodriguez)

Pardners. Paramount (Norman Taurog)

1957 *The Cyclops.* Allied (Bert Gordon)

1958 *The Defiant Ones.* UA (Stanley Kramer)

1959 *Men, Women and Guns.* Universal (Richard Bartlett)

The Alligator People. Fox (Roy Del Ruth)

The House of Terror. Des Fuentes (Gilberto Solares)

The Devil's Messenger (formerly TV series, "13 Demon St.," filmed in Sweden) (Curt Siodmak)

1961 *Rebellion in Cuba.* International (Albert Gannaway)

1964 *The Haunted Palace.* A-I (Roger Corman)

Law of the Lawless. Paramount (William F. Claxton)

Witchcraft. Lippert (Don Sharp)

Stage to Thunder Rock. Paramount (William F. Claxton)

1965 *Young Fury.* Paramount (Christian Nyby)

House of the Black Death. Medallion (director unknown)

Black Spurs. Paramount (R. G. Springsteen)

Town Tamer. Paramount (Lesley Selander)

1966 *Gallery of Horrors.* American General (David L. Hewitt) (Russ Jones co-directed and wrote the script)

Johnny Reno. Paramount; produced by A. C. Lyles.

Night of the Beast. Taurus (Harold Daniels)

Apache Uprising. Paramount (R. G. Springsteen)

1967 *Welcome to Hard Times.* MGM (Burt Kennedy)

Hillbillies in a Haunted House. Woolner.

1968   *Buckskin.* Paramount; produced by
        A. C. Lyles.
        Spider Baby (also released as *The
        Maddest Story Ever Told*). Amer-
        ican General (Jack Hill)
1969   *A Stranger in Town.* National Educa-
        tion Television (Earl J. Miller)
        Fireball Jungle. Americana (G. B.
        Roberts)
1970   *Dracula vs. Frankenstein.* Independ-
        ent-International (Al Adamson)

The Films of Vincent Price

1938   *Service de Luxe.* Universal (Rowland
        V. Lee)
1939   *Private Lives of Elizabeth and Essex.*
        Warners (Michael Curtiz)
        Tower of London. Universal (Row-
        land V. Lee)
1940   *Green Hell.* Universal (James Whale)
        The Invisible Man Returns. Univer-
        sal (Joe May)
        House of the Seven Gables. Univer-
        sal (Joe May)
        Brigham Young. 20th Century–Fox
        (Henry Hathaway)
1941   *Hudson's Bay.* 20th Century–Fox
        (Irving Pichel)
1943   *The Song of Bernadette.* 20th Cen-
        tury–Fox (Henry King)
1944   *Wilson.* 20th Century–Fox (Henry
        King)
        Laura. 20th Century–Fox (Otto
        Preminger)
        The Keys of the Kingdom. 20th Cen-
        tury–Fox (John M. Stahl)
        The Eve of St. Mark. 20th Century–
        Fox (John M. Stahl)
1945   *A Royal Scandal.* 20th Century–Fox
        (Otto Preminger)
        Leave Her to Heaven. 20th Century–
        Fox (John M. Stahl)
1946   *Shock.* 20th Century–Fox (Alfred
        Werker)
        Dragonwyck. 20th Century–Fox (Jos-
        eph L. Mankiewicz)
1947   *Moss Rose.* 20th Century–Fox
        (Gregory Ratoff)
        The Long Night. RKO (Anatole
        Litvak)

The Web. Universal (Michael Gordon)
1948   *Up in Central Park.* Universal (Wil-
        liam Seiter)
        Rogue's Regiment. Universal (Robert
        Florey)
        *Abbott and Costello Meet Franken-
        stein.* Universal (Charles T. Bar-
        ton)
        The Three Musketeers. MGM
        (George Sidney)
1949   *The Bribe.* MGM (Robert Z. Leon-
        ard)
        Bagdad. Universal (Charles Lamont)
1950   *Champagne for Caesar.* United Ar-
        tists (Richard Whorf)
        The Baron of Arizona. Lippert
        (Samuel Fuller)
        Curtain Call at Cactus Creek. Uni-
        versal (Charles Lamont)
1951   *Adventures of Captain Fabian.* Re-
        public (George Marshall)
        His Kind of Woman. RKO (John
        Farrow)
1952   *Las Vegas Story.* RKO (Robert
        Stevenson)
1953   *House of Wax.* Warners (André De
        Toth)
1954   *Dangerous Mission.* RKO (Louis
        King)
        The Mad Magician. Columbia (John
        Brahm)
        Casanova's Big Night. Paramount
        (Norman Z. McLeod)
1955   *The Story of Colonel Drake* (30-
        minute documentary with Price
        enacting role of man who found oil
        in Pennsylvania). American Petro-
        leum Institute (Arthur Pierson)
        Son of Sinbad. RKO (Ted Tetzlaff)
1956   *Serenade.* Warners (Anthony Mann)
        While the City Sleeps. RKO (Fritz
        Lang)
        The Ten Commandments. Paramount
        (Cecil B. De Mille)
1957   *The Story of Mankind.* Warners
        (Irwin Allen)
1958   *The Fly.* 20th Century–Fox (Kurt
        Neumann)
1959   *The House on Haunted Hill.* Allied
        (William Castle)
        The Big Circus. Allied (Joseph M.
        Newman)

352

The Bat. Allied (Crane Wilbur)

The Return of the Fly. 20th Century–Fox (Edward L. Bernds)

1960 *The Tingler.* Columbia (William Castle)

The House of Usher. A-I (Roger Corman)

1961 *Master of the World.* A-I (William Witney)

The Pit and the Pendulum. A-I (Roger Corman)

Queen of the Nile. Max (Fernando Cerchio)

The Black Buccaneer. Max (Mario Costa)

The Last Man on Earth (released in 1964). A-I (Sidney Salkow)

Naked Terror (documentary narrated by Price). Brenner.

1962 *Confessions of an Opium Eater.* Allied (Albert Zugsmith)

Convicts Four. Allied (Millard Kaufman)

Tower of London. United Artists (Roger Corman)

Tales of Terror. A-I (Roger Corman)

1963 *The Raven.* A-I (Roger Corman)

Chagall (26-minute documentary about the famous artist, narrated by Price). Romulus (Laura Venturi)

Twice-Told Tales. United Artists (Sidney Salkow)

Diary of a Madman. United Artists (Reginald Le Borg)

Comedy of Terrors. A-I (Jacques Tourneur)

Beach Party. A-I (William Asher)

The Last Man on Earth. A-I.

1964 *The Haunted Palace.* A-I (Roger Corman)

The Masque of the Red Death. A-I (Roger Corman)

1965 *The Tomb of Ligeia.* A-I (Roger Corman)

City in the Sea (British title: *War-Gods of the Deep*). A-I (Jacques Tourneur)

Taboos of the World (Mondo Cane-style documentary, narrated by Price). A-I (Romolo Marcellini)

Dr. Goldfoot and the Bikini Machine. A-I (Norman Taurog)

1966 *Dr. Goldfoot and the Girl Bombs.* A-I (Mario Bava)

1967 *House of a Thousand Dolls.* A-I (Jeremy Summers)

1968 *The Conqueror Worm* (British title: *The Witchfinder General*). A-I (Michael Reeves)

More Dead Than Alive. United (Robert Sparr)

1969 *The Chautauqua.* MGM (Peter Tewksbury)

The Oblong Box. A-I (Gordon Hessler)

1970 *Cry of the Banshee.* A-I (Gordon Hessler)

Scream and Scream Again. A-I (Gordon Hessler)

1971 *The Abominable Dr. Phibes.* A-I (Robert Fuest)

1972 *Dr. Phibes Rises Again.* A-I (Robert Fuest)

1973 *Theatre of Blood.* United (Douglas Hickox)

1974 *Madhouse.* A.I. (Jim Clark)

The Devil's Triangle (TV documentary).